11-14-66

The American Western Novel

THE
AMERICAN
WESTERN NOVEL

By

JAMES K. FOLSOM

COLLEGE & UNIVERSITY PRESS · *Publishers*

NEW HAVEN, CONN.

MANUFACTURED IN THE UNITED STATES OF AMERICA BY
UNITED PRINTING SERVICES, INC.
NEW HAVEN, CONN.

1385940

For F. K. F.
*Who first showed me the West
and later explained it.*

Acknowledgments

In the preparation of this book I have become indebted in many different ways to many different people. Though particular scholarly debts have been cited in notes and bibliography, it is a pleasure for me to mention once more the work of Henry Nash Smith, Roy Harvey Pearce, W. H. Hutchinson, and the late J. Frank Dobie, whose studies of various aspects of Western life and letters have proved invaluable to me. To Professors Norman Holmes Pearson, Willard Thorp, and William H. Goetzmann my debt is personal as well as scholarly; and to the members of uncounted undergraduate English classes, whose seminars with me were too often wont to take an unexpected turn from the main paths of English literature into the dim trails of Western Americana I would like to express both thanks and apology. To the staff of the Yale University Library—and particularly to Mr. Archibald Hanna, Jr., Curator of the Yale Western Americana Collection and to Mrs. Anne Whelpley, Assistant Librarian of the Yale Collection of American Literature—I am deeply indebted for bibliographical help; and without the aid of a Morse Fellowship, awarded me by Yale University for research and writing, this study would never have been written.

I would like also to express my thanks to Doubleday & Company for permission to quote from "The Ballad of Sam Bass," originally published in *Frontier Ballads*, ed. Charles J. Finger; and to Barthold Fles for permission to quote part of "The Ballad of Jesse James" from *Singing Cowboy*, ed. Margaret Larkin (New York: Alfred A. Knopf, 1931).

For the long monologues which held many a friend and acquaintance in durance vile I hope this study itself will serve as at least partial extenuation; no words can hope to express my debt to my wife for both moral support and patient help.

JAMES K. FOLSOM

Yale University
New Haven, Connecticut

Contents

Contents

The Muse, disgusted at an age and clime,
    Barren of every glorious theme,
In distant lands now waits a better time,
    Producing subjects worthy fame:

In happy climes, where from the genial sun,
    And virgin earth such scenes ensue,
The force of art by nature seems outdone,
    And fancied beauties by the true:

In happy climes, the seat of innocence,
    Where nature guides and virtue rules,
Where men shall not impose for truth and sense,
    The pedantry of courts and schools:

There shall be sung another golden age,
    The rise of empire and of arts,
The good and great inspiring epic rage,
    The wisest heads and noblest hearts.

Not such as Europe breeds in her decay;
    Such as she bred when fresh and young,
When heav'nly flame did animate her clay,
    By future poets shall be sung.

Westward the course of empire takes its way;
    The four first acts already past,
The fifth shall close the drama with the day;
    Time's noblest offspring is the last.

> GEORGE BERKELEY, "Verses on the
> Prospect of Planting Arts and
> Learning in America" (1752).

chapter one

Introduction

One of the most virulent—or perhaps virile—genres of popular modern American art is the Western. On the nation's television screens stories of doctors, psychiatrists, steamboat captains, circuses, and traveling magicians come and go, but always there is a cowboy to be found somewhere. The Western movie is still very much alive, both on the Late Show and in first-run movie houses, and complete with elaborate gadgetry to give the illusion of three dimensions. On the newsstands Westerns of all types and catering to all tastes are readily available in paperback.

Yet when the Western is compared with the other two types of modern American popular fiction—the detective story and science fiction—one peculiarity becomes evident, not so much within the Western story itself as in cultural attitudes toward it; for while the detective story and science fiction have received their share of commentary, the Western is enjoyed in silence. The detective story, perhaps because of certain distinguished practitioners such as Poe and Conan Doyle, is tacitly accepted as a genre with at least the possibility of literary merit. Tired scholars as well as tired businessmen will own up, albeit somewhat shamefacedly, to relaxing with Ian Fleming of an evening after a hard day spent wrestling with Henry James; few, if any, will admit a similar predilection for Zane Grey or, better, for Owen Wister or Eugene Manlove Rhodes. And science fiction, despite an almost complete absence of any work of significant esthetic merit in the genre, has attracted the accolade of book-length studies bursting with high seriousness.

The reason for modern interest in science fiction and the detective story, superficially at least, is not hard to find; for both are genres which are apparently "relevant" to contemporary American culture. This is obviously true of the first, and much pulp science fiction appeals with simple directness to the American fascination with technology—or even gadgetry. Better science fiction, as numerous commentators have pointed out, uses the framework of impossible adventure to discuss the nature of society. Inherent in the theme of confrontation of one culture with another is the moral valuation of the relative merits of each; and serious science fiction quite often concerns itself with a sour evaluation of present society reminiscent in many ways of the radical novels of the thirties. Whatever one may think of the esthetic merits of Ray Bradbury's *Martian Chronicles,* to take a well-known example, its moral purpose is clear, and metaphorical structure typical; for the various chronicles present a history of the loss of Eden in terms of the Earthlings' destruction of the simple, almost golden-age Martian culture. Bradbury's work is certainly among the best modern science fiction, particularly if judged on the basis of moral earnestness; but in a way his concerns are typical, for the genre is almost obsessed with an evaluation of twentieth-century American culture. One could point out that *The Martian Chronicles* particularly—and much science fiction in general—deals with a theme dear to the hearts of writers about the West—the theme of the Last Frontier—and that Bradbury's treatment of the colonization of Mars does not greatly differ from the many novels about the colonization of the West. One *could* point this out, but the fact is that most Americans do not; they tacitly assume that science fiction is relevant while Westerns are escapist. Most science fiction devotees will cheerfully admit that the genre has not lived up to its possibilities; but they will stoutly defend those possibilities as a vehicle for serious literature. The same benefit of the doubt is not given the Western.

Even the detective story has felt the demands of a more sophisticated modern age. The best-known practitioner of contemporary detective fiction, Ian Fleming, has come a long way from his ratiocinative ancestors. It is significant that Fleming's hero—James Bond—is concerned primarily with world affairs. He is a sophisticated connoisseur of exotic drinks and alluring women, and this none too subtle symbolism fixes a great gulf

between him and the meek young men in embassies. The same
superhuman awareness which enables him to perceive immediately the unwelcome presence of an onion in his very dry
martini enables him as well to conquer the knaves who would
frustrate the well-meaning but inept statesmanship of others on
Her Majesty's service. He is one of a few men to whom a
grateful nation allows the privilege of shooting on sight and no
questions asked—a dispensation he shares with many a lawman
who rides the range of the television Western. In both instances,
of course, this is the sheerest fantasy, in Bond's case perhaps
tempered with a bit of nostalgia for the grand old days of gun-
boat diplomacy. But the point is that Ian Fleming is taken at
least quasi-seriously while the television marshal is not; and
certainly part of the reason for this is that he is involved with
world affairs, presented under the aspect of international intrigue
—things which are, we trust, of immense importance to us all.
We may well weep for the innocent days of that amiable
psychopath, Professor Moriarty, who, as nearly as we can tell,
loved a good crime in the same way which gentler folk love a
good game of chess; or, better still, of Poe's famous ape, vicious
it is true, but neither misunderstood, troubled by guilt, nor
vexed with the problem of a social conscience. The modern
practitioner of the detective story cannot be so naive; he must
always take into account the larger picture. His hero's life is
not only fraught with peril but freighted with philosophy; as
he carefully places his bullets to have maximum effect, he thinks
regretfully of the sociological causes which have driven his
victim to a life of crime.

All this is not to say that the detective story and science
fiction are completely without merit; nor is it to suggest that
of all the genres of popular American fiction only the Western
can have any claim upon our serious attention. Rather it is to
point out an interesting double-think about Western story. Most
other genres of popular fiction are assumed to be more profound,
at least in implication, than their writers are in performance.
The whole is greater than its parts, and though various authors
are taken *cum grano salis*, the respective genres are viewed with
sophisticated tolerance. Somewhere, it is felt, sometime, a great
novel will emerge from the often inferior run-of-the-mill pro-
ductions, and this faith keeps serious readers as well as escapists
interested. Yet the Western is apparently not to be included in

this charitable view; it is absolved absolutely from even the possibility of merit.

This tacit denial of the Western's existence is all the more remarkable in light of American interest in so many other things Western. Seminars in "the West" flourish in American universities; commercial and scholarly presses print a constant stream of new historical interpretations of the meaning of the Western experience to American life; and there seems to be no end to the market for reprinted first-hand accounts, from Charlie Siringo to George Armstrong Custer. Yet when the imaginative literary record of the Western experience is approached at all, it is usually peripherally and with condescension. And this even though the reputation of the first great American novelist, James Fenimore Cooper, depends today, and has always depended, on his studies of the West; and though the Western novel today leads a vigorous life which is by no means confined to the sub-literature of the newsstand.

There are many reasons for critical neglect of the Western novel, which though superficially inconsistent, depend upon certain common, inchoate, often only half-formulated assumptions. First, as mentioned above, it is alleged that the Western is an anachronism. Among the perils of the atomic age, stories of Indian raids and cavalry patrols seem to be completely out of touch with the problems facing modern man; and if literature should be a parable of experience, the experience depicted in the Western is too unreal to have meaning today, even granted that it once did. In short, this objection comes down to the allegation that the Western is escape literature, pure and simple. The most that can be said for it is that it gives a harmless retreat from the tensions of modern life to a world of bland adventure where evil and good are easily recognizable, and where the good guy always wins. In support of this assertion it is pointed out that the Western is only very rarely true to the facts of that Western life which it supposedly depicts; and that the landscape of the Western has only a nodding acquaintance with the landscape of the West. As a result, the characters of the typical Western tend toward stereotypes, and the facts of the Western movement are debased into clichés and stock situations.

A more profound statement of this literary objection to the Western novel is that it ignores too many of the facets of human experience with which any art form that claims our serious attention must come to terms. Though—this argument runs—it need not be accepted as axiomatically true that a novel which deals with cowboys and Indians can have no relevance to modern life, yet certainly the very nature of the world of the Western novel is such that it cannot deal with some situations at least which art must interpret. The sexual experience, for instance, is often mentioned as an aspect of life which the Western almost completely ignores.[1]

Many other common critical objections to the Western could be mentioned here, though little purpose would be served by a complete enumeration. What they all ultimately depend upon, however, is a feeling that the picture of western life given by the Western is by and large a false one; considered factually the picture can be shown to be in error, and considered on literary grounds these errors in fact are emblematic of a more profound lack of relevance in the Western novel itself. This criticism is, of course, a particular affront to Americans who—long before Frederick Jackson Turner was to elucidate formally the thesis that the presence of the frontier was the most important single factor distinguishing the American from other peoples—had arrived on their own at the notion that the West was somehow the most expressive part of a culture which likes to think of itself as in all ways peculiarly self-eloquent.

For the distinctively American nature of the American experience has been one of the great themes with which Americans of all times have concerned themselves. From Crèvecoeur's 1782 letter "What is an American?" to Mark Schorer's 1961 biography of Sinclair Lewis subtitled "An American Life," the Americanness of America and Americans has attracted the concern of literary men. And though it is true that there has been singularly little agreement as to just what in fact *is* American about America, it has been just as true that the necessity for defining this American nature has been almost universally understood to be one of the great problems—perhaps *the* great problem— with which the American commentator must concern himself. As a result, a certain coolness in attitude toward the Western is understandable, on the basis that the American life depicted in it can be proved demonstrably false when compared with the "facts" of Western experience.

To add insult to injury, the literary treatment of the West

has always been something in which Americans have had extremely high—and generally unrealized—hopes. If the settlement of the West is in fact the American epic, it is an epic not without a hero, but without a poet. Timothy Flint, writing in 1826 of Daniel Boone, reflects sadly that "this Achilles of the West wants a Homer, worthily to celebrate his exploits,"[2] a feeling which is more or less endemic among American literary critics. Though Flint himself was later to attempt to remedy this situation, the offhand remark in his *Recollections* reveals a very real bitterness; it is galling to reflect that the epic of America finds, as it were, not Homer but Zane Grey as its chronicler. And however strongly the writer of a prize essay in the *Western Monthly Magazine* for 1833 may "firmly believe, that within the borders of our country, in the past and in the present, is an abundance of fine materials, endowed with capabilities of being wrought by the hand of genius into an original, a rich, and various literature," he is distressingly silent about how in fact these fine materials have been used. Both these comments reflect an interesting and ubiquitous attitude in literary criticism toward the West. For both these critics tacitly assume the same point of view mentioned earlier—that the literature of the West must somehow deal with the historical facts of western colonization. In fact, the latter critic goes so far as to mention specifically the peculiar desirability of the West as a literary mine because there "society is in ceaseless motion" and "hence is it singularly free from tameness and dull monotony, those fatal foes to the descriptive novelist."[3] The implied canon for literary criticism here is one which by now should be familiar; that the events of western history—*The Romance of Western History*, as James Hall significantly titles an 1857 collection of anecdotes—are somehow inherently so significant in their own right that they require only straight reporting. If such is the case, it becomes easy to understand on a more profound level the critic's instinctive dislike of the "untrue" quality of actual Western literature.

Indeed, if there is one great theme which runs through criticism of the literature of the West, it is precisely this: because they do not understand the "facts" of Western life, Western writers have been unable to present its meaning. The greatest of Fenimore Cooper's literary offenses, Mark Twain thinks, is the fact that five out of six Indians miss an easy jump into a scow in *The Deerslayer*. Somehow to Twain this proves Cooper's complete incompetence as a novelist; yet, if Cooper had pointed out to Twain that it is even more unlikely that any event whatever could transport a nineteenth-century American to King Arthur's court, Twain would probably have thought the criticism rather monumentally beside the point.

If one asks the writers of Western literature themselves what the nature of the genre is, however, the answer he receives will be somewhat different. For the writer of Westerns is not likely to be so dogmatic about the necessity for realistic use of the materials of Western history as his critic would wish. James Fenimore Cooper, in his Preface to the Leatherstocking Tales, refers to the tales as "romances," as does William Gilmore Simms, who subtitles *The Yemassee* "A Romance of Carolina." Owen Wister, too, uses the term in his Preface to what is probably the most popular Western ever written, *The Virginian.*

The term "romance" when applied to the Western is not without interest, as it had a more definite meaning to nineteenth-century literary criticism than it does to us. One remembers Hawthorne's famous Preface to *The House of the Seven Gables,* in which he discusses the differences between the Romance and the Novel. The Romance, Hawthorne says, presupposes "a certain latitude, both as to its fashion and material," which the Novel does not. The distinction he elaborates is more significant than perhaps at first appears. The Novel, he continues, "is presumed to aim at a very minute fidelity, not merely to the possible, but to the probable and ordinary course of man's experience." The Romance, on the other hand, "while, as a work of art, . . . must rigidly subject itself to laws, and while it sins unpardonably so far as it may swerve aside from the truth of the human heart— has fairly a right to present that truth under circumstances, to a great extent, of the writer's own choosing or creation."[4] The distinction between the two, broadly speaking, is that the Romance is presumed to be relatively free from the necessity of presenting historical "truth" in any particular factual sense, though it may well deal with—and Hawthorne's own practice here is instructive—history as myth, or as metaphor.

Hawthorne's distinction between the Novel and the Romance is not by any means confined to his own beliefs. The idea is something of a critical commonplace in the nineteenth century; William Gilmore Simms had noted earlier another implication of the idea in his discussion of the particular genius of the

Romance in his Preface to *The Yemassee* (1835). *The Yemassee,* Simms insists, is a Romance and not a Novel, and the two forms of literature are very distinct. To the question he raises, "What is the modern Romance itself?" he notes, "the reply is immediate. The modern Romance is the substitute which the people of the present day offer for the ancient epic. The form is changed; the matter is very much the same; at all events, it differs much more seriously from the English novel than it does from the epic and the drama, because the difference is one of material, even more than of fabrication." The material of the Novel, he continues, is "confined to the felicitous narration of common and daily occurring events, and the grouping and delineation of characters in ordinary conditions of society," while the Romance "does not confine itself to what is known, or even what is probable. It grasps at the possible" (pp. 23-24).

To the interesting comparison between the Romance and the epic we will return in a moment; but first let us note the similarity in Simms's and Hawthorne's distinction between the Romance and the Novel. In both men's phrase, the Novel is confined to the "probable"—that is, the everyday world—while the Romance is by no means so limited. The notion is particularly compelling when the fictional practice of the two writers is recalled; for the Romances of both men are very particularly based in history.

The difference between the Romance and the Novel, then, is ultimately one of what questions may be asked from history. Although the truth which the Novel and the Romance reveal is the same, for the "truth of the human heart" is the truth which fills all history, the Novel must present this truth by means of very particular questions of historical cause and effect, while the Romance need not be so narrowly confined.

Behind Hawthorne's and Simms's discussion of the distinction between the Romance and the Novel stands a very definite, though not explicitly stated, idea of the nature of truth. Truth, for an imaginative writer at least, finally is "the truth of the human heart," meaning that the human heart is the basis of history, not the other way around. Hence the Romance in one sense is just as historical as the Novel; indeed, from the Romancer's point of view it may well be more so, for the Novel, he thinks, constantly runs the risk of becoming so involved with meaningless detail as to obscure the truth which all art must in some way reveal. The "facts" of history, in other words, may be so inchoate that they only succeed in confusing the reader by concealing its meaning; as a result, the Novel may well be in a profound sense less "historical" than the Romance, though paradoxically the Romance has less to do with the facts of history. It all depends, as Owen Wister points out in his Preface to *The Virginian,* what questions one asks of history. *The Scarlet Letter, Hugh Wynne,* and *Uncle Tom's Cabin* are all "historical," as is "any narrative which presents faithfully a day and a generation." *The Virginian,* then, is just as historical as any of these, even though it is a "colonial romance" (pp. vii-viii).

Wister's coupling of these four novels is deliberately paradoxical. Each one, he says, is a "historical novel"; it makes no difference that *Hugh Wynne* contains the historic George Washington while in *Silas Lapham* and *The Scarlet Letter* we find only "imaginary figures." Nor, he goes on to say, does the subject of a "historical novel" necessarily have to be contemporary so long as it presents faithfully its day and generation. And also implicit in Wister's list of four carefully chosen books is the critical position that faithful presentation does not of necessity consist of merely relating the sober historical facts of whatever particular generation is under scrutiny. By faithful presentation Wister means something very close to Hawthorne's "truth of the human heart" which all literary endeavor attempts to discover.

The Novel and the Romance, then, are distinguishable only insofar as they represent different methods of elucidating the "truth of the human heart." The truth which they reveal is finally the same. In any particular case, therefore, the Romance may be more or less novelistic in detail, according to the purpose of its author. It can be completely unnovelistic as (to use an example of Simms's) are the novels of Maturin; or, it may be so close to novelistic historical fact as *Ivanhoe.* Hawthorne, whose knowledge of New England history was profound, implies himself that the separation of the novelistic from the romantic elements in *The Scarlet Letter* is not wholly fortunate; and a recent scholar has shown that this Romance is also concretely enough visualized as a Novel for the reader to create from it a street-plan of seventeenth-century Boston.[5] Yet one has to dig to do it, and this is ultimately the point; the Romancer feels that the Novelist runs the risk of being too much bound to the superficies of things to penetrate to their significance. Still, when properly used, novelistic detail can be a useful tool for the Romancer in his own presentation of the "truth of the human heart."

As a result the Romance often, though not invariably, has about it a certain spurious realism which critics are too often prone to see as its heart rather than as an incidental attribute. Is *Moby-Dick*, to take a well-known example, primarily a Romance or a Novel in the sense in which Hawthorne and Simms would use the terms? Obviously it is a Romance, at least insofar as its core is not basically realistic; yet it contains much concrete detail, which critics on occasion have taken for the center of the work, rather than as a device to give a certain believability to a story which is basically not realistic. The difference between the Romance and the Novel is the difference, as it were, between *Moby-Dick* and *Two Years Before the Mast*. *Moby-Dick* is not about the whale fishery in the same sense in which *Two Years Before the Mast* is about the California clipper trade. The "cetology" and the other factual detail of *Moby-Dick*, though Melville visualizes a whaler as clearly as Dana does a clipper ship, are subsumed as parts of a world which is finally not a "probable" one.

Moby-Dick may have taken us rather far afield from the Western;[6] but a similar confusion in terms to that about the Romance and the Novel may also be seen in the common misunderstanding of the "epic," a term universally applied to the novel of the West.

The "epic of the West" has become so hackneyed a phrase as to have lost almost all meaning whatever. Whether this is due to Hollywood or to the inevitable encroachment of time is not ultimately important; but certainly Hollywood's definition of "epic"—that it have a certain vague historical content and horses—is the unthinking definition which comes to most persons' minds when the term is mentioned. Yet the Hollywood epic is not an epic at all, and the difference between it and the traditional epic is not, as is often assumed, one of execution, but rather one of conception. For the Hollywood epic, however badly executed, is ultimately conceived as historical in a very *particular* way. Press releases for any epic film invariably mention the care with which it has been researched, and on occasion this is even true; yet even when it is, there could be nothing further from the traditional epic than the Hollywood version of it. And the difference between the two is precisely what William Gilmore Simms saw in his Preface to *The Yemassee*. The Hollywood epic is, Simms would say, novelistic. It deals with the world of the "probable," a world which is in the last analysis the world of everyday, though presented, it is true, under the guise of grandiose vulgarity. The appeal of the Hollywood epic is ultimately one of fact; it attempts to convince by the repetitive weight of documentary evidence. Who could disbelieve in Cleopatra after seeing a forty-foot-high Sphinx? And especially a forty-foot-high movable Sphinx pulled by hundreds of slaves?

For Simms, however, and for most later writers about the West, the epic is a very different thing. It is, he says, a Romance. It is a story told about history, but it is not necessarily a story constructed of historical details. A fact which perturbs a modern critic of *The Virginian*—that "there is not one scene set on the range among the cattle"[7]—would not have worried Simms; he might even have thought it to be a point in the book's favor. After all, the Trojan Horse never actually appears in the *Iliad*.

Nevertheless, to assume that all the novels about the West form a self-consistent literary method for the interpretation of experience which has always been totally misunderstood by critics would also be unfair. For writers about the West themselves have not been uniformly of one mind about the possibilities and implications of Western story. Though most of them have felt that the Western is a romantic parable, some have taken the contrary view that it is basically a novelistic account of the facts of Western colonization. In the last analysis, this latter group of writers about the West forms one category of the "local color" writers who have played a constant, if minor, role in American literature from its beginnings. The purpose of this type of local-color writing has always been more or less openly conceived as a method of publicizing the facts of American life. Whether writing about the settlement of the West, anecdotes of Southern character, or comic tales of Yankee shrewdness, these writers have assumed that their fiction should memorialize bizarre characters, unusual customs, and strange incidents of American life. Where the romantic western novel has always been fabular, tending toward the parable, this novelistic local-color western novel has always been anecdotal; and where the romantic western novel has tended toward synthesis, the local-color western has tended toward fragmentation and individual statement. The difference between the two, to use an analogy suggested before, is the difference between *Moby-Dick* and *Two Years Before the Mast*.

Yet it must not be forgotten that the romantic western has from its beginnings borrowed freely from the anecdotal material of the local colorists. Cooper's characters come immediately to mind; though his romantic young lovers are often sketchily drawn, such figures as Hurry Harry, Uncas, Chingachgook, and even Leatherstocking himself are as particularly conceived as are the characters of Bret Harte. The real difference between Cooper and Bret Harte—or to take two more nearly contemporary examples, Owen Wister and Bret Harte—in their handling of characters is ultimately to be found not in the way the characters are drawn, but in the way they are used.

Bret Harte's characters, like Bret Harte's world, have no significance beyond the statement of a tricky, anecdotal situation. Harte's real interest, and the real concern of Western local colorists from James Hall onward, is finally to be found in the story he is telling. Untoward revelations, trick endings—in a word, "surprise"—are Harte's real aims; by means of manipulation of the machinery of his tales, he attempts to render his anecdotes memorable. The same trick, somewhat less cleverly used, is familiar to all moviegoers at that point in a Hollywood Western where all seems lost, the wagon train is surrounded, the ammunition running low, the Indians massing for a final charge, when suddenly, far away but distinct, the stirring notes of the bugle inform the beleaguered party that the cavalry has come to the rescue.

What strikes us funny in such a situation is not the fact itself of the cavalry's fortunate arrival—an event by no means unknown in Western history—but that there is no point to the rescue. The same thing depresses us about the often very cleverly handled tales of Bret Harte, or O. Henry, or Will James. It is that the story has no relevance beyond the realm of anecdote. Romantic western fiction, in contrast, though often as anecdotal as the local-color tale, subordinates the events of the latter to some larger purpose. The point may be made clearer by comparing three often-praised works of Western local-color writing: Andy Adams' *The Log of a Cowboy* (1903), Elliot Paul's *A Ghost Town on the Yellowstone* (1948), and John Houghton Allen's

Southwest (1952). All three of these books are written within a completely anecdotal framework; all purport to be autobiographical; each is told in the first person by a narrator not clearly distinguishable from the author. Yet though the books are strikingly similar in format and in material, the differences between them are unmistakable.

Adams' *Log of a Cowboy* is without doubt the most complete and factual account of trail-driving in our literature. It reports a long drive from the Mexican border north through Texas and the Great Plains to a final destination at the Blackfoot Indian reservation in Montana. Almost every incident of trail-driving is faithfully reported in the *Log;* stampedes, river crossings, debauches in the trail towns, methods of handling cattle, as well as all the other colorful minutiae of cowboy life are painstakingly set down by a man who knew them at first hand. The hero of the book, and ostensible narrator of the log, one "Thomas Moore Quirk," almost exactly resembles Andy Adams himself, and the log of his adventures forms a chronicle of Adams' own colorful experiences on the cattle trail. The book, however, is not really an autobiography; except for a few conventional sentiments the character of the author can scarcely be said to enter the book at all. Adams' focus is consistently outward to the world of events, and his book is truly, as the title says, a *log*—that is, a diary of events told in the order in which they occurred. Even when Adams is reporting campfire gatherings where the cowboys swap stories, his focus is completely external. We get only an occasional glimpse of any emotional effect these stories might possibly have had upon Adams or his hero Tom Quirk, and indeed most of the stories are further anecdotes about cowboy life. Though it is true that once the stories revolve around girls left behind, more often the cowboys reminisce about horses they have known, or dogs, or the hazards of the trail. Adams' relation to these stories is also interesting, for he envisions himself as one who reports them for others, not as one who interprets the stories to himself. Almost invariably he listens to the other cowboys tell of their experiences, and copies their stories down for posterity. He is reluctant to tell stories on his own, nor does he report any effect the others' stories had upon him. Never in his record of cowboy anecdote or of cowboy life does he suggest any frame of reference or interest larger than the often fascinating—and often, it must be added, tedious—world of a particular trail drive. Were one to ask Adams his purpose in recounting this trail drive, his answer would be a historical one; *The Log of a Cowboy,* he would say, attempts a report of the facts of a way of life which has vanished.

Elliot Paul's *A Ghost Town on the Yellowstone* is in many ways reminiscent of *The Log of a Cowboy.* Like Adams, Paul was either involved in, or a first-hand observer of, the events he chronicles: the history of the short-lived town of Trembles, Montana, which was founded accidentally in a stagecoach accident in 1907 and became a ghost town fifteen years later. Like Adams' as well, Paul's account is basically anecdotal, though the subject of his story of necessity focuses his anecdotes around the inhabitants of a place rather than the events of a journey. But unlike Adams, Paul is personally involved in the fortunes of Trembles, and the ghost town on the Yellowstone becomes a metaphor for his own coming of age. This can be seen in the quality of the anecdotes Paul tells, all of which reflect personally upon himself. Instead of the various good and bad horses which fill Adams' pages, *A Ghost Town on the Yellowstone* contains only one horse, a miserable little pinto named Crocus because, as Paul tells us, "that early spring flower had been used by the Sioux to poison their enemies" (p. 43). Paul inherits Crocus and finally even manages to train her, as he manages to come to terms with the facts of life in Trembles. Indeed, Paul's trials with Crocus are a metaphor for the basic concern of the book, for Crocus is a particular image of the trials of life in general on the Yellowstone, and ultimately the book becomes a story of how one succeeds or fails in a new environment. In juxtaposition to Paul's adaptability—symbolized by his eventual success with Crocus—stands the stubbornness of a surveyor from Bangor, who knows all about cold weather and will not take advice about sensible footwear, and who loses his toes as a result of his obstinacy; and as a final sardonic metaphor we have the pamphlet put out by the Northern Pacific Railroad describing Montana's beautiful climate, which the inhabitants of Trembles take pleasure in reading whenever the temperature hits sixty below. The point of all this is of course clear; one must learn to adapt to the facts of life, rather than attempt to impose an arbitrary scheme upon them.

John Houghton Allen's *Southwest* is, like the two books already discussed, anecdotal in format. Allen tells a number of stories about the area along the Mexican border, an area he significantly calls the "lost world" (p. 9). Unlike Adams' and Paul's, however, Allen's anecdotes are not necessarily of his personal experience. Though some of the stories he tells are stories from his own life, many more have been told him by older men, and of these stories in turn many have not been part of the personal experience of the tellers. On a literal level, the book has really no organization at all. It is a collection of stories arranged according to what appears at first to be a completely random principle of association of ideas. Even the geographical location of Allen's "southwest" is loosely defined, and the definition is broad enough to allow for the inclusion of relevant anecdotes from Old Mexico and even of the American Civil War. Yet though the book does not confine itself to a particular event or place, it cannot really be criticized as random or diffuse except when it is held up to literal-minded canons of organization. Much more than either of the other two books, *Southwest* is a book with a thesis; and the attitude which Allen adopts toward his material is much more personal than Adams' and more overtly reflective than Paul's.

Allen begins his book by calling attention to the present dreariness of the southwest; the first few pages are filled with descriptions of the land, descriptions which conclude with statements of the southwest's ominous and hostile quality. It is, says Allen, a "lonely land," a "sullen land" (p. 10), a "hollow dismal land," a "stagnant land" (p. 13), an "evil land" (p. 15), and so on. From these descriptions he turns to the new American inhabitants of this "evil land," whom he does not like either; "and I am bitter against the land and these people," he concludes, "because I remember when it was a fine place to live" (p. 17). He then goes on to tell of this older, finer land, the Spanish southwest of his youth, concluding with the significant statement that the stories he will narrate "are a poet's tales, a young man's tales; they were my first loves" (p. 33).

It should be emphasized that the stories which he goes on to tell are not in fact much different from the tales of Andy Adams or of Elliot Paul. Moreover, it develops that the tales themselves are relatively unimportant to Allen, whose final concern is with the ironic contrast between the glorious old times of the Spanish southwest and the degenerate new era of the present American southwest. This explains his choice of anecdotes which, while superficially impressionistic, is actually very carefully selected to develop the ironic contrast between the two periods of history.

So short a summary as the above inevitably does a great deal of harm to the books discussed; for our purposes, however, the differences between them should now be sufficiently clear. What one finds in these three books, really, is a kind of progression on the part of their respective authors in the use of anecdotal material. *The Log of a Cowboy* has no relevance at all beyond the particular world it so accurately describes. Like *Two Years Before the Mast,* with which it has been compared, it attempts an honest, thorough, and unbiased report of the particular facts of a way of life, and the reader who finds it interesting must of necessity be one whose interest is primarily historical. *Southwest,* on the other hand, is finally not a historical book at all in any particular sense. Where *The Log of a Cowboy* is specific, impersonal, and detached, *Southwest* is passionately personal and strives always toward a general interpretation of the meaning of the southwest. For such an interpretation, it matters little whether the anecdotes related are, objectively speaking, "true" or not, and many of the stories Allen tells are admitted fables. In a larger sense, however, these anecdotes are true, for they reveal something about "southwestness" which Allen feels could not be shown through purely factual material. Somewhere between these two books stands *A Ghost Town on the Yellowstone.* In many ways almost as particular as Adams, Paul nevertheless feels uncomfortable in the realm of pure anecdote. Though not so personal as Allen, he feels that his book must have some larger concern than the faithful and accurate reporting of events. The stories Paul tells are objectively true—at least ostensibly, though some of them are a little hard to swallow—but they are arranged in such a way as to afford a more than particular insight into the way in which a man must react in order to face life successfully. The unlikely ghost town of Trembles becomes, in Paul's hands, a little world emblematic of the great world from which it apparently stands so far removed.

If one reads these three books in the order in which I have summarized their respective plots, starting with *The Log of a Cowboy* and ending with *Southwest,* one becomes conscious that the basic difference between them lies in their attitudes toward the historical material with which all three deal. Each book asks the question of how the meaning of the Western experience may best be discovered. Whether the West is best understood in terms of factual anecdotal history or as a metaphorical parable of that history is the real point at issue. In terms of our previous definition, Adams' work is novelistic; Paul and Allen write Romance.

Once this distinction is understood, much of the polemic which surrounds commentary on Western story can be seen in a truer perspective. It is pointless to ask whether *The Log of a Cowboy* is a "better" book than *A Ghost Town on the Yellowstone* or *Southwest*. Adams does not write according to the same standards as the other two authors, and, as the nineteenth century clearly saw, novelistic canons of taste cannot be applied to romantic works of art. No purpose can be served by sneering at romantic western story because it is not true to western life in any specific sense; little is to be gained by wishing Owen Wister were Andy Adams.

And in fact much may be lost; for, if we are to pontificate about the limited success or failure of Western story, we must be very clear about what it has been trying to do. My own position in regard to the novel of the West should by now be obvious. It is, very simply, that the Western has been ignored, condescended to, and maligned largely because the essential nature of Western story has been misunderstood. It has not been sufficiently recognized that this nature is finally unrealistic; that the Western is usually a "myth," or a "fable." The material of this fable is based, at least at one remove, upon American history, but the purpose of the fable is not the realistic explication of a colorful chapter of the American past. It is rather a metaphorical parable of the inconsistencies and contradictions which inhere in the American's paradoxical views about himself, his country, and his destiny. At bottom the Western depicts— often shallowly, sometimes profoundly, but always clearly—the argument which has been with America from the Puritans to the present about what the American experience should be. The question of "What is an American?" is the question the Western novel attempts to answer, though the question is often phrased differently as "What should an American be?" There is of course no answer to this question; art does not give answers to such questions, at least not in any simple way. Yet the Western does attempt to discover what the American is by metaphorical statement of some of the various things he is presumed—or presumes himself—to be. The Western deals in paradox, for the American's view of himself is paradoxical; its material—the Great West—is the material which Americans, rightly or wrongly, have always felt distinguished them from other peoples; and the settlement of the Great West is what tells the American most about himself. The most distinctive fact of American history—the settlement of the Great West—becomes in the Western novel a vehicle which holds in solution the most distinctive fact of the American mind— its obsessive concern with the nature of its own destiny.

A personal anecdote from my own experience may serve to make the point at once more particular and more clear. Some time after the second world war, while a student in Austria, I was invited to have dinner with an Austrian family. The patriarch of this family was an amiable gentleman, a retired industrialist who had spent many years in America and was filled with praise for American ways. He was perfectly clear in his own mind why the Americans had won the war. "We would have won," he said, "had we had such discipline." His notion that, beside the American genius for organization the supermen of the Third Reich were nothing but inefficient bureaucrats, was striking to me at the time. I had not yet discovered Tocqueville's trenchant analysis of the self-deception inherent in American individualism; nor had it occurred to me that there was something profoundly paradoxical in the propaganda war movies I had seen as a youth in which, after the first smashing American victory, a distinguished general would say, "Our men will win because they have been taught to think for themselves," and after the second, "Our men will win because they know the value of teamwork." To both these notions I, and I suppose most Americans, gave un-thinking approval; and yet, when one stops to think of it, the two are at least superficially contradictory.

It is beside the point here to attempt a reasoned assessment of which of these ideas best expresses the truth about the American character, or even if indeed they are as contradictory as they appear. Yet it is worthy of notice that this debate is at the heart of a great mass of literature about the West, most apparently in the innumerable works dealing with the conflict between the cattle baron and the "nesters." Superficially this theme is only blood-and-thunder, an excuse for violence in which the sides are easy to distinguish. One can identify the players without a program, if only because the nesters don't have horses.

Yet the theme is inherently much more profound than this, as Conrad Richter's *The Sea of Grass* and Jack Schaefer's *Shane*, among others, go to prove. In these works, the antagonists in a blood-and-thunder story are given significance as exemplifying two possible ways of life, both representative of conflicting American values, and the range war which ensues as an inevitable result of their conflict is seen as emblematic of inevitable ideological conflict in a people who simultaneously affirm both sets of values at once.

The conflict in the Western novel, in its broadest terms, is an externalized debate which reflects the common American argument about the nature of, in modern parlance, "the good life." It is no accident that the growth, if not the source, of the Western novel is contemporaneous with the Populist-Progressive attack on the excesses of the Gilded Age, nor that the Western accurately reflects this often acrimonious discussion. The American mental hesitation between the values of urban and rural life is mirrored in the Western novel; whether the coming of civilization is good or ill is the burden of Western fiction. Even the world of Western fiction strangely mirrors the Populist attack in party conventions and the halls of Congress. A cynic might point out that there is precious little fact to be gleaned from the highly emotional discussions of the future of democracy which from time to time erupt violently from the otherwise generally placid American moral landscape; a more compassionate observer might say only that, for all this childish joy in facts, the American does not always confuse the good life with the gross national product.

Perry Miller, in his brilliant essay "Errand into the Wilderness,"[8] has mentioned the inherent contradiction in the word "errand." Its denotative meaning, he points out, is "mission"; but combined with this is a contradictory meaning, inherent in the etymology of the word, "to wander," or "to lose one's way." Miller shows that quite early in the American experience both of these meanings come to inhere in the term. Whether in his errand into the wilderness the American has lost his way becomes the burden of Puritan sermons. It is the burden of much later American writing as well, not the least of which is the fictional writing about the West. For the West is unequivocally the wilderness; and it is there that the nature of the errand may best be seen.

When the novel of the West is viewed as a parable, many of

the objections raised to it become relatively unimportant. As a fable the Western is not necessarily an anachronism, for it makes little difference whether the Last Frontier is the Great Plains or the moon. If the Western deals in stereotyped situations, if the characters it draws are unreal, if it ignores or misrepresents particular historic facts, so do all fables. For a fable is not ultimately true to the world of everyday; it is rather a projection upon a stage of personal though universalized virtues and vices, hopes, desires, and fears. The Last Frontier is finally something more than an aspect of the American West; its topography comes to resemble the landscape of the human soul.

A final word about the scope and organization of this study does not seem out of place at this point. Its general purpose will be an examination of the themes, motifs, and implications inherent in the literature of the West. Except insofar as it asks a new evaluation of Western story it will try to avoid, as far as humanly possible, special pleading.

Two things, however, should be kept in mind by the reader. First of all, he should remember that this essay is essentially unhistorical in orientation. It will not, except in passing, concern itself with the relations of Westerns to the West, nor will it spend much time in discussion of the historical development of Western fiction. This is not to say that I find such historical analysis unimportant; nor that I think historical analysis of the growth of Western story is valueless to esthetic literary criticism. In many ways, in fact, the Western may only be successfully approached by way of historical analysis, for from its inception it has been too closely bound not only to the facts but to the conventions of American life. One thinks immediately of the foolish love plots with which many Western stories are at least peripherally concerned. The folkways which surround the sexual mores of one's immediate ancestors always seem ridiculous to a more enlightened era; and the Western is peculiarly vulnerable. Wister's Virginian, for instance, takes his new bride camping; they honeymoon on an island where the Virginian, in the interests of decorum, sets up two separate private swimming holes. To the late Victorian reader this must have seemed ineffably poetic; to us it seems unutterably silly. The stalwart cowboy, to take another example, who rides off into the sunset leaving a weeping maid behind once seemed pathetic, even tragic; to us he seems ridiculous and he may even be, we whisper, homosexual. Conventions, like dogs, have their day, and yesterday's convention is today's whimsy. We find the Victorian lost heir a sadly dated figure; yet with the son oppressed by unmentionable Oedipal longings we admit to more than a chance acquaintance. To the nineteenth-century reader the nester struggling for his rights was a species of the former; the modern Freudian finds a vestige of respectability in this anachronistic theme if it is considered in the light of twentieth-century psychoanalytical theory. Is the nester, then, a type of democratic man fighting for his rights against the tyranny of privilege? Or do we find, in this well-worn theme, a concealed allegory of the male child's revolt against his tyrannical father? Obviously, we find both; also obviously, neither excludes the other. The questions of what these interpretations have in common and how they can be related may only be answered by sensitive historical criticism.

Yet such criticism, valuable as it is, is not the purpose of this study. Nor is a comprehensive coverage of Western fiction an end either claimed or attempted. I have limited myself to a discussion of only those books which seem to me either esthetically significant or important in some other context. The number of Westerns is staggering, and good ones form only a slight proportion of the total. Consequently, I have drawn the material for this study from only the Westerns which interest me, or from authors whom I find intriguing. At the same time, I make no pretense to being an infallible judge in the high court of literature. I have doubtless slighted works of merit; and I am certain as well that I have exalted books which a cooler head would find of indifferent quality. I do not wish to pretend that these faults in this study are virtues in disguise; but the reader may view them more kindly if he keeps in mind the author's purpose, which is not to award ribbons but to suggest criteria for judgment.

With all that has been written about the West, few criteria for judging the Western have been more than suggested. The most common approach to Western story is to focus upon the figure of the Western hero, who is then variously interpreted and explicated. Sometimes he emerges as a modern type of a traditional folk hero, sometimes as a Puritan (or anti-Puritan) symbol of our heritage or of our American feelings of personal and national insecurity, sometimes as quite something else again. But in all cases such an approach to the meaning of the Western through the character of the Western hero contains an implied critical judgment that the most important aspect of Western fiction is revelation of the personal character of its protagonist. Though in many cases this is a just inference, it does not seem to me to rule out other criteria for judgment of Western literature. To my mind the most important other criterion is the one I have suggested above, the idea that the Western is a fable and must be interpreted in terms of parable. In order to suggest the dimensions of Western fable I have felt compelled to discuss the implications of the plots of various novels; since most of the works I draw upon are relatively unknown, I have felt it necessary to summarize them, perhaps at too great length, as it seemed pointless to me to analyze them without presenting them in some detail to the reader. At the same time, in order to keep this study within manageable proportions I have also felt it necessary to limit strictly the number of books discussed. In consequence I have left myself open to the charge of generalizing from insufficient material. For this and for perhaps too great reliance upon plot summary I must ask the reader's indulgence.

One final word. The problem inherent in a proper definition of "the Western" is a difficult one, and I cannot pretend to have thought out a theoretical definition which would magically cover all Westerns and simultaneously exclude all other books. If such a theoretical definition is possible, it is not possible for me. I have contented myself with what I consider a viable, rough working definition. Basically, by "Westerns" I mean the term as commonly used. Westerns, as I have chosen to define them, are those books which deal primarily with the trans-Mississippi West. Most of these books, but by no means all, are concerned with the cattle industry of the Great Plains. I have not felt it necessary to justify my inclusion of books about the settlement of Oregon, or the mining camps of the mountain West, or even about Spanish California if they seemed relevant to the purposes of my discussion. In the interests of space I have eliminated, except for an occasional nod, novels of other frontiers. In many ways this is a purely logical distinction; the sea, as Stuart Chase has pointed out, is as truly a frontier as the Great West, and in the landscape of the mind the Mississippi River is no real barrier. But some kind of definition is necessary to limit a topic so large as the study of Western writing, and in consequence I have fallen back on a geographical limitation where one of thought was not feasible. For perhaps too arbitrary reasons, then, I have generally ignored, if not entirely neglected, the various frontiers east of the Mississippi, my expeditions east of the Father of Waters being, with one exception, in the nature of raids. The exception, I believe, needs no justification. It is impossible to speak of imaginative treatment of the American West without speaking of James Fenimore Cooper. With him, then, we will begin.

1385940

chapter two

James Fenimore Cooper:
The Materials of Western Story

A number of critics have recognized for some time that the supercilious contempt which has relegated James Fenimore Cooper to the place of a capital writer of books for pre-adolescents is misplaced. The revival of critical interest in Cooper and the resultant re-evaluation of his place in American literature have taken many forms. His papers are in the process of being carefully edited and thoughtfully annotated; the Leatherstocking Tales, certainly his best known if not his best work, have been redacted into one volume in the hope of attracting for them a wider audience; his influence on the tradition of later American Wild Westerns of the dime-novel type has been exhaustively traced;[1] and his works themselves have at last been given the sober critical attention which they unquestionably deserve, with the hoped-for result of extending Cooper's reputation beyond those few novels on which it now depends. This last, to lovers of Cooper, is without question the most heartening development of all; for it marks an almost new departure in discussion of Cooper, in which his artistic effort can be assessed as a whole, and in which criticism will not be reduced to a series of ambushes of isolated works.[2]

Whatever the final verdict may be on Cooper's place in the American literary pantheon, it is impossible to deny his phenomenal impact both on his contemporary reading public and on later American literary practice. Always a popular writer, both in America and Europe, his works nevertheless were often critically disparaged; but he at least received the tribute of being slavishly imitated both at home and abroad. In terms of his influence on subsequent American writing—as distinguished from the quite different question of the relative esthetic value of his various works—critics and authors alike have always recognized the paramount importance of the Leatherstocking Tales. Henry Nash Smith has shown the utter dependence of the later dime novel upon Cooper's originals, and has pointed out the incongruities inherent in adapting Natty Bumppo to the somewhat unsympathetic environment of the prairies; yet Cooper's influence on the literature of the West has by no means been confined to the subliterature of Beadle and his dime-novel cronies.

Cooper's importance to and influence on later writing about the West may be considered under two related but distinct heads. The first, and more easily recognizable, is to be found in the machinery of his novelistic practice, avidly picked up by later writers. The figure of the old hunter, obviously modeled after Natty Bumppo; the characters of the young lovers, often separated by wildly improbable romantic difficulties; the general outlines of the typical Cooper plot of wilderness peril and rescue; the emphasis on woodcraft; the figures of the good and bad Indians, and the Indian friend and confidant of the white hero; all these are imitated by Cooper's followers.

This aspect of Cooper's literary influence has long been recognized and, though of unquestioned importance, has already been sufficiently discussed by other critics. The second aspect of Cooper's literary significance has, however, been slighted. Much more basic to Cooper's craft, this legacy to later Western writers lies not so much in his handling of his material as in his attitude toward it, and is of supreme importance to the development of later serious Western fiction, however little it is understood by the dime novelists and the writers of sensational wild and woolly stories in all generations. Indeed, Cooper's most important contribution to later Western story is that he manages to create a way of looking at the events of American history which can make some kind of philosophical sense out of them. And later serious writers, however much they may disagree with Cooper's particular opinions, have found his method of approaching his historical material to be a profoundly workable one.

Cooper's concern, somewhat simple-mindedly stated for the sake of clarity, is to discover some way of interpreting the particular events of history in terms of the meaning of history in general. In order to do this, he realizes, one must first come to terms with the question of how events can be given meaning, with the apparent paradox of giving reflective value to the novel of action. His own approach is generally consistent throughout the five novels of the Leatherstocking Tales and the eighteen years in which they were composed, though he gives the best statement of it to the novel which is at once the last to be written and the first in the series, *The Deerslayer*.

The Deerslayer opens with an offhand statement about the nature of history.

> On the human imagination events produce the effects of time. Thus, he who has travelled far and seen much is apt to fancy that he has lived long; and the history that most abounds in important incidents soonest assumes the aspect of antiquity. In no other way can we account for the venerable air that is already gathering around American annals.[3]

In terms of Cooper's novelistic practice this quotation is of supreme importance in a number of not immediately evident ways. First of all, it suggests a way of using events to give "the effect of time," and is a wonderful practical answer to one of the great problems facing the early nineteenth-century American romancer, who felt that antiquity was necessary to the proper exercise of his craft, and simultaneously felt that he should write about America, a land without a past. Hawthorne's Preface to *The Marble Faun* states the dilemma clearly; this novel is set in the old world rather than the new, for "no author," says Hawthorne, "without a trial, can conceive of the difficulty of writing a romance about a country where there is no shadow, no antiquity, no mystery, no picturesque and gloomy wrong." Hawthorne accepts as axiomatic that history is necessary to give events meaning; and from this it follows that events in a land with no history cannot be more than sensational.

Stated thus baldly the idea seems rather silly; but Hawthorne's concern with antiquity reveals a more profound concern about the nature of historic cause and effect. His point is that an event cannot be seen to be significant until its results are known, and its results cannot be known until the passage of time has made them evident. How to make American events significant by applying to them a historic perspective? That was the problem.

The solutions tried were numerous, and generally unsatisfactory. One could, of course, as Hawthorne did, write about the few parts of America which actually did possess antiquity, mystery, and picturesque and gloomy wrong; but this eliminated most American material, and especially the "incomparable materials"—in Emerson's phrase in "The Poet"—of "the western clearing, Oregon and Texas." Or one could appropriate history not rightfully one's own, as did Longfellow when he wrote of Hiawatha. This was not too satisfactory either, for antiquity itself was unimportant if it was not relevant to American life. However belligerently Timothy Flint might affirm that to a reflective mind the mounds built by the prehistoric Indians gave as much food for thought as did "ruins, ... baronial castles, and monkish towers"[4] no one would believe him. For modern Europe descended directly from baronial castles and monkish towers; but the modern American and the mound-builders were not even collateral relations.

Cooper's practice, however, suggested a different approach by emphasizing that event rather than time was of primary importance for creating a historical perspective. The passage of time was significant only insofar as it of necessity produced the passage of event. But in a land where events move rapidly, a real history is created even without the passage of a great amount of time.

If one keeps Cooper's distinction between time and event clearly in mind, much in his own and later novelistic practice becomes clear. First, the primary importance of event serves to justify the exciting and often melodramatic plots of his own novels as well as of many later Westerns. If a "venerable air" is desirable in a novel, and if this venerability can be achieved through the swift passage of event rather than the slow passage of time, the more action the better. At the same time, the use of action to create a "venerable air" resolves the problem of how a novel which deals primarily with events can be given philosophical significance, and makes it possible for an author to write a blood-and-thunder tale which is also reflective. By using events in the way Cooper suggests, one may reconcile the novel of action with some kind of respectable philosophical end.

In a less general sense, Cooper's distinction permits a certain reflectiveness on the part of his characters which would be out of place in a novel more immediately concerned with the sensationalism of events. Just as events can become venerable without being remote, so can a man become venerable without being old; and such a man—if he is a literary character—can not only act with decision in the events into which he is thrown, but can reflect upon their meaning without himself seeming incongruous or anachronistic.

Properly used, this device can enable the author, either through the presence of a character or through his own personal interpolations into the narrative, to develop a peculiar double perspective toward his material, by which he is at once involved in his story's action and at the same time an observer of its meaning. But Cooper's insight goes one step further; he clearly understands that such a perspective implies that the Western story must be elegiac in mood; if it is an epic, it is an elegiac epic.

The almost virtual necessity for novels dealing with Western materials to be elegiac in tone is one of Cooper's most important insights, and incidentally explains much of his own novelistic practice. The character of Natty Bumppo himself is a case in point. In the first of the Leatherstocking Tales to be written[5]— *The Pioneers*—Natty Bumppo is already conceived of as a man with the venerability of age. In this story he actually is old— he admits to seventy-one years—but in the later tales his venerability remains unchanged no matter how young he may be. Indeed, in none of the three tales published before 1840 is Natty Bumppo young in years, nor, significantly, are either he or Chingachgook personally involved in the plots of romantic love of the respective tales; and in the two remaining, which detail Chingachgook's and Natty Bumppo's respective love stories, Cooper has so controlled his mood and the implications of his theme that the Tales turn out to be not about romantic love at all, but about its inevitable passing. Even when they are lovers Natty and Chingachgook are "old," an incongruity which has been recognized—and often overemphasized—by many of Cooper's critics.

In this regard it is worth mentioning that the individual Leatherstocking Tales without exception conclude with some kind of elegiac scene. Particularly the novels always end happily; the specific wrong which has given the plot its impetus has been righted and on the level of event all has turned out for the best; yet Cooper is never satisfied to leave the particular "happy ending" unqualified. The dominant note at the end of each Tale is always one of melancholy. *The Pioneers* offers the most striking example. The plot of this novel, without question one of Cooper's creakiest and most wildly improbable, ends with a mood—on one level at least—of universal harmony: the young lovers are reconciled with Judge Temple, whose apparent villainy turns out to have been due only to misunderstanding, and with his blessing they marry. But to this scene of general benevolence Natty Bumppo forms a striking exception. His history is sharply contrasted to the good fortune of the other characters, with whom he stands in total contrast. During the course of the novel the apparent alienation of the other characters is found to conceal bonds of real affection: not so with Natty who, at the beginning of the story, had been committed to a life near Templeton (Cooperstown) by loyalty to old Major Effingham and friendship for Chingachgook, but by the end is bereft of all his friends and, no longer tied by any human bonds to Templeton, must leave for the Great West. His departure, itself emblematic of the major theme of the Leatherstocking Tales, is symbolically emphasized by the burial of Chingachgook on the site of their own burned cabin. And when he leaves, he himself makes the point specific. Though urged to stay by the promise of being left free to hunt undisturbed in Judge Temple's woods, he refuses. Such woods, he says, "be nothing to a man that's used to the wilderness. I have took but little comfort sin' your father come on with his settlers; but I wouldn't go far, while the life was in the body that lies under the sod there [Major Effingham]. But now he's gone, and Chingachgook is gone; and you be both young and happy" (p. 474). The woods are gone, his friends are gone, and Natty himself, no longer at home in Templeton, must leave.

The elegiac tone of this scene is unmistakable, and Cooper has made it even more explicit by placing in Natty's mouth a speech which is an almost traditional *ubi sunt*, in order to emphasize the dominant motif of the action. Nor is this concluding scene of *The Pioneers* an isolated instance, though the presentation of this scene is less subtle than similar scenes in other of the Tales. In *The Prairie*, the device is obvious; the entire book in general and the last section in particular form a requiem for Leatherstocking. *The Last of the Mohicans* is reminiscent of *The Pioneers*. It ends with the death of Uncas, and a lament for the Mohican people by the old Indian prophet, Tamenund: "My day has been too long. In the morning I saw the sons of Unamis happy and strong; and yet, before the night has come, have I lived to see the last warrior of the wise race of the Mohicans" (p. 423). In *The Pathfinder* as well, Natty Bumppo, crossed in love, retires into the wilderness.

The most interesting use of this final elegy, however, may be seen in the curious ending of *The Deerslayer*. This novel, the first in the series but the last written, is unique among the Tales in that both Chingachgook and Natty Bumppo are participants in, rather than spectators of, the love plot. Like the rest of Cooper's tales of young lovers, Chingachgook's story ends happily; the end of the action of *The Deerslayer* finds him an accepted suitor. Yet the novel does not end with this; Cooper concludes the story of Chingachgook's courtship with a sudden glimpse fifteen years into the future, when he, his son Uncas, and Natty Bumppo again visit the region of their adventures. In the intervening fifteen years, we discover, Chingachgook's wife has died; and the remnants of his first warpath are either rotting or have disappeared. Chingachgook's and Natty Bumppo's feelings are again summed up in an elegy: "Chingachgook and his friend left the spot with melancholy feelings. It had been the region of their first War-Path, and it carried the minds of both to scenes of tenderness as well as to hours of triumph." They leave "to rush into new adventures, as stirring and as remarkable as those which had attended their opening career" (p. 572), in which, we should keep in mind, Uncas will be killed; their final return, later still, to the scene of their first warpath is as old men. The scene of *The Deerslayer*, as Cooper specifically reminds us, marks both the place of Chingachgook's first warpath and of his grave.

The pervasive elegiac mood which fills the Leatherstocking Tales is much more than a concession to the contemporary popular taste for sentimentality. It is essential to Cooper's mode of perception into the meaning of his subject. It serves to explain, though esthetically it may not completely justify, the superficially incongruous love plot in each of the Leatherstocking Tales. For the love plot in each Tale, like the plot dealing with war and physical danger, is to Cooper's eyes symbolic of the events of history considered without historic perspective; it is not, in his phrase, "venerable," nor does it have "the aspect of antiquity." Particular events, in Cooper's view, may turn out well, but the trend of history is tragic. The young lovers may marry, but we remember that Chingachgook has also married, and that his wife and son are dead; and though Natty Bumppo and Chingachgook are mighty warriors, their own prowess ironically dispossesses them from their heritage.

This method of perceiving the meaning of Western story through an elegiac perspective on the events of history is Cooper's great particular legacy to later writers in the Western tradition. Though sometimes merely a superficial device, at its best it becomes the vehicle for profound insight into various ironies of the historic process. Much more often than not the later frontiersman is conceived as the last man of some particular way of life, and often, like Cooper's heroes, he sees history in melancholy terms. The *ubi sunt* is his characteristic habit of speech: "'What's the use of improvements? When did cutting down trees make deer more plenty? Who ever cotched a bear by building a log cabin, or twenty on 'em? Who ever found wild buffalo, or a brave Indian in a city? Where's the fun, the frolicking, the fighting? Gone! Gone!'" soon becomes almost the archetypal utterance of the literary frontiersman.[6]

In more specifically Western story the influence of the Leatherstocking Tales is recognizable in the often-presented figure of the last cattle baron, protecting his domain against encroaching settlers; or that of the last Indian, like Chingachgook mourning the passing of tribe and kindred; or the last cowboy driven from his range, hoping for a land where "the old trails are the same, . . . and I can spread my loop without getting it caught in a fence-post." "How many of 'em would like to see the country as it was?"—whoever "they" may be—becomes a justification for telling Western stories which is stronger even than the compulsion to record—often shrilly—the facts of life in the old days; and the motto for one book, "Oh, how I wish I had the power to describe the wonderful country as I saw it then," has been the inspiration for many.[7]

Cooper's influence on later Western story, however, is not only limited to his insight into the implications of melancholy manipulation of characters; it is his view of the nature of history and of the ironies inherent in it which becomes of the greatest symbolic importance to later writers about the West. Of all early writers in the Western tradition, Cooper is the one to see most clearly that characters in Western story are only of secondary importance. Hence he manages on the whole to avoid successfully the series of trivial and pointless anecdotes which so many writers and critics find the only possible justification for writing of the West. Indeed, even Cooper's two most carefully developed characters, Natty Bumppo and Chingachgook, are of primary importance not as flesh-and-blood persons but as personified statements of general themes. The relationship between the two is more than a statement of the nature of friendship; this friendship is in turn seen as a symbol of the ironies of history and at the same time as an elegiac comment upon them.

Since the twin figures of Natty Bumppo and Chingachgook constantly recur in later Western fiction, their relationship ought to be analyzed at some length. To begin with, we should note that the long and occasionally tedious conversations between the two are representative of a moral debate—in Cooper's own terms—about the nature of "red gifts" and "white gifts."[8] Natty Bumppo typifies the potentialities of "white gifts"; Chingachgook, "red." Both men become representatives of the potentialities of their two distinct ways of life, the values of which are shown in a double way. The first is by means of the plots of the various Tales, in which Chingachgook and Natty are placed in opposition to various inferior types of whites and Indians—the latter generally, but not invariably, the dastardly "Mingoes." The second is by means of the running didactic argument which fills far too many pages of the Tales in which the two men discuss the nature of these opposed "gifts."

Without question this intellectual preoccupation with the nature of the distinction between red and white gifts is important in establishing the relationship of the two men toward each other and toward society. Yet this is only one aspect of the complex relationship between them; for Chingachgook is a tragic figure in his own right, and not merely a handy exemplum of red gifts to which Natty can refer in his long-winded arguments.

Readers of Cooper have long known, though too often overlooked, the fact that he uses a very specific chapter in Indian history as the background of the wars between Mohicans and Mingoes in which Chingachgook and Natty are involved. A brief recapitulation of this history seems appropriate here, since its importance to the thematic structure of the Tales has not fully been recognized, nor does Cooper anywhere systematically explain it.

The conflict between Mingoes and Mohicans is the last chapter of a long struggle which had begun before the settlement of the whites in America.[9] The two sides to this dispute were the two Indian peoples of the Iroquoians and the Algonkians. During the fourteenth and fifteenth centuries the Iroquoians had invaded upper New York from the West and gradually succeeded in driving out the resident Algonkian tribes, most particularly the Mohicans, from land which was theirs by right of hereditary possession. At the same time the Delawares, a larger Algonkian confederacy located to the east along the Atlantic seaboard, became engaged in conflict with the whites, who were encroaching upon their territories. The Algonkians, as a result, were caught between two fires. On the west, the Iroquois gradually gained ground, slowly driving the Mohicans eastward; on the east, white encroachments weakened the Delaware confederacy so badly that it could no longer aid in the battle against the Iroquois. Eventually both the Mohicans and the Delawares were completely defeated, and the whites and the Iroquoians reigned supreme over their ancestral territories. For his own thematic purposes Cooper places Chingachgook and Uncas at that point in the history of the long battle between the Iroquoians and Algonkians when the victory of the former was completely assured. (Indeed, Uncas was historically the last of the Mohican chiefs, though his biography was much different from Cooper's fictional treatment of it.)

In the figure of Chingachgook, placed as he is in a moment in historic time where he must both participate in and be a witness to the disintegration of his people, Cooper has made a thematic foil to Natty Bumppo. For though the two men are approximately the same age, Chingachgook is far the more "venerable." Even as a young man things have happened to him which make his perception more historic than Natty's; and his presence in the first four volumes of the Tales serves as a constant reminder of the ultimate futility that will result, whether they will it or not, from his and Natty's endeavors. Though Cooper becomes more subtle in his conception of the ramifications of this theme, in broad outlines his conception of Chingachgook is evident even in the first of the Tales to be written,

The Pioneers. Conventionally seen in the beginning of the book as a melancholy survivor of a dead race, by its end Chingachgook has achieved a kind of tragic grandeur. His death scene, at the end of *The Pioneers,* is a symbolic statement of the novel's major theme, and Natty Bumppo's bitter requiem for him—"Flesh isn't iron, that a man can live forever, and see his kith and kin driven to a far country, and he left to mourn, with none to keep him company" (p. 437)—reflects accurately his opinion of the gifts of a race which can cynically rob a man of his birthright by whiskey and then offer him Christian consolation for the good of his soul. Chingachgook dies true to his own gifts, renouncing at one and the same time the rum and religion which have made him, as he had earlier put it, "a Christian beast" (p. 185). The world as it was had been good enough for him in life, and he asks no better after death. "He is old and stiff," Natty reproaches Mr. Grant, the imperceptive minister who is worried about the state of the dying Indian's soul; "and you have made the game so scarce and shy, that better shots than him find it hard to get a livelihood. Now he thinks he shall travel where it will always be good hunting; where no wicked or unjust Indians can go; and where he shall meet all his tribe together ag'in" (p. 438). In short, he will go to a land remarkably like his own country before white gifts had "civilized" it, and his death song represents his final opinion of Judge Temple and the goodly folk of Templeton. *Desertum faciunt et pacem vocant,* as Tacitus said of the Romans: They make a desolation, and call it peace.

The second of the Tales to be written, *The Last of the Mohicans,* explores this theme of *The Pioneers* much more explicitly. For the real subject of this novel, as the title makes clear, is a broadly historical one, the destruction of the Delaware nation. Throughout the novel the curiously ambivalent title becomes more general in reference. Most immediately, of course, it refers to Uncas, the son of Chingachgook, who is last in historic succession of the Mohican chiefs. By the end of the tale, however, the reference has become twofold in application, including at once Uncas and his father, for upon Uncas' death Chingachgook ironically inherits the title which had before been a description of his son. But by this point the title no longer specifically refers to either character; it has become elevated to the description of a historic process—the final extermination of the Mohican nation. The development of the novel has been from the examination of particular character to the study of a universal historic process, and this progression is mirrored in the ambivalent reference of its title.

Through the figure of Chingachgook, in sum, Cooper is able simultaneously to universalize and render explicit the problems raised through the character of Natty Bumppo. The irony of Natty's character as a "man between" has often been noticed; he is invariably depicted as the good servant of a society in which he himself cannot live. Every victory which his side "wins" succeeds in further civilizing the wilderness in which Natty alone can exist. His particular success leads inevitably to his ultimate failure.

Not until later in his life, however, does Natty himself realize this. Only in *The Pioneers* and *The Prairie* has his particular historic optimism given way to the somber realization that he will never be at ease in Zion; but through the figure of Chingachgook, Cooper is able to give a perspective on the tragic nature of history which is superior to Natty's. In *The Deerslayer,* the first of the Leatherstocking series, Chingachgook and his people are already fighting with their backs to the wall. Natty offhandedly remarks, at one point in the novel, in explanation of who Chingachgook is, that "If he had his rights, he would be a great chief; but, as it is, he is only a brave and just-minded Delaware; respected, and even obeyed in some things, 'tis true, but of a fallen race, and belonging to a fallen people." He goes on, imperceptively, to mention how " 't would warm the heart within you to sit in their lodges of a winter's night, and listen to the traditions of the ancient greatness and power of the Mohicans!" (p 19). For the young Natty these are only stirring anecdotes; but for Chingachgook they already have a deeper significance.

In one way, then, Chingachgook parallels Natty. The history of the Leatherstocking Tales is from one point of view the story of the progressive alienation of the two men from society through the ironic workings of the historic process. But though in many ways parallel, Chingachgook and Natty are not identical; for Chingachgook is the more universalized figure. While Natty is only one of many frontiersmen, Chingachgook is the last chief of a once great people. Consequently every action of his is of more than merely individual significance. In *The Deerslayer* and *The Last of the Mohicans*, while Natty's involvement is only personal, Chingachgook's represents the last desperate strategems of a people fighting vainly for survival; and his presence in the Tales universalizes Cooper's picture of the historic process.

Chingachgook is important in another related way to the general scheme of the Leatherstocking Tales: he is the primary foil by which Cooper investigates a problem which is to become of supreme importance to later Western fiction—the nature of law. Two of the Tales—*The Pioneers* and *The Prairie*—deal very explicitly with this problem, and even in those Tales which do not primarily concern themselves with the nature of law the legal metaphor is not far to seek. Part of the irony of Chingachgook's situation is that he is a man with unimpeachable right to the land of which he has been bereft. Both interlopers—whites and Indians—have no legal claim to his property. The title of the whites is perhaps better, or at least more sophistically defensible, for the Delawares have ceded their land to them by treaty. The whites' methods of obtaining these treaties might not stand too close scrutiny, but at least the white men are within the letter of the law, if not its spirit. The Mingoes, in contrast, have no shade of legal justification for their encroachment upon Delaware territory except for the ancient and honorable principle that might makes right. They are the stronger party, and argument with them is useless.

Just how far Cooper wishes to push his comparison between outlaw Indians and legalistic whites is a matter of question, but from Chingachgook's point of view it is an academic question at best. For the result to him—whether through white chicanery or Indian force of arms—is the same. He is defrauded of his birthright. Significantly as well, he is defrauded by Indians morally inferior to him; for the Mingoes in Cooper's pages are as dastardly a set of rascals as could well be imagined. It goes without saying that this is a gross calumny upon the Iroquois confederacy, which, historians tell us, succeeded in establishing a stable political system based upon the principles of federal union. Or possibly Cooper's irony cuts deeper than critics have recognized.

In any event, the general history of the extinction of the Delaware people as symbolized through the particular figure of Chingachgook poses the dilemma of the basis for law which

The Pioneers and *The Prairie* specifically investigate. In *The Pioneers* law, though seen in terms of a specific incident, is discussed in terms of two conflicting abstract moral "rights." Specifically, these are presented in the novel in terms of Natty Bumppo's "right" to shoot game on land owned by another. Judge Temple, in one of Cooper's finest ironies, has loftily granted Natty the right to hunt on land which, by right of possession, Natty had owned much longer than the judge. The first time the conflict is mentioned, Cooper draws our attention to the paradoxical nature of the Judge's "permission." When he reproves Natty for what he considers unwarranted hunting, Natty replies, "There's them living who say that Nathaniel Bumppo's right to shoot on these hills is of older date than Marmaduke Temple's right to forbid him" (p. 12). Of course, if Natty's right is older than Judge Temple's, Chingachgook's is older than either, and in fact Natty has here put his finger on a very precise legal distinction often used to justify, by appeal to higher law, white appropriation of Indian lands. This is a careful discrimination which the Indians, as Timothy Flint puts it, "were not sufficient civilians to distinguish," between "the right of empire and the right of soil."[10] The right of empire, according to this distinction, is the right which a government has over its territories; it is, say, the right which the United States has to the lands within its boundaries. The right of soil, in contrast, is the personal right of any individual to use whatever property he owns in any way he chooses; it is the right of a farmer to plant crops, of a rancher to raise livestock, of a miner to dig for gold on his own land. In case of conflict between these two rights, according to early nineteenth-century legal casuistry, the claims of the right of soil are basic, and those of the right of empire must give way before them. The Indians did not understand this distinction, and assumed that the right of empire was the basic right, and that it gave them the right to prescribe how the "empire" itself might be used. Consequently, when the white man destroyed the woods in order to plant crops, the Indian did not accept his right to do so.

The difference ultimately is one of conception of the nature of property. For the white, private property was supreme; for the Indian, property was conceived as communitarian, as belonging to the tribe, and insofar as he recognized the right of soil at all it was only as the right of the individual to hunt on property owned and shared by everyone. This distinction is clearly the one which lies behind the argument over hunting in *The Pioneers*. Judge Temple assumes the primacy of the right of soil; Natty, of the right of empire. But Chingachgook stands in the background as an example of the way the conflict is always settled. In actual practice the argument is not decided on the basis of *a priori* merit, but on the pragmatic basis that possession is nine points of the law. If possession is the primary principle of law, any arguments about the right of empire and the right of soil become purely academic, for in this very principle the right of soil is tacitly understood to be supreme. Hence any moral arguments about the nature of right are, practically speaking, irrelevant even if—as Cooper at least speculatively suggests—the claims of the right of empire are indeed the morally just ones. This explains why, when Natty Bumppo and the Judge argue over the nature of right Natty invariably wins. But his victory is always a victory of words alone; win or lose, the argument has already been decided.

Through this argument over the nature of law Cooper reinforces his profoundly tragic view of history. For he sees clearly, in terms of this legal metaphor, that the right of empire cannot be divorced other than logically from the right of soil. The right of soil implies the right of empire, for on the way land is used depends the way of life of its possessors. A land cleared of trees and planted with crops, though it will support farmers will not support those who live by hunting, as Natty points out time and again in *The Pioneers*. The right to farm and the right to hunt are mutually incompatible, and the stronger side—the farmers—will inevitably prevail. Natty's simple requiem for his dead friend marks his realization of how little right has to do with law, and how powerless morality is when confronted with force. For by the end of *The Pioneers* Natty has finally arrived at the "historic" view which only Chingachgook had previously possessed. He can at last see that the meaning behind the events of his friend's life—and of his own—is that history favors not the just but the strong, and that law is an expression not of morality, but of force.

This distinction between the right of empire and the right of soil, though often differently stated, becomes one of the great conflicts in later Western fiction. As it usually appears in Western writing, the argument becomes one of the conflict between possession and ownership, or between ownership and use. A typical theme, for instance, is that of the conflict between the cattlemen and the sheepmen. Neither one of these groups "owns" the range. Their possession is ultimately only by right of soil— the right to use the range to graze their livestock. In theory there should be no conflict between the two interests except that of the equitable sharing of available range. Such however is not the case. Sheep, it is alleged by the cattlemen, graze so close to the ground that they destroy the range for cattle. Hence, once sheep are admitted to the range the cattlemen are doomed. The two interests cannot exist together. As a result, any law which legislates the equal rights of sheep and cattle interests with apparent fairness, in fact discriminates against the cattlemen, in exactly the same way that in Cooper's works Indian treaties which cede equal use of land to the whites discriminate against the Indians.[11]

A more common theme than the conflict between the cattle and sheep interests is the running quarrel between the cattlemen and the nesters which is the basis for much Western fiction. This typical story expresses a more basic conflict than that between the cattle and sheep interests, and this perhaps explains why it plays so prominent a part in fictional treatment of the West. For the cattlemen and sheepmen, however much they may detest each other personally, are in theoretical agreement about the basic right to graze freely on the open range. Anathema to both parties is the moral position represented by the nesters that a man can fence off one hundred and sixty acres and call it "his." Once the nester has fenced the land, neither cattle nor sheep may graze freely on it. If there are enough nesters to fence in all the land—or, as usually happens, all the water holes—the cattle and sheep interests must perforce be driven out. The question, in sum, becomes one of how the land shall be used, rather than which of two opposing interests shall use the land in a manner both would theoretically approve.

The conflict between the homesteaders and the cattlemen is, transposed to the Great Plains, exactly the conflict over "clearings" Cooper presents in *The Pioneers*. In both cases the debate focuses upon two mutually incompatible points of view, and, by presenting the ideological conflicts between them, attempts a metaphorical assessment of the historic process. Of more specific interest, however, to return to our discussion of law in

The Pioneers, is the way in which each party tries to seek legal justification for its actions. Significantly, as in Cooper, the law finally reflects not the morally correct course of action but the particular economic and social interests of the stronger party.

Conrad Richter's *The Sea of Grass* forms an interesting case in point. The book opens with a courtroom scene in which a number of cowboys are acquitted of the charge of running a homesteader off his land; the cattle interests are in power and no jury in the county will send cattlemen to prison. Toward the end of the book Jim Brewton, the cattle baron, is again haled into court on charges of destroying homesteaders' property; by now the homesteaders are the stronger group in the territory, and he is convicted. In neither trial are the rights and wrongs of the particular case presented as of any real importance. Clearly in both cases the law reflects nothing more than the wishes of the dominant party.

In sum, the terms of the debate which pervades later novels of the West about the future of America tend to follow very closely Cooper's earlier formulation. More specifically, the legal terms of this argument are presented in a way which mirrors almost exactly the earlier nineteenth-century controversy over the right of empire and the right of soil. Nearly always there are two antagonistic parties in this quarrel, one of which thinks in terms of "ours," and another which thinks in terms of "mine and thine." The Indians' warfare with the encroaching whites, the cattlemen's struggles with the nesters, the mountain men's opposition to the settlers, are among the many fictional ways in which this clash of interests is presented.

Yet such plots, with their often mechanical and convention-ridden statement of these two opposing points of view, by no means exhaust its possibilities in Western fiction. On a slightly more abstract level, the sexual plot of the Western is often visualized in the same terms. As Cooper so clearly saw in *The Pioneers* and elsewhere, the ultimate taming of the frontier is beautifully symbolized by marriage. Elizabeth Effingham, *née* Temple, bidding farewell to Natty Bumppo at the end of *The Pioneers,* is the first clearly visualized statement of a ubiquitous later image in Western fiction. *The Virginian* ends with a marriage; when the bride comes to Yellow Sky the old way of life, aptly symbolized by a bachelor, must go; even *Destry Rides Again* concludes with the hero's succumbing to the lure of

matrimony and shortly thereafter hanging up his gun. Though
at times, it is true, this matrimonial image is nothing more than
a meaningless convention, inherently it is a way of underscoring
the significance of many books about the West. For the bride
has one thing in common with the nesters; both are emblematic
of the death of the older, more primitive way of life of the cattlemen. Quite often the woman is seen in exactly the same terms in
which settlers are elsewhere described; she thinks of "mine"
where her husband thinks of "ours." As an old song has it,
"Don't fence me in"; both the nester and the bride are emblems
of the disappearance of free range.

The presence of women on the frontier is important in another
way to Cooper's view of the nature of law. Women in Cooper's
pages need to be protected; they are a particular example of the
general group which he often refers to as "the weak," and hence
their presence implies the necessity for some order to watch
over them. Cooper's fiction abounds with ladies who have gotten
too far away from the protection of society and to whom, as a
result, all kinds of untoward things happen. Each of the
Leatherstocking Tales except for *The Pioneers* concerns itself
at least peripherally with women who, for one reason or another,
are placed in some kind of wilderness peril which would have
been avoided had they remained behind in the settlements.[12]
Such women, of course—as "the weak" in general—must be rescued or protected, and in Cooper's world they become emblems
for the necessity of some kind of law, even though this law
may not, abstractly considered, be completely fair or just.

Of all the Leatherstocking Tales *The Prairie* is the one which
most thoroughly explores the necessary dependence of society
upon law. Whereas in *The Pioneers* Cooper had addressed himself to a discussion of the moral basis of law, arriving at the
conclusion that law cannot claim a basis in abstract justice, in
The Prairie he turns to a different if related question, the
absolute necessity of law to society. Though it may be unjust,
though it is often unfair, still it cannot be dispensed with.

It is true that *The Prairie* does not single-mindedly concern
itself with this theme, for in many ways this novel is reminiscent
of the concerns Cooper had previously investigated in *The
Pioneers*. The conflict between the Pawnee and the Sioux for
control of the prairie, for instance, recalls the history of the
earlier battles between the Delawares and the Mingoes; and

Cooper remarks that the outcome of the struggle will be the same—the whites will finally take it all. In this regard, the mention of the Louisiana Purchase which opens the novel is of interest, and Natty stresses the point explicitly in a conversation with Hard Heart, the chief of the Pawnee. Hard Heart has queried the justice of selling the Indians' lands without consulting them. "Where were the chiefs of the Pawnee-Loups when this bargain was made?" he asks, to which Natty replies, "Right enough—right enough, and where were truth and honesty also? But might is right, according to the fashions of the 'arth; and what the strong choose to do, the weak must call justice" (pp. 219-20). This could almost come from *The Pioneers;* but its explicit nature if nothing else serves to show that this question is not Cooper's ultimate concern in *The Prairie.*

This difference in emphasis between the two novels is also clearly stated at the beginning of *The Prairie* when Natty meets Ellen Wade in the encampment of Ishmael Bush's party. He tells her that she had left behind her in the settlements a friend who was "always bound to look to the young and feeble." She, not understanding his drift, asks who this friend is; he replies: "The law! 'tis bad to have it, but I sometimes think it is worse to be entirely without it." For, he goes on significantly, "the law is needed when such as have not the gifts of strength and wisdom are to be taken care of" (p. 23). This statement could well stand as a motto to *The Prairie.*

That the law may be unjust to some had been amply shown in *The Pioneers;* that some kind of law is nevertheless a necessity everywhere is shown in *The Prairie.* Again, Cooper's implication is tragic, for at no time in either book is the law presented as at all desirable in itself. The best that can be said for it is that it serves as a protection of the weak against the strong, a shield to save the impotent many from the rapacious few.

The plot of *The Prairie* centers around the figure of Ishmael Bush, a man who has crossed the "Big River" in order to escape the law. Ishmael had killed a deputy sheriff who had tried to evict him from land on which he had squatted, and he had gone west to escape apprehension. In a sense this places him in a position similar to Natty, who had also metaphorically been dispossessed and had come west to avoid civilization. There is, however, one real difference in their situations; for Natty had come west alone, while Ishmael Bush had brought with him a party consisting of his family and a few others. In the course of the story Asa, Ishmael's son, is murdered by Abiram, Ishmael's brother. This forces upon Ishmael the necessity for acting in accord with some kind of law even though ironically he had hoped to escape law altogether by leaving it behind in the settlements. He discovers, of course, that this is impossible, for he has misunderstood the nature of law. Law is not the kind of thing one can leave behind in the settlements, but is a necessity wherever there is more than one human being. As Natty says, man's "natur is the same, be he born in the wilderness, or be he born in the towns" (p. 283). In sum, law is a necessity arising from the imperfections in the character of man and not, as Ishmael Bush had first thought, an extraneous tyranny applied to him from outside. Ishmael himself expresses his recognition of the necessity for law by executing Abiram in accordance with Old Testament legal theory of an eye for an eye, after which he and his party return once more to the settlements.

As this discussion should by now have made clear, I find it difficult to accept the present critical consensus that Cooper is somehow or other on the side of progress. The whole burden of the Leatherstocking Tales, it seems to me, makes quite the opposite point, that the course of history is a disaster. Because history reflects the basic evil in the nature of man, absolute morality in Cooper's world is always doomed to defeat, for man creates law and society in his own image, and that image is imperfect.

If we keep in mind the fact that Cooper's final concern is to comment upon the nature of man in general rather than the facts of frontier history in particular, much of the argument over the relative merit of red gifts and white can be seen in a different perspective. It has been insufficiently noticed that, to Cooper, man's nature is everywhere the same, and his gifts are trained into him by society. Neither red gifts nor white can change the basic imperfections of his nature. Natty's own comments on the difference between red and white gifts always metaphorically make this point. To white men he affirms the superiority of certain red gifts; to the Indians, the superiority of certain white ones. But his total view does *not* come to the position that, when taken in a lump, one set of gifts is superior to the other. Nor does it come to the position that either red or white man is basically an admirable creature. Cooper's view is much more tragic:

history, which reflects the imperfect nature of man, is a record not of man's consistent success but of his successive failures.

An insufficient recognition of this fact has kept many commentators from a clear understanding of the role which Natty himself plays in the Leatherstocking Tales. Natty is, Cooper tells us in the Preface to the Tales, conceived as a creation who possesses the "better qualities" of both white and red life. He is not, in short, a flesh-and-blood man. Morally he represents a condition unattainable by ordinary humanity, a combination of both red and white "gifts." His nature, to paraphrase, is *not* the same as other men's, though Cooper has drawn him so realistically that he does not have the coldness or abstractness of a typical allegorical figure. Cooper indicates Natty's superior nature by giving him only superior human gifts, unalloyed with the gift to do evil which is a necessary result of the imperfect nature of our common humanity; and Cooper removes him from society, placing him between red men and white, so that Natty's comments may be upon the failures of both.

This detachment from society is another aspect of the "venerability" of Natty Bumppo mentioned above. Cooper must remove Natty as far as possible from direct involvement in the world about him in order that he may more objectively comment upon it; for his perspective is the unbiased and clear perspective of history upon the confused world of event.

From Natty's historic perspective, the world he sees about him gives no particular cause for rejoicing. The changes he observes, whatever others may think of them, record no more than the inevitable unfolding of man's imperfect nature. Wherever he looks, in the forests of Old York or the prairies of the Great West, he sees that the fact of history is change; but that this change is representative of moral progress he wholeheartedly denies.

Perhaps in this respect he is an expression of his creator's often analyzed aristocratic views. But whether he is or not, in him Cooper has created one of the most profound literary commentators on the nature and potential of American democracy, and his criticisms strike to the heart of the most cherished shibboleth of American life. For that better society which Americans believe they will realize somehow, somewhere, in some distant future, Natty says has already been irrecoverably lost.

When Cooper himself looks about at the American scene he,

like his character, is impressed with the same fact which has astonished commentators of all eras about the United States; the magnitude of change. But that any particular part of this change is necessarily representative of progress he doubts. In his Preface to *The Pathfinder* he remarks the great transformations of the West which have occurred in his own lifetime. "That great results are intended to be produced by means of these wonderful changes," he sums up, "we firmly believe; but that they will prove to be the precise results now so generally anticipated, in consulting the experience of the past, and taking the nature of man into account, the reflecting and intelligent may be permitted to doubt" (pp. v-vi).

The way in which the nature of man qualifies his ideals is most profoundly shown in Cooper's discussion of law and justice. As Cooper sees it, the two are by no means synonymous. Law is a necessity to society, but this by no means makes it an unequivocal good. Though in the best of all possible worlds it may be necessary, even in the worst of ideal ones it would not be required. The workings of the law in the Leatherstocking Tales are always to be taken on balance; never a positive good, at times they are a positive evil. And this is Cooper's point. In its very nature law must be imperfect, for it is an expression not of man's strengths but of his weaknesses. The record of human striving, law is subject to the same limitations which warp the course of history. For man's "gifts are not equal to his wishes," as Natty says in *The Prairie*. "That he would mount into the heavens, with all his deformities about him, if he only knew the road, no one will gainsay, that witnesses his bitter strivings upon 'arth" (p. 283). But he does not know the road, and his bitter striving can lead him no closer to heaven. He may change, but he does not progress.

As a result, the chronicle of man's impact upon the wilderness becomes at last the history of his self-deception. It is a record of brave hopes and of how they are not realized. It is elegiac in tone, for it celebrates the greatest of man's defeats, the conquest of his ideals by his humanity.

No summary such as this can hope to do more than suggest some of the aspects of Cooper's genius. Nor would a thorough explication of the Leatherstocking Tales, even if space permitted, be to the point in the context of our present discussion. But hopefully this short survey has suggested the most important aspects of Cooper's influence on later Western story.

It is, I think, no exaggeration to say that every major theme of the Leatherstocking Tales is picked up by later writers about the West. Whether any particular writer happens to agree with Cooper's philosophical, political, or ideological conclusions—whether, indeed, my own reading of Cooper is not hopelessly eccentric—is not really the point at issue. For Cooper's conclusions are not really what is significant to later writers, who by no means generally either accept or agree with them. His major importance to them, as I have tried to indicate, lies in his discovery of a viable method for the interpretation of Western history which is potentially more profound than the mere reportage of sensational event. Cooper's method of narration is one later writers can use to obtain a perspective on the facts of the American western movement which can render them capable of symbolic and philosophical interpretation.

The clearest example of this may be seen in the character of Leatherstocking himself. Here Cooper has seized upon a fact of American history which he has transformed into a statement of the nature of a general American dilemma. He has taken the sober case-history of a pioneer and universalized it into a statement of the contradictions inherent in the very nature of pioneering. Where he goes beyond the treatment accorded the theme of the pioneer by earlier writers is precisely in his ability to universalize not only his pioneer but the implications of the theme of pioneering.

Leatherstocking owes a great deal of his being to the figure of Daniel Boone who, since John Filson's 1784 account of him in *Kentucke,* had been assumed—for literary purposes at least—to be the epitome of the pioneer character. By 1823, when *The Pioneers* appeared, he had been the subject of numerous prose accounts and one long narrative poem modeled on *Paradise Lost,* all of which depended very closely on Filson's historical summary of Boone's life. But all these accounts, the best of which was Timothy Flint's *Biographical Memoir of Daniel Boone* (1833)— exactly contemporaneous with Cooper—had assumed that the significance of Boone's life was somehow bound up with the recounting of his adventures. These adventures ultimately were of importance in a didactic way. They showed the providential order which had, for its inscrutable but all-wise purposes, sent the pioneers westward. "Thus we behold Kentucke," says Filson, "lately an howling wilderness, the habitation of savages and wild beasts, become a fruitful field."[13] The purpose behind the narration of pioneer history was to show the triumph of democracy.

Cooper, however, understands far better than Filson and the writers who follow his lead that the real significance of the figure of the pioneer is more profound than this. The conversion of a howling wilderness into a fruitful field may well be a fact of history, but the meaning of this fact lies behind the mere description of the process. And, as Cooper explains the process of civilizing the howling wilderness, he sees that it can best be apprehended in terms of conflicting and paradoxical ideologies. His Leatherstocking, unlike Filson's and Flint's historic Boone, is not particularly enraptured of the civilizing process; for, from a moral point of view, the future can at best bring nothing better than the present.

Indeed, there is a considerable implication in the Leatherstocking Tales that change may very well be for the worse, for man's increasing ability to transform the world about him may in itself have drastic implications. Cooper's particular criticisms of the American experiment in colonization of the frontier seem to be primarily social rather than moral ones. Morally, the Mingoes or the Sioux are about on a par with the white despoilers, as far as their will to do evil goes. Their ability to do harm, however, is much more limited. Their only crimes are against other human beings, and even here their power to wreak destruction is less than that of the whites. Moreover, they cannot destroy the riches of nature with the same facility as the white men. The Indians, though they may have the will, have not the capacity to destroy possessed by the good people of Templeton who, in some of the most powerful scenes in *The Pioneers,* ruthlessly lay waste to nature. The Indians in Cooper's tales can destroy only themselves, but the whites can destroy themselves and nature too, and Cooper suggests that here is the real danger to America; for once the forest is cut down and the game exterminated, they are gone for good. At that point it is a little late to lament their loss—but it just may be true, as Natty tells Obed Bat in *The Prairie,* that "the garden of the Lord was the forest then, and is the forest now, where the fruits do grow and the birds do sing, according to his own wise ordering" (p. 232).

chapter three

The Sea of Grass

The idea that the Great West is, in Natty Bumppo's phrase, "the garden of the Lord," is a notion by no means confined to Cooper. Though Natty himself had serious reservations about the ideal nature of the prairie—for him the garden was the forests of "old York" before they had been cut down—his basic assumption that the Garden of the Lord consisted, in general terms, of the natural world before it had been blessed by civilization is one which is held in common by many later writers about the West. The idea has a long polemical—and at times quasi-respectable—history in American thought. In part it represents a conscious propaganda effort to counteract the idea that the West was, as the alternative myth had it, "the Great American Desert"; and it reflects as well a much more venerable debate about man's relative happiness in society or in a state of nature.[1]

Western fiction as a whole, following Cooper's lead, tends to present these two related debates about the nature of the frontier itself and of life upon it in terms of polarized points of view. The great "fact" of American history—the presence of the frontier, whether it be specifically conceived in terms of the Garden of the Lord or the Great American Desert—becomes in Western fiction a symbol about which two conflicting groups of characters have two diametrically opposed sets of ideas. One of these groups consists of those who, following Natty Bumppo, wish to leave the garden as it is. This faction is an anti-progressive one, both in its ideas and usually in the social position in which it finds itself in the fictional world of any particular story. The other group consists of those who, following Judge Temple and others of Cooper's civilizers, wish to improve the garden. Quite often this group is conceived as the party of the future, just as the anti-progressive faction is conceived as the party of the past, though such is not invariably the case.

Writers who are in general sympathetic to the view that history or life was somehow better in the good old days and who, as a result, tend toward the opinion that history is an ironic tragedy, are—not surprisingly—inclined to see the defeat of the old by the new as emblematic of moral as well as purely historic decline. But this by no means exhausts the thematic possibilities inherent in the interaction between these two points of view. Sometimes, in literature of a more anecdotal cast, the conflict is no more profound than a statement of how one side succeeds in putting something over on the other, as in the occasionally amusing, often tiresome, stories in which a dude is the butt of a joke perpetrated by those in the know; but more frequently the difference is presented, as it is in Cooper, as an emblem of some more basic concern for which the ideological conflict between the two opposed factions is only a metaphor.

In poor Western fiction the conflict between these two polarized points of view is predictably didactic, faithfully mirroring the hoary Enlightenment argument about whether man is happier within society or outside of it. Such fiction adds nothing new to this debate. It is true that the noble savage in such literature is occasionally at least superficially original. Unlike his continental forebears, he is not always an Indian; but though he may be, and often is, a frontiersman, a prospector, a romantic desperado, or a cowboy, he has to hand the tried-and-true traditional weapons of his intellectual ancestors—a quiver of clichés which he lets fly at a defenseless society.

Yet even in poor Western fiction this Enlightenment argument has an immediacy which gives it a different quality from its European counterpart. For in America there was always the chance that the argument might be taken seriously and interpreted in a literal fashion. However sympathetic an Enlightenment Londoner might feel to the theoretical position represented by Peter the Wild Boy, there was little danger of his resolving Peter's criticisms of civilized ways of life in any pragmatic way. In America, contrariwise, running off to the Great West was a distinctly practical alternative if life amid the corruptions of society were to become too unbearable, and one which was in fact indulged in by a great many people, not all of whom by any means were of that multitude of silent dispossessed who make up the majority of colonists in all times and of all countries. The early life of a President of the United States gives a clear and not particularly unusual example of how a philosophical principle might very easily be turned into a pragmatic course of action.

The ubiquitous argument in Western fiction, then, over what to do with the Garden of the Lord reflects a certain practical concern in America of which the often very similar European debate over the relative ideal philosophical value of primitive or social life is almost entirely devoid. Nor is the immediate relevance of this debate confined simply to discussion of the possible alternatives facing any particular individual who might relinquish his settled way of life to go West and grow up with the country. For the question of what to do with the Garden of the Lord is a question which affected—and to some extent still does affect—the future of American society at large. The very intensity of the concern in America, which is by no means confined to the pages of Western fiction, emphasizes the real importance that Americans attach to this question. In Europe, in contrast, the Enlightenment debate over the relative worth of primitivism always smelled rather strongly of the scholar's lamp. Nothing could be more indicative of the difference than Dr. Johnson's refutation of the rhetorical question of an English officer who had allegedly said of his experiences in America: "Here am I, free and unrestrained, amidst the rude magnificence of Nature, with this Indian woman by my side, and this gun, with which I can procure food when I want it: what more can be desired for human happiness?" To which Dr. Johnson crushingly replied: "Do not allow yourself, Sir, to be imposed upon by such gross absurdity.... If a bull could speak, he might as well exclaim,—Here am I with this cow and this grass; what being can enjoy better felicity?"[2]

Unlike Dr. Johnson, Americans would not find the question so absurd, nor would they find the truth of the matter so easily attainable. But the basic difference between Dr. Johnson and most Americans is not so much one of philosophical disagreement as of practical relevance. Traditionally Americans have felt and, however wrongly, still feel that they have the option to choose for or against society, albeit perhaps only in peripheral ways. As a result, the choice is not so simple to them as it was to Dr. Johnson, nor can the alternatives clearly be stated in terms of good and bad. Deeply committed in practice to an often fuzzily defined ideal of "progress," they are equally committed to a quite different theoretical position that the good life must be found somewhere outside the "rat race." Their often pathetic and occasionally absurd attempts to reconcile these two ideals may well seem amusing to the disinterested or unsympathetic observer: the stockbroker who discovers true wisdom at the knee of his Indian guide, the harried commuter attempting a rediscovery of the serenity of Walden Pond on his half-acre lot in Suburbia, and other kindred absurdities are a recognized part of contemporary demonology. Yet the supercilious commentator often fails to recognize that such phenomena reflect an endless internal debate about how best to live one's life, nor does he take sufficient cognizance of the fact that the American approaches this perennial philosophical problem from a rather singular point of view which is reflected in American primitivistic literature and which sets that literature distinctly apart from its European relations. For European primitivistic literature is an eccentric offshoot from a traditional preoccupation of Western philosophy, the study of how one organizes his mind in order to preserve its inner tranquility against unpleasant external facts which he is powerless to change. The preoccupation of American primitivistic literature, in contrast, is quite different; it is an exercise not in philosophical resignation but in the study of practical alternatives which the American hopes will make the outer world conform more closely to his inner wishes.

As a result, American primitivistic literature generally does not have the static quality of European. In particular, the literature which concerns itself primarily with the theme of the settlement of the Great West rarely turns into the sterile traditional philosophical debate over whether one is happier within society or out of it; rather it concerns itself with how man may best change (or not change) the world around him in order to make it a more desirable place to live. Consequently this literature does not content itself with the mere statement of different academic points of view about man's role *vis à vis* society, but concerns itself much more with the practical relevance of these viewpoints to life in the external world. Where primitivism traditionally had been a statement of man's reservations about a social order which he was powerless to change, the literature dealing with the settlement of the Garden of the Lord is typically a study of man's hopes that he may shape the course of history.

This typical attitude in American literature about the settlement of the Great West is a basic thematic concern in the works of A. B. Guthrie, Jr., one of the best contemporary authors now writing in the Western tradition. In many respects Guthrie's work bears a striking particular resemblance to Cooper's. The old mountain man Dick Summers, a major character in *The Big Sky* (1947) and *The Way West* (1949) (the first two volumes of Guthrie's Western trilogy which concludes with *These Thousand Hills* [1956]), is a close relative of the old Natty Bumppo of *The Prairie*. The sprawling, episodic plots of all three novels are strongly reminiscent of Cooper, as are various particular devices—characters who turn up in more than one book, for instance, and families whose descendants become characters in later works—which Guthrie uses to give unity to his individual works and to his trilogy in general. Like the five Leatherstocking Tales, Guthrie's trilogy is in a very real sense one book, and Guthrie's subject, like Cooper's, is the settlement of successive American frontiers, concluding with what each considers the "last frontier."

To emphasize Guthrie's similarity to Cooper is to run the risk of implying that Guthrie has been a mechanical or unoriginal imitator of "the master." Such is most emphatically not the case. As, hopefully, the following discussion will make clear, the particular resemblances between the two authors are due more to similar attitudes each brings to his material than to philosophical agreement about the metaphysical nature of the Garden of the Lord. For the two authors are not ultimately in accord over the ideological significance of the civilization of the last frontier. Guthrie, especially in his two later books, is much less pessimistic than Cooper; where Cooper's view of the course of civilization grew darker in his later works, Guthrie's grows more optimistic. The affinities between the two authors, then, are those of craft rather than of philosophy.

Guthrie's history of the frontier begins, in *The Big Sky*, with the story of Boone Caudill, who runs away from his home in

Kentucky after a family quarrel, hoping to find an uncle of his who is a trapper beyond the Missouri. After sundry adventures he arrives in St. Louis, where he and Jim Deakins, a friend he had met on the road, take jobs as deck hands on a keelboat bound up the Missouri River on a fur-trading expedition. Also aboard are an old mountain man, Dick Summers, and a young Blackfoot squaw, Teal Eye, whom the traders hope to return to her relatives and thus buy immunity from Indian attack. This ingenious plan is thwarted when Teal Eye escapes; soon after, the keelboat is attacked and everyone killed except Boone, Jim, and Dick Summers. The three survivors throw in together and, under the guidance of Summers, Boone and Jim are transformed from tenderfeet into mountain men.

The next section of *The Big Sky* describes the almost idyllic life these three live, trapping in the mountains and coming together with the other mountain men for the trappers' annual rendezvous. Though it is true that furs are getting scarcer every year, and that every year as well there is less room for the individual mountain men because the great American Fur Company has a monopoly on the trade and successfully keeps the price of pelts down, still these are happy times. The three men are congenial, though temperamentally very different: Jim is gregarious, delighting in the sociability of the trappers' rendezvous and the summers which he spends in the settlements; Boone is introspective and moody; and Dick Summers is a cheerful stoic, accepting life as it comes, while still maintaining his ability to comment upon it.

This idyllic existence, however, contains within it the seeds of its own destruction, and one by one the three men are driven from it. Dick Summers is the first; he grows too old for the hardships of the mountain man's life and retires to some property he owns in Missouri which he hopes to farm. For the other two the end of the idyll is more abrupt. Boone hopes for a greater happiness by first finding and then living with Teal Eye, in a situation reminiscent of the one mentioned previously to which Dr. Johnson took such violent exception. Nor is Boone's experiment more successful than Dr. Johnson would have prophesied; his and Teal Eye's child is born blind, and Boone, who wrongly suspects Jim of having seduced Teal Eye, kills him and returns to the settlements.

Boone is no more at home in the clearings, however, than was

Natty Bumppo, and in a brilliant series of ironic vignettes Guthrie shows how Boone's years in the wilderness have rendered him unfit for civilization. His trip east is an ironic inversion of his first escape, ending with his return to the home from which he had originally run away. He finds that he cannot stand the confinements of society nor the dullness of life in the settlements. The complacent attitude his relatives and old acquaintances have toward him—symbolized by a mindless and conventional "nice" girl who stands, in opposition to Teal Eye, as a metaphor of life within the social order—alienates him, and in a splendidly conceived scene of renunciation he reasserts his independence from the trammels of civilization by seducing the hopeful bride and again escaping to the wilderness.

From his home in Kentucky Boone flees to Dick Summers' farm in Missouri where he finds Summers married to a nagging wife and unhappily tilling the soil—another pointed comment about the price society exacts from its members. Boone and Summers reminisce about old times, and Boone confesses to the murder of Jim. In the concluding scene Boone, now a man with no home either in the clearings or in the wilds, once more leaves society—but this time he has no place to go. "It's like it's all sp'iled for me now, Dick—Teal Eye and the Teton and all. Don't know as I ever can go back, Dick. Goddam it! Goddam it!" (p. 386), he says as he leaves.

So cursory a summary of *The Big Sky* is unfortunate in many ways, most important of which is that plot summary perforce eliminates all evidence of Guthrie's greatest literary ability, his gift for the re-creation of history. One of the most important factors in the esthetic success of *The Big Sky* and of his later novels is Guthrie's peculiar talent for evoking the emotional spirit as well as the factual substance of certain periods of the past. Part of this talent is undoubtedly due to his remarkable industry as a researcher—*The Big Sky* and *The Way West* at least may profitably be read as fictionalized historical study—but more important is an ability Guthrie shares with Cooper, the skill of calling forth a certain mood from his historical raw material which he can apply to the sprawling plot and multitude of characters of the episodic novel. Like Cooper, Guthrie unifies his story by means of the consistency of his attitudes toward his material rather than by the mechanical means of a well-made plot. In *The Big Sky* this is a real strength, for it gives to the novel a looseness in detail which is eminently believable, while at the same time saving it from pointlessness.

Plot summary of *The Big Sky* does serve to emphasize at least one of the novel's thematic concerns, however, a concern which Guthrie shares with Cooper—the theme of the alienation of the hero from society. Even when allowances are made for the different ways of telling a story in the early nineteenth and mid-twentieth centuries, *The Big Sky* is still strikingly like the various novels in the Leatherstocking Tales in this particular regard. The novel's final scene, for instance, is generally reminiscent of the endings of the Leatherstocking Tales, and specifically reminds one of the final scene of *The Pioneers.* Boone himself, in fact, is not unlike Natty Bumppo in many respects. He has, as does Natty, the "gifts" of both red and white men, and like Natty also he stands apart from both societies. Unlike Natty, however, Boone wishes to belong to one society or the other, while Natty had been happy beyond all social order. But this difference is more apparent than real. Where Natty had had a close friend—Chingachgook—so does Boone have the company of Jim and Dick Summers, and the passing of happiness in both the Leatherstocking Tales and *The Big Sky* is linked symbolically with the dissolution of the bonds of friendship.

Where Guthrie most significantly differs from Cooper is in his presentation of another theme which both men have in common, the theme, broadly stated, of the specific irony of human endeavor. It has long been recognized that Cooper conceives of Natty Bumppo's whole fictional career in terms of one great irony, for Natty's actions in the Leatherstocking Tales are symbolically self-destructive: everything he does metaphorically destroys a part of himself by eliminating forever a piece of the only place where he can live—the wilderness. In the Leatherstocking Tales, however, this theme is usually subordinated to some other preoccupation and, at least as far as Natty is concerned, is not made overt. Though Natty may inveigh against the excesses of civilization, though he may lament the passing of the Delaware nation, though he may violently defend one set of "gifts" against another, or the whole concept of "gifts" against those who do not understand it, he never recognizes his responsibility for his own alienation. Nor, as Cooper presents him, is Natty conceived as personally responsible for the ironies of the historical process in which he finds himself enmeshed.

In this regard, no figure could be in greater contrast to Natty Bumppo than Guthrie's Boone Caudill, who is a very specific agent in his own tragedy. Boone's misfortunes are brought about by his own impulsive actions which, Guthrie suggests, writ large are what determine the ironic course of history; when Boone states that his world has been spoiled we as readers recognize, even if he does not, that he has been the cause of his own ruination. He has no one to blame but himself.

As a result, while the irony of Natty Bumppo's historic position is largely implicit in the Leatherstocking Tales, the irony of Boone's historic position in *The Big Sky* is much more explicitly developed. More than Natty, Boone is a *conscious* agent in his own dispossession. For instance, at one point in the novel—in a kind of capsule Leatherstocking Tale—he acts as guide to a man who wishes to find a way across the mountains to Oregon. He has no illusions as to why this man wishes to reach Oregon. "When country which might support so many actually supports so few," the man, Elisha Peabody, tells him at one stage in the journey, "the inhabitants have not made good use of the natural possibilities." In case Boone had missed the point Peabody goes on to make it specific. "That failure surely is justification for invasion, peaceful if possible, forceful if necessary, by people who can and will capitalize on opportunity" (p. 278). Boone does not doubt the desire of colonists to reach Oregon; he simply has no belief in their eventual ability to do so.

Indeed, Boone's greatest weakness in his perception of the external world is precisely this inability to assess the magnitude of change. For him the world exists in a constant idyllic present, and though he sees it alter around him he refuses to recognize its transformation. When on his first trip west he meets his Uncle Zeb, Boone does not believe the old trapper's words. The country, Zeb says in exact anticipation of Boone's own later statement, is "sp'iled," and the prognosis for the future is even more gloomy. "The beaver's nigh gone now. Buffler's next. Won't be even a goddam poor bull fifty years ahead. You'll see plows comin' across the plains, and people settin' out to farm" (pp. 150-51). With such visionary ranting Boone has no patience, nor can he accept the course of history when he sees Uncle Zeb's prophecy beginning to come true.

Around Boone, however, the world of the mountain men is a world in flux. The buffalo do grow scarce and the beaver are trapped out. Those who are older, like Uncle Zeb and Dick Summers, see the trend of history clearly and, like Natty Bumppo, their habitual form of speech is an *ubi sunt*. At the trappers' rendezvous the conversation always turns to the glories of the good old days when the beaver were plenty and the trappers themselves young and vigorous. Boone cannot understand this, even though the fact of change forcibly intrudes into his own tight personal world when Dick Summers announces that he is too old for the mountains and must retire to civilization. In Boone's world no one can grow old, for age is an admission of mutability.

Boone's refusal to admit that things change is emblematic of a more basic lack of perception, his refusal to accept the idea of responsibility. Just as he cannot arrive at any understanding of his true position in an external world of flux, neither can he relate the results of his past actions to his present situation in his personal life. Hence when his and Teal Eye's baby is born blind he is unable to attribute this apparently gratuitous blow of fate to the "clap" he had brought with him from St. Louis. Nor can he admit the possibility that the baby's red hair comes from his own ancestry (his grandfather, he discovers on his trip to Kentucky, had been red-haired); it must be related to the present fact that Jim is red-haired.

Just as Boone cannot relate his own personal past actions to his present situation, neither can he understand how his life as a mountain man contributes to the eventual civilization of the country. His world, consequently, is a world of inexplicable coincidence and misapplied analogies. Since he refuses to admit the very existence of the past, much less the fact that the past can shape the present, and that the present shapes the future, he is trapped in time without the perspective of history, and hence understands neither himself nor his world.

In *The Big Sky*, then, the ironic course of history and the imperfect nature of men are seen to be functions of one another. Man cannot find a "new life" for himself on the frontier because he brings his "old life" with him. For this reason his ability to change the world is limited; the most he can hope to do is to understand it.

The only character in *The Big Sky* with any understanding of the world around him is Dick Summers, and his running commentary on the action of the novel gives the reader a sense of historic perspective on the confused world of event. His final consolation to Boone stands not as moral to the story but as description of the ironies of history and of life. "I don't guess we could help it," he says: "There was beaver for us and free country and a big way of livin', and everything we done it looks like we done against ourselves and couldn't do different if we'd knowed. We went to get away and to enj'y ourselves free and easy, but folks was bound to foller and beaver to get scarce and Injuns to be killed or tamed, and all the time the country gettin' safer and better known." The only thing left for the mountain man to do, he concludes, in an ironic recapitulation of what Boone had already done, is "to hire out for guides and take parties acrost and sp'ile the country more" (p. 385).

To take parties across and spoil the country more becomes Dick Summers' own occupation in the next novel of the series, *The Way West*. This novel, much more easily summarized than *The Big Sky*, details the fortunes of an emigrant train on the journey from Missouri to Oregon. The story is told from multiple points of view, most important of which are those of Summers and of two new characters, Lije Evans and his son Brownie. The framework of the novel is essentially chronological: Guthrie begins *The Way West* in Missouri with a few chapters describing the organization of the train and suggesting the various reasons for the "Oregon fever" which motivates the emigrants; he then follows the emigrants across the plains and over the mountains to Oregon. After the train once leaves Missouri the chapters usually record some incident of the hardships of the trail, and the novel as a whole turns into a roll call of various possible disasters and of how they are met, until the emigrant train finally reaches Oregon.

It is as a fictionalized history of a universal wagon train that *The Way West* may most profitably be interpreted. Guthrie successfully resists the lure of sensationalism which mars so many chronicles of the pioneers, rightly seeing that the romantic perils of the trail were really the most insignificant encountered by the emigrants. The Indians are more a nuisance than a real menace to a large and well-armed wagon train, though they are inclined to steal and may prove dangerous to an isolated individual or small party; the natural hazards of swift rivers and steep mountains are surmountable by the native ingenuity of the pioneers. The real hardships, Guthrie suggests, are the unexpected ordinary nagging worries which the emigrants had hoped to leave behind in Missouri. For example, the wagon train is convulsed by a power struggle over who should be the leader. The forms of election (after considerable politicking for votes) are duly gone through, and the worst possible candidate is chosen. Though he is later forced to resign in favor of Lije Evans, the resulting bitterness periodically erupts and finally splits the wagon train into halves, one of which heads for California under the leadership of the former captain. In addition people die in unromantic ways, from rattlesnake bites or fevers. Nor are the pioneers all honorable and courageous; the train includes a motley crew of miscellaneous weaklings among whom are numbered a cowardly sadist and a seducer. As in *The Big Sky*, the perils faced by the characters are not the predictable external ones of hostile Indians but a series of unexpected crises from within.

The major concern of *The Way West* is to present the pioneers' discovery of their ability to cope with the new demands of life on the road. First they learn to discard those vestiges of civilized life which have no application to their changed circumstances. The first to go, or rather to be seriously modified, is the fascination with forms of government with which the emigrants are preoccupied. Laws are passed to cover a variety of possible hazards. For some unknown reason, for instance, it is decided to shoot all the dogs in the train, though opposition to this regulation prevents its being put into effect. More amusing is a brilliant satiric scene in which the question of whether buffalo chips ought to be used for fuel is solemnly discussed and finally approved by vote. The point, of course, is that the pioneers have no choice but to use buffalo chips.

In place of reliance upon the forms of government the pioneers gradually learn to adapt to the demands made upon them by the journey, and to govern themselves effectively without undue concern for the details of parliamentary procedure. Symbolically this training on the trail will fit them for their new life in Oregon, and Guthrie strongly implies that the hardships which they have undergone and the resourcefulness they have learned will enable them to begin a superior society in the West. Their old life, along with their useless baggage and their old customs, has been left behind them somewhere along the trail.

Though *The Way West* is in many ways an arresting story, it is not so successful a novel as *The Big Sky*. Part of the fault is technical: the technique of narration through multiple points of view which Guthrie had used successfully in the earlier novel simply does not work so well in *The Way West*. In *The Big Sky* there had been only three major characters, all of whom were similar in perception, but in *The Way West* there are many more, few of whom think alike or view the world about them in a like manner. Thus the multiple points of view in *The Way West* tend to diffuse the force of the novel, an effect they had not had in *The Big Sky*. Contributing further to the diffuse quality of the novel is the chronological method of telling the story. *The Way West* never quite transcends the form of a fictionalized guidebook, and hence becomes regrettably predictable. As a result, though particular scenes stick vividly in one's mind, the novel as a whole does not have the force of its predecessor.

More important than these technical flaws is Guthrie's more basic failure to control the implications of his historic parable. We are asked to believe that in some way the train, upon its arrival in Oregon, has been purified by the hardships it has undergone on the trail, and that hence Oregon will be a place superior to Missouri. This is strongly emphasized in an unfortunate scene where the dissident faction of the train—containing most of the "bad guys"—splits off from the main body to go to California. Unfortunately, even in terms of the novel itself this is difficult to believe. For one thing, the hardships of the trail have little direct relevance to the new life in Oregon, which will be much more like the old life left behind in Missouri than it will be like the rather unnatural existence of the emigrant train. Though some individuals may have been morally uplifted by the journey across the plains, one finds it difficult to accept the idea that the whole tone of nascent Oregon society will have been noticeably altered, even though the most obviously undesirable elements may have gone to California.

This weakness of the novel is underscored by the running philosophical debate throughout the book between Dick Summers and Lije Evans. Guthrie clearly intends Evans to represent the highest potentialities of the pioneer character. He begins as a likable but lackadaisical farmer on whom, during the trip, greatness is unwillingly thrust. He first becomes a reluctant voice in the affairs of governing the train when he thwarts enforcement of the dog extermination order. Later on he is made, against his wishes, captain of the train, and succeeds in leading it to its final destination. In a sense, the story of the pioneer is symbolized in Evans, who without seeking authority rises successfully to meet every challenge. Unfortunately the problem in Guthrie's presentation is that Evans' character does not really develop; rather Evans comes to realize the possibilities for greatness in himself which everyone else had seen all along. Throughout the book people take to Lije for reasons he, but unfortunately not the reader, is at a loss to understand. Consequently, though a great deal of *The Way West* must of necessity consist of scenes in which everyone waits around for Lije to find the way out of some dilemma, Guthrie sacrifices much of the inherent interest in such scenes by making it perfectly clear that Lije has everything under control and, when pressed, will come up with the proper solution. Since all but the dissidents in the train are also of this opinion, the suspense on which any such scene must depend for most of its effect is lost. The reader also has the uneasy suspicion that Lije would have done just about as well in Missouri as on the trail, and that his whole symbolic education is not the inevitable consequence of his experience of pioneering so much as the natural result of his superior abilities; and that he would have used these abilities whether or not he had ever gone West.

Throughout the trip across the plains Lije engages in a running argument with Summers, hoping to convince him of the desirability of settling in Oregon. Summers likes Lije, and for a while it looks as though Lije has talked him into joining the other emigrants. Just before they arrive in Oregon, however, Summers slips away one night to go back to the mountains. Since Summers' approval of Lije is one of the major devices by which Guthrie makes the reader also approve of Lije, Summers' disappearance seriously damages the structure of the novel. The function of the journey to Oregon in *The Way West* had been as a kind of symbolic purification; various undesirable, immoral, and incapable elements of the train had been symbolically purged by death or by turning back or by splitting off. Summers' departure from the train, though undoubtedly true to life, weakens this symbolic pattern, for when the character with whom we have been asked to sympathize and to some extent identify turns his back on Oregon we are inclined to follow him.

These Thousand Hills follows the fortunes of Lat Evans, the grandson of Lije Evans of *The Way West*, who moves from Oregon to Montana. In broad outline, the plot of the novel tells of his arrival in Montana at the end of a trail drive, of his friendship with the cowboys and especially with the likable and worthless Tom Ping, of his subsequent decision to settle in Montana and to start his own ranch, of his meeting with a beautiful prostitute named Callie who lends him $1000 which he gambles into a stake sufficient to begin his ranch and whom he later abandons, and of his marriage to a respectable girl and the final success of both his home life and his ranch. Lat Evans, like his grandfather in *The Way West*, must "find himself" among the confusing values of a new environment, and his attempts to do so form the basic thematic preoccupation of the novel. The failure of *These Thousand Hills*, which is the weakest of Guthrie's Western trilogy, is that the contradictory values among which Lat must choose are not only seen in external terms, but become external values. While in *The Big Sky* the world of history had been presented as an expanded metaphor of man's internal weaknesses and contradictions, in *These Thousand Hills* the Montana frontier becomes a kind of allegorical orchard hung with deceptive fruit, into which Lat is turned to pick whatever he will. The one fruit not to be found in the garden is that of the tree of knowledge, and as a result Lat's discovery of the good life turns into a resounding affirmation of conventional values. It is understandable, if deplorable, for a young man to take up with a prostitute; it is even legitimate to borrow her life savings to risk on a horse race, the proceeds of which one uses to establish his own fortune; but one should not marry her, and if one's closest friend loses his head and marries a prostitute—as Tom Ping does—one should show his moral disapproval by staying away from the wedding. One marries a "nice" girl, the relative of an important man, and one resolutely advances toward the Jehovah-like eminence of owning the cattle upon a thousand hills by single-mindedly using only those opportunities which can advance one's fortune. In such a fantasy world, of course, the prostitute whose love one uses as a means of economic advancement is eventually seen to be an unworthy mate; the friend who marries against the dictates of prudence lives to rue the day; and one's respectable bride miraculously develops into the quintessence of heart's desire.

The world of *These Thousand Hills* is unintentionally ironic. Supposedly a parable of man's coming to terms with the sham of respectability, the novel is actually a story of ingratitude, and of how ambition can drive one not only to do evil, but to justify his actions on the basis of the very morality of appearances he supposedly condemns. Though at the end of the novel Lat's pride is humbled when he discovers that he is an illegitimate child related to a man he despises, and his reputation in the community is compromised when it is revealed that he had at one time been a vigilante, none of this matters very much. He still has cattle upon a thousand hills and he returns to his forgiving wife, secure in the knowledge that love conquers all.

The inferiority of *The Way West* and *These Thousand Hills* to *The Big Sky* is largely explained by their relatively superficial presentation of the process of history. They abandon the tragic vision of *The Big Sky*—that, as Natty Bumppo had put it, man's "gifts are not equal to his wishes"—in favor of a facile optimism which makes history "prove" the inevitability of progress. Nevertheless it should not be overlooked that all three novels have in common their basic theme of man's quest for the good life in the Garden of the Lord. Each chronicles man's attempt to find or make a world more closely approximating the land of heart's desire. In their complete dependence upon this theme all three are typical of the generality of literature which concerns itself primarily with the settlement of the West.

It is not particularly surprising that the theme of the search for the good life in the Garden of the Lord is a basic preoccupation of novels about pioneering, but it is perhaps not so evident that this theme is by no means limited to such novels. One other genre of Western fiction to concern itself almost exclusively with this theme is the story of the search for precious metal— usually, but not invariably, gold.

Almost without exception stories about the men who moil for gold take their departure from one of two related basic plots, both of which, though varied in detail, are in outline pretty much the same wherever they appear. The first of these is the story of the miner or prospector who spends his life vainly searching for a fabulously rich strike (or occasionally a lost mine) which he never finds. This story has a perennial fascination based on the common human desire to get rich quick and, if possible, without any actual work. The story is usually told from the point of view of some solid citizen who refuses to become involved in any such madcap scheme and is justifiably virtuous in pointing out its foolishness. Though the plot can be, and often is, used only as a vehicle for telling in a new format the age-old parable of the ant and the grasshopper, it is sometimes developed more sensitively. In such stories the miner's quest becomes a symbol for the search after some kind of ideal, and the burden of the story is a description of how devotion to an unrealizable ideal incapacitates one for even qualified happiness in the everyday world.

The second plot is the exact converse of the first, and potentially much more interesting. It is the story of the man who strikes it rich. Like the first plot, this one also is generally used as a vehicle for sententious moralizing, but it can be more intriguing and more profound; for when subtly handled, stories of those who strike it rich reveal the irony that what man thinks he wants is not in fact what he wants at all. When insensitively handled, this theme deteriorates into the commonplace platitude that material success does not bring happiness, but when more perceptively presented it turns into an expanded rhetorical question: Can one buy happiness? This of course is a pervasive American theme, by no means confined to literature about the West—*Walden* comes immediately to mind—which explores the question of whether, when the external conditions of one's life are changed, happiness must inevitably follow. In sum, the parable of the miner who strikes it rich finally develops into the story of whether happiness can be defined in external terms, a theme we have already seen in *The Big Sky*; for the successful miner, just as did Boone in that novel, "gets what he wants."

A brief explication of Clifford M. Sublette's *The Golden Chimney* (1931) may make the point clearer. This novel is conventional in conception, though considerably better in execution than most sensational tales dealing with the discovery of gold. It recounts the fortunes of one Marcellus Bassett, a refugee from a fundamentalist upbringing who has gone west to make his fortune and who, at the beginning of the story, is down on his luck. He is a blacksmith in a sleepy little Colorado town and his wife takes in washing. With all their labor they can barely make ends meet, until Marcellus strikes a fabulously rich "chimney" (a vein of mixed gold and silver) on a supposedly worthless claim. The rest of the story recounts Bassett's growing material prosperity and corresponding moral decline. He first blossoms out in the expected status symbols: he affects a Prince Albert coat, drives a smart team of matched bays specially imported from Kentucky, and moves into a large and pretentious house. To match these outward and visible signs of his new affluence he takes to himself a vulgar mistress, the widow of an acquaintance of his from whom he had bought another mine and who, after numerous vicissitudes, has ended up in an exclusive house of prostitution in Denver. Things predictably go from bad to worse: Bassett begins to believe in his myth of himself as a shrewd man of affairs rather than what he really is, a person who has been incredibly lucky. He speculates in various wild schemes, all of which turn out disastrously; for one reason or another he alienates his friends; he divorces his wife, only to discover that his mistress has run off with one of his trusted henchmen; and at the end of the novel, a ruined and solitary man, he dies of an apoplectic stroke.

This bald synopsis makes *The Golden Chimney* sound tedious in the extreme. Actually such is not the case; the novel is not so pat as a plot summary makes it appear, nor is the obtrusive symbolic moralizing quite so heavy-handed. The convolutions of the plot, which appear in summary as merely ingenious, are rigidly subordinated to the theme, and hence give the effect of inevitability rather than of captious accident or thinly disguised moral platitude. The search for gold in *The Golden Chimney* becomes emblematic of man's refusal to understand himself. Rather than take the trouble to discover what his real wishes are, Bassett assumes his trials will miraculously cease with the acquisition of wealth; but, because he refuses to ask himself what he wants of wealth, his fabulously rich mine only intensifies his problems.

The great weakness of *The Golden Chimney* lies in Sublette's handling of the character of Marcellus Bassett, his protagonist. Though a blacksmith by trade, Bassett's ancestor is not so much Longfellow's manly smith as Markham's man with the hoe. Brother to the ox that he is, Marcellus does not engage our sympathy, nor can his internal conflicts be readily dramatized. His essential humanity is best demonstrated not by his foolish dependency upon a blowzy mistress or his mistaken impression that he is a financier of judgment and vision, upon which aspects of his character Sublette relies too heavily, but by subtle revelations of his longings, of which we have unfortunately too few. The best of these is the desire for comfort which Marcellus defines to himself as the ability to buy sardines, for which he has a taste, whenever he wants them. "I reckon me an' Connie [his daughter] c'n have all the sardines we want, now," is his first, and best, comment upon his discovery of the golden chimney (p. 78).[3]

A more interesting novel than *The Golden Chimney* is Dorothy Gardiner's *The Golden Lady* (1936); unjustly forgotten today, this novel is one of the very best stories of the mining frontier. It combines both the stock plots mentioned above: the heroine, Vanny Swenk, is possessed on the one hand of a supposedly fabulously rich mine—The Golden Lady—which turns out to be worthless; yet on the other hand she achieves the desires of Marcellus Bassett when she marries the richest man in the mining settlement, whose wealth has come from rich mineral claims. Vanny, who is the first child born in the little mining settlement of Duke's Gulch, is given as a birthday present the title to The Golden Lady mine. Supposedly incredibly rich, this mine is actually filled only with small pockets of gold, each of which leads the miners on to a futile search for the vein which all are sure lies imbedded in the rock just a few feet beyond where they are digging at the moment. Throughout Vanny Swenk's childhood her mother skimps to pay the taxes and improvements on the mine rather than give up title to it, secure in the belief that some day, when they once strike the vein, it will become valuable. Vanny's mother, who had been a prostitute in Leadville before coming to Duke's Gulch, is firmly wedded to the idea that the pursuit of money is identical to the pursuit of happiness, and not only does she keep title to the mine but spares no effort to turn Vanny into a great lady, that is, in her definition, the kind of woman who can marry a rich husband. Though mining The Golden Lady does not pay off, Vanny's mother strikes it rich in her other enterprise when Vanny is successfully married to Eliot Trask, the wealthy, though elderly, owner of the most valuable mines in Duke's Gulch.

Vanny's marriage to Eliot symbolizes the plight of someone who, like Marcellus Bassett, has every material thing and yet is unhappy, a metaphor which becomes explicit when Eliot dies, leaving Vanny wealthy in her own right but with no human ties. On a later trip to England she meets a young baronet who wishes to marry her, but she refuses him—not because of any sentimental attachment to Eliot's memory but because she feels she is "not a lady" and that his family would despise her as a fortune hunter. Her lover is killed in France in the first World War and she realizes her mistake when his family treat her as though the two had been engaged.

Ironically, during the war her mining interests had been making money—even The Golden Lady had produced a small pocket of gold—and after the armistice she is at once more isolated and more wealthy than she has ever been. This hollow prosperity lasts only until the Great Depression, however, when her investments prove worthless and she must return, practically penniless, to Duke's Gulch. All she has, outside of a pittance from government bonds, is the title to The Golden Lady, and at the end of the novel she is again working it, hoping to strike it rich once more.

The ironic theme of *The Golden Lady* is first touched on at the beginning of the novel when Vanny is given title to her worthless mine. Throughout the book her identification with this mine is made more explicit; Tandy Hickman, the man who has given it to her, is the first to identify her as "the golden lady," and she herself eventually comes to accept this ironic identification as true. The development of this identification exemplifies the novel's theme; from a rather obvious symbol for what one should not do to be happy, The Golden Lady develops into an ironic metaphor for mining itself. The barren mine, identified with the barren heroine, becomes emblematic of the self-defeating quest of men who conceive of themselves always in terms of what they possess rather than of what they are. The moral heroes of *The Golden Lady* are those who are not concerned with mining; that is, those who are superior to the struggle for possession which motivates the other characters. In most particular contrast to Vanny stands Miss Alice Frazer, a housekeeper at the Trask home who is engaged to teach Vanny ladylike deportment. Not until late in the book do we discover that Miss Alice had once been a nobleman's wife and had run away from him to America where she could live with the man she loved. Miss Alice's symbolic renunciation of the world's gifts stands in explicit contrast to the frantic attempts of others to possess them, and there is no doubt at all with whom the author's sympathies lie.

Finally, then, *The Golden Lady* is about two contrasting sets of values. The first are those of acquisition, represented by the miners and symbolized by the worthless mine and the heroine whose barrenness is identified with it; the second, those of human worth, are represented by Miss Alice and her lover and by Tandy Hickman who had renounced the scramble for wealth by giving The Golden Lady to Vanny and who, though pathetic and ridiculous at least in the world's eyes, has a certain dignity. Vanny's own inability to seize love at the price of renunciation of worldly goods symbolizes at once the weakness of those who define happiness in terms of material success and the self-defeating nature of that acquisitive spirit which represents for Dorothy Gardiner the most glaring deficiency in American society.[4]

In *The Golden Lady* the search for happiness turns out negatively. Unreal ideals of wealth and happiness must, Dorothy Gardiner suggests, be reinterpreted in order to conform more closely with life as it actually is. Such a conclusion forms the theme of another novel, Susan Ertz's *The Proselyte* (1933).

At first glance *The Proselyte* seems to have nothing whatever in common with *The Golden Lady,* for it is a story not of the Colorado mining frontier but of the Mormon migration to Salt Lake. The protagonist, an English girl named Zillah Purdy, marries a Mormon missionary, Joseph Hewett, whom she had heard preach in London. She converts to Mormonism—she is "the proselyte" of the novel's title—and eventually the two of them move to America. They travel to Salt Lake City by handcart[5] where Joseph takes a second wife (an attempt at plural marriage which turns out badly when the girl runs away with a Gentile) and becomes a respected Church official. Later, they are sent from Salt Lake to found another settlement which is soon abandoned because of Indian troubles. Joseph is finally shot and killed from ambush by a man whom he had caught stealing bread many years before when the handcart pioneers had been starving on the trail. After his death Zillah returns to her old home in England, only to find that she is a stranger in her own country. Her real home, she discovers, is no longer in England but in Zion, and at the end of the novel she and her son return to America.

The Proselyte, though flawed in many respects, is a novel of much more than passing historical interest. Its faults are obvious and no point is served by glossing over them. Like a great many novels which paint a broad historical picture it is marred at times by the characters' being woodenly moved about to satisfy the demands of history rather than the probabilities of their fictional lives; more serious, perhaps, is the fact that there is little suspense in the novel and no real conflict: even the antagonism between Joseph and the man who eventually kills him is never explicitly developed.

Yet with all its flaws *The Proselyte* is an impressive achievement. It is one of the very few novels about Mormonism which is neither Gentile polemic nor Mormon apologetic. Though Susan Ertz is on the whole a sympathetic observer of Mormonism, she does not feel called upon to apologize for every stupidity of every Saint, nor does she feel obligated to make the Church the only repository of virtue. Consequently her picture of Mormon history, though sometimes factually in error, has about it the air of truth. Her purpose, she says in the brief preface to the book, is not primarily that of historical documentation; for though the novel deals with historical materials, yet she specifies that her purpose in writing is to reveal "the truth that lies hidden behind the facts" (p. [v]). All in all, she succeeds admirably: the unpleasant facts about both Mormon and Gentile conduct are sympathetically presented without special pleading, and the novel rarely deteriorates into propaganda.

One of the major reasons for this is that the truth Susan Ertz hopes to discover behind the facts is not the truth of whether or not the Mormon revelation is truer than the Gentile. The book is not about the relative superiority of one revelation to another, but rather about the process of conversion considered independently of the question of what one is converted to. The story of *The Proselyte*, as the title suggests, is that of the inner development of Zillah's conversion from symbolically considered Gentile values to Mormon ones, a conversion which is not completed by her nominal acceptance of the tenets of Mormonism but by her eventual inner understanding of what these tenets signify. In this more profound sense her conversion is not completed until the very end of the novel, when she symbolically renounces the Gentile world for Zion.

The process of conversion, as it is presented in *The Proselyte*, is one of gradual renunciation, symbolized by Zillah's reluctant acceptance of the superficially unpleasant facts of the Mormon world. For these she must give up the Gentile values toward which, until the conclusion of *The Proselyte,* she yearns. When we first meet her, an adolescent girl, she is—or thinks she is—in love with Henry Persons, the heir to Gaillards, a rich English country estate. She has no hope of marriage "above her station" to Henry, but he does not treat her in the fate-worse-than-death way which such a stock situation apparently demands. Henry is a sympathetic person—even Joseph thinks him a fine man—who represents in the novel the very real attraction of the things of this world. Hence Zillah is never quite at ease in Zion, and her conversion depends upon her ability to accept the often unpleasant realities of life symbolized by her marriage to Joseph and by her growing commitment to the Church, and to choose them even above the attractions of Gaillards.

From the beginning of the novel the history of Zillah's life is a story of struggle against constantly more difficult trials. She leaves her comfortable home with her parents for the life of a missionary's wife. Often there is not enough to eat, and her first baby is born dead. This apparent time of tribulation comes to an end when Joseph is allowed to return to Salt Lake City (always referred to as Zion in the novel) with his wife. In order to reach Zion, however, they must march across the prairie, and the poverty of a missionary's life is exchanged only for the greater horrors of the trail. Zillah's remark that "if being a Mormon means always being dirty and uncomfortable, I wish I wasn't one" (p. 102) takes on growing significance as the story progresses; for this in fact is one of the things that being a Mormon means. On the dreary trek across the prairie all she wishes is to sleep in a bed again, and Joseph keeps up her spirits by promising her that things will be different in Zion. But things are not different in Zion, for Zion is a raw frontier town filled with ordinary folk. Zillah wishes that the Saints looked "more like the selected people of the Lord" (p. 187), but they appear to be just like everyone else. In addition, once Joseph and Zillah are comfortably settled in Zion, Joseph takes a second wife, an eventuality which Zillah had feared more than all else. Even the hoped-for bed proves delusory, for Joseph and Zillah are sent to found a new settlement, and for the relative comforts of Salt Lake, where Zillah could at least play the piano, are substituted the hardships of life on the frontier. In addition to the ordinary difficulties of establishing a new community the settlers are faced with Indian trouble, and one of Zillah's sons is killed when warfare breaks out. Finally Joseph himself is killed, and Zillah is bereft of everything which she had hoped for at the beginning of the novel. Apparently all reason for remaining in Zion is gone, and she returns to England. Only there does she realize the hold Zion has upon her, a pull which is stronger than the most easy life the Gentile world can offer, symbolized by the kindly and benevolent Henry Persons and his beautiful estate Gaillards, home—as its name suggests—of gaiety and mirth. In the compelling metaphor which concludes the book, Zillah renounces England for "that bit of stony, barren ground, and that pile of stones in the wilderness" (p. 359) where her husband is buried.

At the end of *The Proselyte*, Zion is no more attractive than it was at the beginning; in contrast to the luxury of Gaillards stands the barren grave in the wilderness. And this is precisely the point of the parable, for Zillah's original ideal of Zion had been unreal. She had expected Zion to be Gaillards miraculously transposed to the Great Salt Lake, and easily accessible. She had found the way to be difficult, and at the end of the book realizes that if what one really wishes is gaiety and mirth he should stay at home.

This explication of *The Proselyte* should make clear its relation to the considerable body of Christian literature which concerns itself with the necessity of asceticism for spiritual purification—a theme, by the way, which is never far below the surface of Western story. The novel's ascetic quality is emphasized in the symbolic nature of that Zion which Zillah seeks. For Zion has a double aspect: on the one hand stands the temporal Zion of the Church Militant, Salt Lake City and its inhabitants; on the other, the eternal Zion of the Church Triumphant, for which the first is only a symbol. An address in the former does not posit residence in the latter; for the riches of the earthly Zion can be delusory. Like the riches of the mine, they bring disaster to those who do not understand their significance, and whether one finds Zion or El Dorado makes little difference if one does not know how to use the riches he discovers.

Zion becomes, therefore, a symbol in many ways analogous to the symbols we have already mentioned in other novels of the West which, like *The Proselyte*, explore the theme of the quest for the good life in the Garden of the Lord. Nevertheless there is a very real difference; for while the earlier symbols for the good life had been superficially attractive, the temporal Zion at least has little to recommend it at first glance. In *The Golden Lady* the ideals of wealth and power, and in *The Big Sky* the ideal of the free, open life of the wilderness are apparently inviting, however shabby or ironic the virtues they symbolize may eventually turn out to be. In *The Proselyte* the case is quite opposite: pleasure and comfort are all to be found in England, and though virtue and possibly happiness as well may ultimately be found in Zion, still its beauties are not to be discovered at the first casual glance.

Here again Zion is typical of an immense body of Western literature in which life in the West is assumed to be unattractive and dismal rather than romantic and beautiful. This literature has been generally ignored, yet it is by no means either rare or esoteric. The unattractiveness of God's country is quite often the point of departure, as it is in *The Proselyte*, for an exploration of the nature of the good life, since to many people's eyes the West did not appear even superficially attractive. In their view the only way to make God's country habitable was to make it as like the East as possible, preferably without delay.[6]

A specific disagreement between those who would leave the West as it is and those who would change it is at the heart of the conflict between Natty Bumppo and Judge Temple in *The Pioneers*, though Cooper is by no means the only one of his contemporaries to explore the problem. Of all his contemporaries, however, Cooper is the most significant, in terms of later novelistic practice, for the way in which he symbolizes the debate. The concluding scene of *The Pioneers*—mentioned above—where Effingham and his new bride sentimentally watch Natty Bumppo disappear into the West, is the first clearly articulated image of what is later to become a major theme in the Leatherstocking Tales and in most subsequent writing about the West. This is the theme that the untamed West, whether because of its physical danger, hardship, or psychological peril, is unsuited to female inhabitants. The particular scene at the end of *The Pioneers* reappears constantly in Western fiction (everyone can recognize its bastard progeny in the well-worn scene which concluded many an old Western film: the hero, given the choice of an attractive girl or an attractive horse, invariably chose the latter); but the thematic statement for which it is an image is more important than the scene itself. In a general way each of the four later Leatherstocking Tales is concerned with the perils of bringing women to the frontier, a theme implicit in *The Pioneers* as well, and symbolized by the specifically frontier perils of the forest fire and the panther which threaten Elizabeth Temple.

In later Western fiction the removal of peril is seen as the prerequisite for feminine life on the frontier; or, in other words, a modicum of civilization is needed before women can be safely brought to the wilds. This in turn implies that the feminine view of the frontier will normally be negative, and that woman's literary place on the frontier will be as an agent of civilization. In literary terms, then, the debate over what to do with the Garden of the Lord is often presented in terms of contrasted masculine and feminine views of frontier life.

A simple articulation of this theme may be found in Dorothy Scarborough's novel *The Wind* (1925). The heroine of this story, Letty Mason, is an eighteen-year-old Virginia girl who comes from a sheltered and genteel Southern home to the raw Texas frontier. She is unable to adapt to the hardships of frontier life, marries unhappily, is seduced by the only apparently sympathetic male character in the novel, whom she later shoots, and finally, in the climactic scene of the book, goes mad and runs out into the waiting wind.

To summarize the Gothic plot of this story is to make it sound scarcely worth taking seriously; the novel's real strength lies in its carefully thought-out and generally skillfully developed symbolic structure, for *The Wind* is a study in symbolic opposites. On the most elementary level, the wind itself stands in opposition to Letty; "Long ago," writes Dorothy Scarborough, the winds "were wild and free, and they were more powerful than human beings." More than that, they were specifically "the enemies of women," for "they saw in them the symbols of that civilization which might gradually lessen their own power." Women were the agents for whom men worked to "increase their herds" and "turn the unfenced pastures into farms, furrowing the land that had never known touch of plow since time began" (pp. 2-3), and hence the wind is their inevitable enemy. Less concretely, then, the wind becomes a symbol for the frontier life before the advent of civilization, and its symbolic values of wildness and freedom are emphasized by the wild black stallion to which it is often specifically compared. As the book progresses, each of the two symbolic polarities—Letty, emblematic of "woman" on the one hand, and the wind on the other—gathers about itself a series of subsidiary symbols. The wind, the sand, the drought, and other miscellaneous symbols emblematic of life in Texas are placed in opposition to woman, the home, and the pleasant life in Virginia from which Letty had come. The wind, we are specifically told, is the hardest thing for a woman to bear on the frontier, and Letty is also fond of recalling her life in Virginia where the wind had no dominion.

Finally, then, the metaphorical opposites of Letty and the wind become symbols for the process of colonization or, in terms of the novel's symbolism, the bringing of land under the plow becomes an emblem for the replacement of "Texas" by "Virginia." When the land is finally civilized the wind will be vanquished, but until that time Letty herself can have no home in Texas.

Related to this symbolic structure is the omnipresent sexual symbolism which fills the book. In opposition to the metaphor of genteel home life in Virginia is placed the more elemental purely sexual metaphor of the wind, seen first as a great black stallion, an obvious symbol of sexual power; later, more explicitly, Letty hears the wind "wailing" about her house "like a lost soul, like a banshee, like a demon lover" (p. 167), images which constantly reappear. Against this elemental force Letty has only the home as a barricade. In Virginia this might have been enough, but in Texas the house is only a tarpaper shanty about which the wind prowls and into which it drives sand at will. Just as her home is not proof against the wind, so Letty herself is not proof against Wirt Roddy, who seduces her in a powerful scene while a great storm rages outside. The two are at least symbolic partners, for Letty is driven to Roddy by the wind: "The wind! The wind! Don't let the wind get me!" (p. 311) she cries as she goes to him. Her hope is futile, however, for the wind does get her. The explicit sexual imagery in the scene when she "gives herself" to the wind makes perfectly clear the metaphor of the demon lover whose elemental force has broken down the safe conventionalities of the home. "With a laugh that strangled on a scream," Letty "sped to the door, flung it open and rushed out. She fled across the prairies like a leaf blown in a gale, borne along in the force of the wind that was at last to have its way with her" (p. 337).

In *The Wind* Letty, and by extension woman in general, is clearly visualized as inimical to the frontier. The frontier itself, however, though it is symbolized in elemental sexual terms, is not presented as specifically masculine. Men in *The Wind* are the agents by which the "womanly" work of colonization is accomplished and hence both are in a sense on the same side. Such is not true of many novels which concern themselves with colonization, in which masculine and feminine attitudes toward the West are clearly contrasted. Such a distinction is at the heart of Edna Ferber's *Cimarron* (1930), one of the best modern treatments of the theme.

Cimarron is a novel based upon the events of the Oklahoma land rush. It follows the fortunes of Yancey Cravat and his wife Sabra, who emigrate from Kansas to Oklahoma. Sabra, like Letty in *The Wind,* is the descendant of an aristocratic Southern family which had moved to Kansas after the Civil War. Though they had lived in Kansas for two decades, the family had remained proof against Western values and are representative, at the start of the novel, of an island of civilization amidst what they at least consider the barbarities of Wichita. Yancey in contrast had originally been a Texan, and though neither rough nor crude is an explicit representative of Western virtues as opposed to the Southern virtues of Sabra and her family. Sabra's family look on him as wild and irresponsible, albeit likable enough, and cannot understand his enthusiasm for the newly opened, desolate Oklahoma territory to which, at the beginning of the novel, he is about to take Sabra. When the two arrive at Osage, the raw boom town in which they are to settle, the differences between them are made even more explicit. Yancey establishes a newspaper in which he is fond of championing unpopular notions, largely for the uproar they cause. Since, as it turns out, he is also a redoubtable gunman who can back his words with a well-placed bullet, the free expression of radical ideas becomes a heady feature of life in Osage. It is one of the few, for Osage is desolate and life there grim and sterile, at least to Sabra's view, and this contrast between her and Yancey's attitudes toward life in Osage becomes a metaphorical statement of two diametrically opposed opinions about life on the frontier.

These differences in attitude are by no means purely academic, but are translated into action. Yancey personifies the spirit of the man impatient of things as they are, and to him the West offers a golden opportunity to make a new beginning "as unlike the old as possible." In consequence he is a relentless champion of moral right against all right-thinking opinions based upon customary injustice. He is fond of moral crusades; his newspaper defends the rights of Indians and the character of Dixie Lee, the notorious madam of the local bawdy house. Sabra and "the other virtuous women of the community" set about in contrast to make "this new frontier town like the old as speedily as possible." The outcome of this struggle is foreordained. Yancey, "with his unformed dreams" never has a chance against what Edna Ferber specifically calls "the indomitable materialism of the women" (pp. 166-67).

The notion of the feminine position as a materialistic one in opposition to masculine idealism may strike the reader of this study as odd, especially if he is accustomed to the quite opposite symbolic structure of much romantic literature in which woman is habitually conceived as giving cheerfully and without thought of recompense whatever metaphorical "all" strikes the author's fancy. Though few authors are as uncompromising in their view as Edna Ferber—part of whose purpose in *Cimarron* as well as of many of her other writings is to satirize unmercifully what she considers the ludicrous excesses of American materialism— the idea is implicit in most Western literature. The Leather-stocking Tales again come to mind; in contrast to Natty Bumppo, whose only material desire is for his trusty rifle, stand the various good women of the Tales, all of whom marry both wisely and well. Natty's symbolic renunciation of "clearings" is largely a renunciation of material success, and of those who, like Judge Temple, inherit the wilderness and bring to it the new values of material improvement.

The notion that material improvement, prosperity, happiness, and moral worth are inseparably bound together is one of the basic moral premises underlying the nineteenth-century debate over the right of empire and the right of soil which is one of Cooper's most lasting legacies to Western writing. *The Big Sky* gives another example of the same implicit sexual identification of the feminine with the materialistic. The joys of civilized life are symbolically offered Boone in the person of the nice girl he should marry and for whom he should renounce his wild frontier ways and settle down to serious farming. The same theme appears again and again. Owen Wister's Virginian, content at first with his fine horse Monte, discovers that the lure of womankind brings with it the necessity for economic advancement; the same theme is at the heart of the argument over "wages" in Arthur Miller's *The Misfits*, to mention only one other of many possible examples.

In *Cimarron* neither the masculine idealism of Yancey nor the feminine materialism of Sabra represents a position which Edna Ferber can affirm without qualification. Yancey, though undoubtedly in the right of the argument, can find no way to translate his idealism into a program of practical action; however much he may weep for Zion he is incapable of realizing it. Sabra's materialism is no better an alternative; for it does not represent a clear-sighted recognition of the necessity to compromise ideals in order to realize them even partially in a flawed world, but rather a complete denial of any idealism at all. Sabra does not only find Yancey's visionary notions to be impractical, but scornfully rejects even their speculative wisdom.

That both these positions are incomplete Edna Ferber suggests through the fates of her two protagonists. Yancey's idealism becomes less realizable as Osage grows toward the embodiment of Sabra's idea of "progress." Yancey, the perpetual frontiersman, is forever searching for new frontiers in which he can realize his impossible world, only to be constantly frustrated and to die a penniless derelict. Sabra's fate is more ironic. The proponent of material success, she succeeds far beyond her wildest dreams; she attains to wealth, power, and political office, becoming by the end of the novel another example of the by now familiar figure, the person who "gets what he wants."

Yet, rather predictably, all her success does not buy happiness, and through the story of her and Yancey's two children Edna Ferber suggests how materialism unleavened with idealism is self-defeating. The boy Cim marries an Indian—much to his mother's horror—and, even more ironically, an Indian fabulously rich from the oil leases on the tribal lands. The girl Donna also translates her mother's materialism into an ironic success by calculatingly becoming the mistress of an elderly oil millionaire whom she cold-bloodedly marries for his money. Yancey's two great idealistic crusades have been translated into action, and Sabra discovers that idealism may be ignored only at one's peril.

Much of the powerful effect of *Cimarron* is clearly a result of

Edna Ferber's presentation of her two protagonists, with both of whom the reader's sympathies partially lie. In complete agreement with Yancey's principles, he nonetheless realizes that in any given situation he would probably act like Sabra. The external world of *Cimarron*, like that of many other Westerns, becomes a metaphor for the dilemma of human beings who simultaneously affirm two contradictory and mutually exclusive points of view, represented in the story by contrasting masculine and feminine attitudes toward the colonization of the West.

Care should be taken here, as in the discussion of most aspects of Western fiction, against taking symbolic points of view literally. The difference between masculine and feminine perceptions into the meaning of the frontier experience need not necessarily be accepted as a psychologically tenable distinction between male and female character. It is more successfully interpreted as a literary device which makes possible a more compelling statement of different attitudes toward progress. For the statement of these different attitudes a feminine point of view is not absolutely required, nor does the fact that a certain consistent point of view is expressed by a female character necessarily imply that women in the real world would inevitably hold such a position. Indeed, women are not absolutely necessary to the presentation of these two differing points of view, but the attitude which they are conventionally made to represent *is* required. The values represented by a stable society must in some way be introduced into any fictional exploration of the significance of the frontier, if only to throw into greater relief the contrasting values which the frontier represents.

An interesting example of the presence of conventionally assumed feminine values in a story in which there are no feminine characters may be found in Bret Harte's familiar tale "The Luck of Roaring Camp" (1868). This sentimental story tells of the birth of a child in a mining camp. His mother, a prostitute named Cherokee Sal, dies and the boy is raised by the denizens of Roaring Camp, only to drown, with two of his protectors, when all are swept away in a flash flood.

To modern taste "The Luck of Roaring Camp" seems overly sentimental, and whatever merit it may possess is drowned with the baby in the maudlin ending. The most interesting feature of the story is not to be found in the pathetic account of the rough miners with hearts of gold but rather in the values represented by the foundling child. For in order to bring him up properly, the miners decide that they must turn Roaring Camp into a closer imitation of Eastern civilization, and this process is very specifically seen as one of renouncing conventional masculine values for (equally conventional) feminine ones. Harte is at his best in telling of the "regeneration" of Roaring Camp, that is, of its symbolic renunciation of Western values for those of civilization. First the cabin in which the baby is kept is cleaned out and whitewashed, then repaired; new furniture is imported; those who wish to hold the baby are made to wash first; shouting and profanity are prohibited within earshot of the infant, though "vocal music, . . . being supposed to have a soothing, tranquilizing quality" is permitted; one song in fact, sung by an expatriate English sailor, becomes "quite popular as a lullaby"; it is "a lugubrious recital of the exploits of 'the Arethusa, Seventy-four,' in a muffled minor, ending with a pro- longed dying fall at the burden of each verse, 'On b-oo-o-ard of the Arethusa.'" News of Roaring Camp's regeneration is carried to the marveling outer world by the expressman, who tells an unbelieving audience in Red Dog, a rival and unreformed city, that in "Roaring" "They've got vines and flowers round their houses, and they wash themselves twice a day" (pp. 9-12).

It is true that this is all a little overdone—Harte's major esthetic failing in all his work is a congenital inability to let a good thing go—but it is still effective. More to our point is the fact that the miners' symbolic change of heart is presented in terms of their acceptance of conventional feminine values at the price of masculine ones. Roaring Camp is simultaneously civilized and feminized; or perhaps it is better stated that civilization and feminization are represented in interchangeable terms.

A better story than "The Luck of Roaring Camp" is Stephen Crane's "The Bride Comes to Yellow Sky" (1898), in which the passing of the frontier is also symbolized by the arrival of a woman on the scene. The many ingenious and often subtle explications of this story have tended to ignore the fact that Crane's purpose is mirrored in the story's title; for the tale is a metaphorical presentation of the process of history, a process exemplified by the symbolic action of the story, the bringing of woman to the frontier. The confrontation between Scratchy Wil- son and Jack Potter which concludes the story ends with an appeal to the bride. When Scratchy learns that Potter is married he must admit that the quasi-serious quarrel the two had carried on so long is "all off now" (p. 285). As in the analogous situation in "The Luck of Roaring Camp," Crane's story concludes with a symbolic replacement of conventionally assumed masculine values by equally conventionally assumed feminine ones.

Where "The Bride Comes to Yellow Sky" differs from "The Luck of Roaring Camp"—as well as from *Cimarron* and *The Wind*—is in its less mechanical handling of these two points of view. For while the other works had contented themselves more or less with some statement of the nature of these contrasting metaphorical perceptions into the meaning of frontier life, "The Bride Comes to Yellow Sky" relates them explicitly to a larger concept of history. The esthetic effect of Crane's story does not depend primarily upon our understanding of the difference between these two points of view, but upon the symbolic confrontation between Scratchy and the bride which becomes a symbol of the course of history. Hence in this story we are asked to accept without explication the "fact" that the bride and Scratchy stand for two different attitudes toward the West; we are told that this difference exists, but what it specifically is, is never mentioned.

In many ways "The Bride Comes to Yellow Sky" may be read almost as a fictional statement of Frederick Jackson Turner's frontier hypothesis. Like Turner, Crane focuses upon the frontier as the area most significant to American life. Like Turner as well, he sees that the most important factor in American democracy is the impact of a more advanced state of civilization upon the frontier. Finally, Crane and Turner are in agreement that the difference between life on the frontier and the civilization which succeeds it lies in the latter's greater complexity. In "The Bride Comes to Yellow Sky" this is clearly reflected in the sexual metaphor of the replacement of Scratchy by the bride. Throughout the tale Scratchy is described in terms of naiveté. He is, as the barkeeper of the Weary Gentleman saloon says, "kind of simple" (p. 281), and in his simplicity is unable to understand the facts of that complex life represented by the new estate of marriage. "In the presence of this foreign condition," Crane reminds us at the conclusion of the story, "he was a simple child of the earlier plains" (p. 285), and before this complexity the simplicity of the frontier must yield.

The notion in "The Bride Comes to Yellow Sky" that the feminine point of view is not only different from the masculine, but representative of greater complexity, is by no means confined only to Crane; it is inherent in whatever stories concern themselves with the advent of civilization in terms of the metaphorical distinction between men and women. Often, as in "The Bride Comes to Yellow Sky," the greater complexity of the feminine point of view is also associated with the idea of growing up. Scratchy Wilson is not only simple, but childlike; and the bride is not only complex, but adult. The coming of the bride to Yellow Sky, then, is also emblematic of a much-discussed American literary theme, the symbolic story of coming of age.

The theme of coming of age is never far to seek in Western fiction. At times ineptly handled, it becomes on occasion an admirable vehicle for presenting either or both of two related parables, the maturing of an individual or of society. Not surprisingly, coming of age in such parables is metaphorically associated with sexuality, and the presence of woman becomes a symbol for maturity. The point of view the woman represents in such stories is of necessity more complex than the simple one of the childlike male. What sets the Western apart from most other treatments of the theme of coming of age is that it offers an almost unique opportunity to combine the theme of personal maturing with a statement of the nature of the course of history. The Western hero personally and the country which he represents both "grow up" in such a story. Yellow Sky repudiates Scratchy's gun in favor of Potter's bride.

The peculiar appeal of the theme of growing up in the Western must be explained by the fact that the reader of Western story is ambivalent in his own attitudes toward maturing. From the standpoint of the child who lives somewhere in every adult, maturing is not an unqualified blessing, as many children's books bear eloquent witness; but however much the adult may give way on occasion to the wish to be a child again, he usually resists the impulse as unworthy of him. He cannot stay forever in the nursery with Pooh or on the island with Peter Pan. He must, now that he is a man, put away childish things. He must turn resolutely away from Scratchy's gun to embrace the bride.

On a non-personal level, however, he need do no such thing. He may sincerely believe, however foolishly, that the modern complexity of life represents a falling away from the simplicity of an earlier day and may long to return to a more elementary manner of life. In any case, even if he believes new ways to be preferable to old, he will confess that old ways had something in their favor. He may believe in progress, while at the same time readily admitting that it must be taken on balance. The Western manages, by identifying personal maturation with social progress, to capitalize upon the individual reader's ambivalence. Personally the individual would accept the bride in lieu of Scratchy without much hesitation; but in a historic rather than a personal context, is he so willing to reject the position Scratchy represents?

The possibilities for tragic irony inherent in the literary identification of the theme of acceptance of feminine values with an explication of the course of history may clearly be seen in Conrad Richter's brilliant novel *The Sea of Grass* (1937). The historical plot of this novel concerns itself with the well-worn theme of the struggle between the nesters and the cattlemen for ownership and use of the prairie. When the story opens, the cattle baron, Jim Brewton, runs cattle upon a huge range on the sea of grass. Onto this range the nesters are encroaching, and Brewton becomes involved in a range war when he tries to run them off. At first the nesters are powerless, for the cattle interests control the sea of grass and no jury will convict cattlemen charged with running nesters off their land. Opposed to Jim Brewton in this struggle is the new district attorney Brice Chamberlain, who is making political capital by defending the nesters and thus representing himself as the champion of the rights of the oppressed common man against the abuses of privilege. Chamberlain is of the opinion that God is "clearly on the side of the settlers" (p. 88), and that Jim Brewton is therefore of the devil's party. Since God has clearly manifested His will, Chamberlain can do nothing else than implement it; he aids the Divine Purpose by changing the law in order to make it a more effective agent of revelation. He is successful in his work; he succeeds in stripping the sea of grass from Brewton and opening it to colonization.

Up to this point *The Sea of Grass* is a conventional statement of the dramatic possibilities inherent in the clash of two conventionally conceived opposed points of view. In this respect it is typical of, though far better executed than, the general run of Western novels which describe the perennial conflict between the cattlemen and the nesters. But onto this conventional conflict Richter grafts another concern: in terms of the moral law to which Chamberlain so confidently appeals, which one of these points of view is right?

Both Brewton and Chamberlain are convinced that their side is allied with some higher purpose, and Chamberlain claims to have had a sign which, when properly interpreted, should convince all doubters; for heavy rains have fallen on the normally dry sea of grass, symbolically blessing the efforts of the new colonists.[7] Brewton is not sure that the Divine Will is so easily read; he tells the soldiers who come to protect the nesters from the cattlemen, "You can keep the nesters from being blown away, but God Himself can't the prairie!" (p. 80). It turns out that Brewton is right; when the dry years come again the nesters are forced out, but in the meantime they have destroyed the sea of grass, the only thing which will grow upon the prairie.

Onto this chastening exploration of the course of history is grafted the story of Jim Brewton's personal fortunes, a story symbolized by Lutie, the woman he marries. At the beginning of the novel the narrator of *The Sea of Grass* is sent into town to meet the train on which Lutie is arriving from the East. Lutie's arrival is symbolically identified with the arrival of Brice Chamberlain and the nesters, for at the same time Chamberlain is vainly attempting to win a conviction of some of Brewton's cowboys who have run a nester off his land. From the first Lutie is not at home on the sea of grass. She plants trees around the great bare ranch house in a gesture which is at once a symbolic defiance of the prairie and an affirmation of her desire to make the West as much like the East as possible. She hates the sea of grass and its loneliness, preferring the civilized East where, as she says, "there's life" (p. 41). Her renunciation of the frontier for civilization is further symbolized by her choice of Chamberlain, whose mistress she becomes, over Brewton. She eventually leaves the ranch, though Chamberlain has not the requisite courage to face Brewton in a gun battle and lets her leave alone. He never joins her, for in his personal life as in his career he is responsible ultimately only to himself.

Behind her Lutie leaves her children, one of whom, Brock, is Chamberlain's son. As he grows older he comes to resemble the unpleasant features of both his parents. Like his mother he wants "to be where there's excitement and people" (p. 121) and like his father he will not accept responsibility for his actions. He runs away rather than face his punishment for cheating at cards, becomes a desperado, and is eventually brought to bay by a posse. He takes refuge in a cabin and Chamberlain, now a judge, is asked to come and talk him into surrendering. Chamberlain ignores the request; Brewton goes in his stead and the wounded Brock dies in his arms.

Brock's fate is representative of the fate of the sea of grass which, in a large measure, he personifies. Both are destroyed by the forces of progress: Brock's character is eroded by his identification with the false values of civilization, and his literal and symbolic identification with Chamberlain links his own destiny with that of the prairie. The conflict between Brewton and Chamberlain for the boy's allegiance (Brock's parentage is never explicitly attributed to either man, though the implication is clear that he is Chamberlain's son) is emblematic of the struggle between the two men for control of the sea of grass, and the conclusions of both struggles are symbolically linked: the sea of grass finally reverts to Brewton after it has been destroyed, and Brock too returns to him in death. The question of Brock's parentage and the question of the ownership of the sea of grass are symbolically decided only after both have been destroyed. Brock dies in Brewton's arms and on his tombstone the name Brock Brewton (rather than Brock Chamberlain) "is carved in unequivocal letters that all who ride may read" (p. 148).

In Richter's view the moral difference between Chamberlain on the one hand and Brewton on the other lies in the greater sense of responsibility of the latter. Chamberlain considers nothing but his own welfare: he champions the cause of the nesters only to advance his political fortunes and refuses to accept any responsibilities toward either the sea of grass or its inhabitants; similarly he washes his hands of his responsibilities toward Lutie and Brock. Brewton, in contrast, is always responsible to something larger than his own personal fortunes; he sees himself as a steward rather than an owner, and the responsibilities of his stewardship extend to Brock and Lutie and the sea of grass. In the contrast between these two men we see once again the conflict we mentioned earlier between two points of view, one of which (represented by Chamberlain) thinks in terms of "mine and thine" and the other (represented by Brewton) which thinks in terms of "ours." Significantly, the feminine point of view represented by Lutie takes sides with Chamberlain.

Whether or not one wishes to accept Richter's point of view in a literal historical sense—whether, that is, one believes that the civilized world is morally less responsible and more self-seeking than the frontier—is quite irrelevant to the different question of how one explains the powerful esthetic effectiveness of *The Sea of Grass*. The novel's success is partially due to Richter's stylistic competence; for, in marked contrast to many Westerns, this book is beautifully written. More important is Richter's uncanny ability to breathe life into the hoary clichés of Western fiction with which the book is filled. At the heart of the novel is the familiar theme of the struggle between cattle-men and nesters; Lutie, the visitor from the East, closely resembles the conventional mail-order bride; Chamberlain is a city slicker whose smooth exterior conceals a cunning and diabolical character; he is also a lawyer, the stock Western villain; Jim Brewton is a beautifully articulated example of the familiar figure of the "last man," and his habitual manner of speech is the oratorical *ubi sunt;* Brock's tragic history is a typical cowboy's Rake's Progress; Brewton even hopes to settle the conflict over Lutie by a gun duel, but Chamberlain, coward that he is, refuses to fight. To say that these characters and situations are commonplace is to belabor the obvious; what is not so obvious is the fact that they have a real emotional impact when properly used by a sensitive writer. Like Cooper, whom in many ways he resembles, Richter understands how the narration of event may be transformed from sensationalism to revelation.

But the esthetic success of *The Sea of Grass* depends mostly upon the figure of Lutie. Beautiful, capricious, willful, she represents at once that maturity and complexity which the simple child of the plains covets, yet before which he stands abashed. She must be bought, not merely possessed, and her price is high, for to enjoy her one must renounce the Garden of the Lord. It is not an easy choice.

It has probably already occurred to the reader that the historical plot and the romantic plot of *The Sea of Grass* have, when considered in a coldly rational light, very little logical connection with one another. There is no particular reason at all why the historic development of the West need be considered in terms of specific human growth and development. The analogy between Western history at large and the personal fortunes of the major characters of Richter's novel is rationally as unconvincing as are most analogies which attempt to trace a logical relationship between the individual and society. Yet emotionally the idea is intriguing, for the human being likes to think of history as a metaphor for his own fortunes writ large. The rich ironic complexities of *The Sea of Grass* depend upon the fact that this analogy between the individual and society is *not* true, and that the reader recognizes this, however much he would like to think that his own destiny is directly related to the purpose of a large and grand historic process. The reader's own unresolved attitudes toward his personal place in society and his general place in history are expressed through the interaction of a romantic and a historical plot which have no logical connection but which are conventionally assumed to be related. As a result, the reader finds an expression within the novel of the various ambivalent points of view which he himself may have toward his own experience.

In *The Sea of Grass,* then, we find a subtle method of presenting the ambiguous and often self-contradictory points of view which we have seen as the basis of other literature about the settlement of the Garden of the Lord. Though the survey of such literature in this chapter must necessarily be incomplete and fragmentary, hopefully it has served to explain, at least to some extent, the perennial fascination which this theme holds for Americans. The American would find the story of the colonization of the West of no particular interest were he not himself so unsure of how his life ought to be led, and did he not have real emotional commitments to contradictory points of view—represented in the Western conventionally through the antagonistic values of civilization and the frontier. Were the American not convinced that the good life is to be found somewhere, he would not have such a desire to roam to and fro over the allegorical Western prairies in search of it; yet were the happiness he seeks all to be found in one symbolic place he would not feel the constant need to keep searching. He wanders tirelessly between the contrary symbolic virtues of civilization and the frontier; at home nowhere, his search for happiness is a constant endeavor to discover a place of permanence in a world of change.

chapter four

Good Men and True

At this point, before continuing with our analysis of the treatment of the settlement of the Great West, it is well to take time for a closer look at the denizens of the Garden of the Lord. In this and the next chapter, then, we will examine the Western hero and his sometime antagonist, sometime friend, the Indian. Both these figures have been much analyzed, and further discussion seems, at least at first glance, to be superfluous; yet the Western hero and the literary Indian have generally been considered in a context more or less divorced from the literature in which they appear. Consequently they have usually been interpreted as emblems of some larger concern in American thought without, in my opinion, due consideration of their roles within a specifically literary tradition.[1] Such interpretations ignore the marked difference between real cowboys and their fictional counterparts and, more to the point, tend to become somewhat supercilious in their contemplation of Western fiction on the grounds that it is not "true to life." The criticism is perfectly legitimate; the cowboy hero is not true to cowboy life, nor does the literary redskin by and large bear more than a nodding resemblance to the anthropologist's Indian. Yet the implicit inference drawn by such critics—the notion, based on realistic canons of taste, that a portrait which is in some factual sense unreal must categorically be inferior—is often unjust. In this chapter I will attempt to assess the role of the cowboy hero in Western fiction, concerning myself primarily with his place in American literature rather than discussing him in some larger ideological context of the American character in general.

Most critics who have felt at all compelled to comment upon the character of the Western hero have also felt that they ought somehow to apologize for him. In a way this represents a real critical awareness that the cowboy hero is out of the ordinary. Like all non-realistic figures he is subject to caricature or abuse on the basis of realistic criteria, and many of his conventional literary excesses can be interpreted as representative of something either ludicrous or unsavory.

It has been so generally reiterated as to have become by now almost an axiom, for instance, that the literary cowboy lives in an asexual world which in many ways mirrors the presexual fantasies of the immature; this is certainly partially true, but the critic who seizes upon this fact as a means by which the Western can be dismissed as "unreal" misses another larger point. For the theme of a great many Westerns, as the preceding chapter hopefully made clear, is the impact of the fact of sex upon a conventionally assumed presexual environment. The bride who comes to the West, the difference between male and female points of view, and many other phenomena are clear exemplifications of a larger sexual theme in Western literature. Even the scene which conventionally concludes many Westerns, in which the cowboy settles down to a life of matrimony, is not always due merely to the sentimental conventions of popular fiction. For though Scratchy Wilson may not marry, Jack Potter does, and the theme of marriage in "The Bride Comes to Yellow Sky" becomes as a result larger than the personal fortunes of any one character in the story. The confusion of the themes of Western story with the attitudes of particular characters has constantly plagued criticism of Western literature.

More important than this has been a general misunderstanding of the conventions of the Western hero's behavior, which have again been interpreted on the basis of a misapplied (and often factually mistaken) realism. The cowboy's fondness for his horse is a case in point. He tends to be overly enamored of his noble steed rather than developing the mature responsible love of human male for human female (or at least this is the allegation; the truth is not quite so simple); much has been made, on the basis of this, of his preadolescence and even of his unhallowed sexual drives. The cowboy's supporters have rushed to his defense. Not so, say they, for in real life the cowboy had to depend upon his faithful steed, for whom he often had unbounded respect and admiration. The chaste kiss planted on the horse's nose, according to this interpretation, is nothing more than a symbol of gratitude for services rendered.

Possibly. The realistic defender of cowboy story, however, gets into greater difficulty when he attempts to explain some of the more ludicrous aspects of the tradition of his hero's excessive kindness to animals. Walter Gann's *The Trail Boss* (1937), for example, details the mutual fortunes of one Bill Sanders and a steer named Sancho. Bill becomes fond of Sancho, one of the chattels of the ranch for which he works, and takes him under his special protection. After various adventures, Sancho is captured by the bad man of the story, a desperado named Ben Harte, who drowns him in an attempt to ride him across a river.[2] This act rouses the normally lethargic Bill to fury, and he tracks down Harte and turns him over to the sheriff. With the thousand-dollar reward money he builds a statue as a memorial to Sancho near the place where that noble animal had met his untimely end.

More incredible, and in many ways even sillier, is the animal plot of Robert Ames Bennet's *Branded* (1924). This story tells of the respective fortunes of two rivals for the affections of the heroine of the story, a young lady rancher. The plot is complicated by the presence of old Gotch Ear, a she-wolf who is living off the ranch calves. Gotch Ear is finally tracked down by the two rivals and shot, but one of her cubs is spared because the heroine thinks she is too cute to kill. The captive cub gradually turns into a one-girl wolf, of whom the heroine becomes extravagantly fond. The "bad" rival, realizing this, is wont on occasion to work the wolf over and blame the damage on the "good" rival. Finally the "good" rival, for reasons which never become quite clear, turns the wolf loose and the rest of the story details his winning of the heroine and his simultaneous hunt for the released wolf (named Splay Foot), who finally dies in the best tradition of *noblesse oblige*, having at one stroke killed the villain and saved the child of his successful rival, with whom the villain had absconded.

These two stories, which though of abysmally bad quality are not particularly unusual in conception, serve to prove rather decisively the impossibility of expecting the cowboy hero to act in any way more than superficially at one with "real life." The literary cowboy's love for animals reflects a convention—

possibly based at one remove upon the facts of real life in the West, or more likely aimed at the sentimental tastes of feminine readers of Western story—rather than an attempt at realistic portrayal of Western life. This particular convention may well be absurd, and most critics have recognized it as being so, but its foolishness is due not to its lack of realism but to the fact that the convention itself has no significant relationship to the story in which it appears.

It cannot be too strongly emphasized that the main "fact" of the literary cowboy's fictional life is that it is circumscribed by a series of conventions, some superficial, others more profound. If the reader realizes that even at his most apparently realistic the cowboy hero is actually conceived within a framework of conventions, he may be more inclined to judge a particular Western hero more charitably. For there is nothing necessarily suspect about literature which is highly conventionalized; but one cannot apply to such literature the same criteria which one would use in judging a work which purports to be realistic. The apparent realism of some Western fiction has caused unwary critics to assume that the genre is, or ought to be, a realistic one, and to attribute the weakness of inferior Western fiction to the fact that the writer does not know enough about the facts of Western life; actually, the success of any particular Western is much better assessed on the basis of how well the conventions which surround the story's protagonist serve to deepen and intensify the meaning of the parable.

As an example we may glance briefly at another convention which has often mistakenly been taken literally, and which has caused innumerable readers to balk at Westerns; the impossibly priggish morality of many a Western hero. At times, as in Zane Grey's *The U. P. Trail* (1918), the straight-arrow quality of the protagonist renders a book completely laughable. *The U. P. Trail,* for instance, recounts the adventures of a young engineer for the Union Pacific Railroad who, at one point in the tale, goes down the primrose path. He loses all his ambition to get ahead on the Railroad, takes to drinking and gambling, and even meets the beautiful madam of a house of prostitution. But fortunately, no matter how low he sinks, he never associates with "those camp women" (p. 204), as he self-righteously assures his commanding officer when he finally pulls himself together and returns to a position of responsibility with the line.

The impossible virtue of Grey's hero is echoed in another convention which becomes ridiculous when insensitively handled—the superhuman cunning of the Western hero. Frank H. Spearman's Whispering Smith, the protagonist of a once-famous Western novel of the same name (1906), is a case in point. Smith is fond of telling other characters what a first-class troubleshooter he is (though he always speaks diffidently and in a low voice so that no one will think he is bragging), and the other characters are equally fond of repeating his stories to each other. He is, we are told, exceptionally capable with a six-shooter and has already subdued numerous undesirables in other places. Such in fact turns out to be the case. He is indeed a very proficient gunfighter and succeeds in chastening without much difficulty the unruly elements of the population with whom he is faced. Unfortunately, by the time the showdown actually occurs the reader couldn't care less what happens.

It should be emphasized, however, that the fault in these two novels is not primarily a fault within the conventions themselves, but rather an esthetic failure on the part of the respective authors to grasp the significance of their materials. A chaste hero does not necessarily have to be silly, nor is a redoubtable gunfighter by definition a meaningless convention. Both can be accepted on the level of metaphor or symbol, however impossible they may appear in terms of realistic canons of taste.

All this is not to justify the foolish use of various conventions in numerous Westerns. Sancho the pet steer, Splay Foot the noble wolf, Zane Grey's priggish hero, and Spearman's tedious pistol champion are all unutterably silly. But this is not because the characters are unrealistically conceived, but because their conventionality is not shown to have any relation to the meaning of the various works in which they find themselves.

The first thing we must ask, then, about the cowboy hero is what his actions—absurd as they may well seem on occasion—signify in terms of the particular parable in which he exists. To start we must mention one aspect of his behavior which has been noted by many critics, the fact that he has more "insight" than the non-Western hero with whom he is always either implicitly or explicitly compared. He may not be any better educated than his non-Western adversary, but he understands more. Indeed, in many cases his understanding is seen as a direct result of his lack of formal knowledge, and his intuitive grasp of the meaning of things is placed in contrast to the pedantry of his more learned adversary. This tradition is a long and honorable one in the Western. A clearly articulated example of the conflict between the two kinds of knowledge may be found in the long discussions between Natty Bumppo and Obed Bat in *The Prairie;* and, as this example shows, it is one of the basic concerns of the ubiquitous later theme of the "dude" who goes west to discover a land in which his civilized values seem to have no relevance.

In origin this is a romantic notion, a corollary to the idea of the superiority of one raised in the country among the beneficent effects of nature to one whose moral growth has been stunted by the deprivations of the city. In the Western, however, the theme is handled in an atypical manner, more emphasis being placed upon the Westerner's craft and understanding than directly upon his moral worth. At bottom, of course, the two ideas are difficult to separate; for the traditional romantic hero's greater insight into moral values may well give him a certain pragmatic advantage in at least the romantic world at large. Yet where traditional romantic literature tends to focus more directly upon the moral worth of the hero which occasionally reflects upon his insight into the world at large, the Western focuses upon the hero's resourcefulness and capability in the external world and from this implies his perhaps greater moral worth. One should not lose sight of the fact that the difference is one of literary emphasis rather than of basic philosophical disagreement. However superficially unlike they may seem, the ethereal heroine of *Green Mansions* (to take a clear example), at one with the beasts of the field and the fowl of air, and Owen Wister's stalwart Virginian, equally at home in a cutthroat game of poker or hanging rustlers, are close relations. Both possess the gift of insight into the world in which they find themselves, and this gift sets them apart from the observers (the narrators of both novels) who are at a loss to understand the nuances of meaning of the world in which the heroes so easily move.

The convention of greater insight into the world which the Western hero possesses almost by definition may most easily be seen in the work of Owen Wister, for Wister's basic fictional preoccupation in his Western writing is to present the character of that cowboy hero who penetrates more deeply into the meaning of things than do others. From the time of his first attempt to define the essence of the cowboy hero, the only limitedly successful short story "How Lin McLean Went East" (1892), through the rest of his fictional career, Wister again and again defines the unique character of the Western hero as precisely this ability to interpret the facts of life insightfully. Indeed, the various anecdotal short stories which Wister put together to make his first Western novel, *Lin McLean* (1898), form a kind of *Bildungsroman* of the Western hero. At the beginning of *Lin McLean,* Lin is conceived as a likable young man well on the way toward becoming a worthless drifter. The first story in the book, a rewritten version of the earlier "How Lin McLean Went East," metaphorically sets the stage for the rest of the novel. It details Lin's amusing attempt to get East to see his brother in Massachusetts and the scenes of his nostalgically remembered happy childhood. First he loses all his money gambling, then strikes up with an old friend with whom he goes prospecting (unsuccessfully), wanders all over the West, finally wins a fast horse in a gambling game, which he successfully races and, with the money, goes back East. This is the story of "how" Lin McLean goes East, and Wister's point lies in the very circumstantial nature of the plot. For at the beginning of the novel McLean can do nothing purposefully.

McLean's discovery of purpose is coincidental with his discovery of insight into life. From an unhappy marriage into which he drifts more or less because he has nothing better to do, he moves to friendship with a street urchin he meets on a trip to Denver, and finally to a happy marriage with a girl who, unlike his first wife, is conventionally out of the ordinary but basically profoundly suitable. McLean's discovery of the difference between the apparently attractive and the really desirable is emblematic of his growing ability to cope with the realities of life by seeing beneath surface appearances.

Lin McLean is not a particularly successful novel, largely because Wister was unable to combine the various stories which were put together to make the book into a unified whole, and as a result the story is too fragmentary to give much of a total effect. Perhaps more important is the fact that the romantic plot has little real relation to McLean's being a Western hero. The love plot concerning two women, one apparently attractive yet evil, the other less attractive but profoundly good, between whom the hero must choose is a well-worn convention of many a sentimental novel; Wister has only shifted the drawing-room to the Western plains. Still his basic concern is evident, and McLean's search for control of life by penetrating through the superficies of things to an understanding of their meaning becomes the central concern of Wister's later fictional Western heroes.

A more successfully conceived hero than Lin McLean is Wister's Scipio LeMoyne, who appears as the friend and confidant of the Virginian in the novel of that name, and as the hero of several short stories in his own right. Like the Virginian, Scipio is a man who sees beneath the surface of things and moves by indirection. He is perhaps best conceived on his own in the story "Happy-Teeth," another anecdote of slight profundity but considerable interest in its portrayal of the insight of the typical Western hero. This story tells of the conflict between two rival storekeepers on an Indian reservation. One of them, "Happy-Teeth," is a parlor magician who delights in astonishing onlookers with various feats of legerdemain, the exhibition of which he is wont to conclude by protruding his tongue on which are displayed his false teeth. The other, befriended by Scipio, is unable to compete with Happy-Teeth's political influence—for Happy-Teeth has friends in the Indian bureau who support his storekeeping venture—and his store suffers as a result. The climax of the story comes when Scipio convinces Happy-Teeth to have a magic show for his Indian customers by way of attracting them to his store. The idea seems a good one, and accordingly the magic show is given; but what Scipio had neglected to mention is the fact that Indians have a superstitious dread of magic. The magic show ends with the Indians in precipitate flight from the store to which, we are informed, none of them will ever return again.

The point of the story, of course, is the demonstration of Scipio's superior knowledge which enables him to dupe his rival by making a trap into which he falls. Even the metaphor of "magic" which defines Scipio's rival serves to make the ironic point. For the real magician of the piece is not Happy-Teeth but Scipio, whose insight enables him to control the world in which his rival thinks he is so thoroughly at home.

Without question, however, Wister's most successful depiction of the cowboy hero is to be found in *The Virginian* (1902), the only novel of his which is at all widely known today. Since the Virginian himself is in many ways the sire of most later Western heroes, Wister's novel is worth examination at length. The fact that the title of the novel is the sobriquet of the story's protagonist is a point of some significance, for *The Virginian* does not develop according to conventional methods of plotting; rather Wister constantly introduces the reader into ever more subtle examples of his hero's ability to see through and to solve problems. Hence the subject of the story is really the character of the Virginian and not the sundry adventures which make up the novel's plot. The reader is asked to examine the character of the hero rather than lose himself in the miscellaneous action which fills the book. Wister organizes the reader's perceptions into the meaning of the novel by means of a first-person narrator closely modeled on himself. This is a favorite device of Wister's, not always too successfully used; but in *The Virginian* it works very well, for the reader's insight into the complex character of the Virginian is guided by that of the narrator, himself an Eastern dude at the beginning of the novel who, as the story progresses, develops an increasing insight into the meaning of the West and hence into the character of the Western hero.

Our first sight of the Virginian comes in a series of a few short vignettes which emphasize his proficiency in various Western skills of which Wister, and we, have no conception. We first see him roping a horse which no one else can get a lariat on, and his skill in horsemanship becomes a metaphor for his skill in other not strictly Western fields of endeavor in which he is a master and Wister a complete tyro. Wister's inability to understand the facts of life in the West is the second point emphasized by the first scenes in the novel; for his trunk has gone astray, and he suggests to the Virginian—who has been sent into town by his employer in order to convey Wister to his ranch—that they might drive out to the ranch and then drive back into town for the trunk the following morning. From an Eastern point of view this seems a perfectly reasonable suggestion; but Wister is unaware that it is 263 miles to Judge Henry's ranch.

Other happenings in the town of Medicine Bow serve to emphasize the contrast between Wister and the Virginian. Wister is unable to understand why the Virginian is cold to his overtures of friendship, and yet how, on the other hand, he can allow his old friend Steve to call him a "son-of-a——." But Wister develops respect for the Virginian when he discovers what a capable manipulator he is of the world about him, for the principles on which this world moves are a complete mystery to Wister. Two events, prefigurations of the Virginian's later role in the novel, show his greater "insight" into this strange Western world.

The first of these is a long practical joke in which the Virginian succeeds in convincing a drummer who has offered to share his bed that he is prone to occasional nightmares from which, if awakened, he is likely to prove violent. The Virginian had already bet his friend Steve that he would have a bed to himself— accommodations in Medicine Bow were so crowded that the visitors had to double up—and his besting of the hapless drummer both wins the bet and underscores the Virginian's manipulative ability.

Though this particular practical joke is neither especially humorous nor a marvel of subtlety, Wister's purpose in including it is clear. For the Virginian manages throughout the novel to get his way by seeing beneath the surface appearances of things, and quite often the measure of his insight is his ability in tall story or practical jokes.

The second event in Medicine Bow important to the later development of the novel is the Virginian's lovemaking to the woman who runs the local restaurant. Here again the Virginian's success is placed in explicit contrast to the failure of the Eastern drummers, for though as Wister says "impropriety lurked noiselessly all over her" (p. 46), none of the drummers is able to elicit any sympathy from the attractive restaurant-keeper. The Virginian, however, succeeds where the others fail, and his prowess in love foreshadows his later success with Molly Stark, the heroine of the novel, whom he also wins where all others fail.

These instances of the Virginian's inevitable success are summed up in the poker game in which he engages in Medicine Bow. He is playing against Trampas, the later villain of the novel, from whom he wins heavily. Trampas tries to rattle the Virginian by means of slighting references to "amatures," but the Virginian does not lose his equanimity; however, when Trampas pushes his luck by trying to hurry the Virginian's bet—"Your bet, you son-of-a——," he says, the Virginian replies by drawing his pistol and retorting with the best-known line in Western fiction: "When you call me that, smile!" (pp. 27-29).

This short vignette, though notorious, has received insufficient critical notice. It is significant first of all that the Virginian's game is poker rather than faro or craps or any of the other common Western games of chance. For poker is a strange game in which winning depends not only upon the hand one holds considered in relation to some abstract mathematical standard of possibilities, but upon judgment of a number of relatively imponderable factors, most important of which is an understanding of the way in which one's opponents will behave. Poker, as everyone knows, is a game of "bluff" in which the "facts" about who has what cards are hidden beneath the misleading exterior of the "poker face." Good cards alone do not win at poker.

The game of poker, as Wister develops it, becomes a metaphor for the world of man, where realities are also not easily seen because of deceptive appearances. Like the game of poker, the world is also a game of "bluff," and the man of insight will do best in both. Significantly, the Virginian places little faith in the idea of luck, though he is successful both in love and at cards, two fields in which luck is usually assumed to play an important role. For the Virginian the idea of luck is nothing more than an unsatisfactory explanation for apparently inexplicable phenomena; a man who can see beneath the surface can dispense with the notion of luck.

In the first scenes of the novel at Medicine Bow, then, Wister presents us with a series of apparently unrelated events, all of which go to show the Virginian's superior insight into the world around him, and to hint very strongly that this superior insight gives the Virginian a great degree of control over it; the remainder of the novel presents to the reader the measure of the Virginian's control.

The Virginian's superior insight is most successfully presented in the story of his running quarrel with Trampas, and the final intellectual showdown between them combines the themes of the practical joke and the game of bluff which were first developed at Medicine Bow in the early pages of the novel. In the course of the book Trampas comes to work at Judge Henry's ranch along with the Virginian. At one point Judge Henry sends a crew of men, with the Virginian in temporary charge, to deliver a trainload of beeves to the stockyards at Chicago. The Virginian is also supposed to bring the crew back intact to Judge Henry's ranch, lest the ranch be left short-handed. The assignment proves routine until the returning crew hear reports of a rich gold strike and Trampas tries to get them to desert Judge Henry and follow him to the mines. The struggle for dominance takes the form of a tall-story contest between Trampas and the Virginian. The dissident faction has managed to discredit the Virginian through Wister, his friend, by telling him a tall story which he believes. Trampas, flushed with success, tells another to the Virginian himself, concluding, "You've been running too much with aristocrats" (p. 183). The Virginian bides his time.

A bridge has washed out just before the station where the mutineers plan to desert for the mines, and there the Virginian makes his play. He tells a truly masterful tall-tale about the former frog ranches at Tulare which, according to him, made a fortune by raising prize bullfrogs for restaurants in the East. He manages to lure the mutineers into speculation about whether there is more money in frogs or in gold and then squashes their hopes by telling how the frog industry vanished. The Tulare frog ranchers, he says, played a thoughtless joke on two big Eastern buyers who, in revenge, killed the market. They "wiped frawgs off the slate of fashion," as the Virginian picturesquely puts it: "Not a banker in Fifth Avenue'll touch one now if another banker's around watchin' him."

Of course the whole story is a complete fabrication; there never was a frog industry at Tulare. But the Virginian's story has won the duel of wits and the erstwhile mutineers give him their allegiance. They go with him; the idea of deserting with Trampas for the gold fields is forgotten. "Frawgs are dead, Trampas," the Virginian concludes, "and so are you" (p. 200).

The most interesting aspect of this duel of wits between Trampas and the Virginian lies in the fact that the real conflict between the two men is never made explicit. Both men attempt indirectly to win the allegiance of the mutinous crew, and the struggle between the two, like their earlier struggle in the poker game, becomes a battle of "bluff." Trampas, in terms of the poker metaphor, makes the same mistake both times; he calls the Virginian's bluff unaware that it is backed by a strong hand. The Virginian in both cases understands Trampas's weakness, and

wins both games by a similar play; he forces Trampas into
"calling" him by pretending his hand is weak.

The observers of the game of bluff as well may be divided into
those with insight and those incapable of seeing beneath the
surface. The mutinous cowboys, for whom the game is played,
understand what is going on beneath the surface; the Indians
lounging around the stalled train, though they understand
nothing of what is going on, immediately sense that the Virginian is "the great man"; and a marvelous dialogue takes place
between one of the passengers and his wife. He, understanding
something of what is really at stake, sends for her to come and
hear the story; when she arrives where the Virginian is gulling
the mutineers, she is unimpressed.

> "Why, George," [she says] . . . , "he's merely deceiving them!
> He's merely making that stuff up out of his head."
> "Yes, my dear, that's merely what he's doing."
> "Well, I don't see why you imagined I should care for this. I
> think I'll go back."
> "Better see it out, Daisy. This beats the geysers or anything
> we're likely to find in the Yellowstone."
> "Then I wish we had gone to Bar Harbor as usual," said the
> lady, and she returned to her Pullman (p. 196).

In the statement of the good lady who wishes she were in Bar
Harbor we recognize the incomprehension of the typical dude,
that is, of one who cannot or will not see beneath the surface
of Western life. The moral landscape of the West, as her husband
obliquely tells her, is of considerably more interest than Old
Faithful.

The point is made again when Wister, at Judge Henry's ranch,
tells the story to the Judge and some guests, among whom is
an obnoxious itinerant minister named Dr. MacBride. The Judge
and most of the guests are not only amused by the cleverness
of the story but are filled with praise for the Virginian's psychological acumen. Not so Dr. MacBride, who says pompously:
"Am I to understand that these—a—cow-boys attempted to
mutiny, and were discouraged in this attempt upon finding
themselves less skilful at lying than the man they had plotted
to depose?" On one level this is a perfect description of what
had actually happened, but the tone of Dr. MacBride's comment
betrays the fact that he is a victim of that lack of perception

which all Easterners first have upon their arrival in the West. Like the lady in the Pullman, he does not see the point of what is going on; and like the greenhorn Wister who earlier could not understand why the Virginian let Steve call him a "son-of-a——," Dr. MacBride is put off by what he considers the questionable taste of the proceedings. Molly Stark, the girl whom the Virginian will later marry, understands better the reasons behind the Virginian's conduct. "It wasn't that George Washington couldn't tell a lie," she tells Dr. MacBride. "He just wouldn't. I'm sure if he'd undertaken to he'd have told a much better one than Cornwallis" (pp. 226-27).

The above examples by no means exhaust the various devices by which Wister shows us that superior insight which renders the Virginian equal to any occasion, "the only kind of equality," says Wister, "which I recognize" (p. 202), but hopefully they make the point of Wister's conception of the Virginian as a man with "insight" sufficiently clear so that further examples are unnecessary. In conclusion, however, we might look at the one time in the novel when the Virginian explains his own view of insight. He and Wister are discussing another character in the novel named "Shorty," a perennial ne'er-do-well who is placed in explicit contrast to the Virginian. Throughout the book, while the Virginian prospers, Shorty's fortunes consistently decline, and he ultimately comes under the influence of Trampas, who finally rewards his lack of understanding by murdering him. Of him, the Virginian says:

> "Now back East you can be middling and get along. But if you go to try a thing on in this Western country, you've got to do it *well*. You've got to deal cyards *well*; you've got to steal *well*; and if you claim to be quick with your gun, you must be quick, for you're a public temptation, and some man will not resist trying to prove he is the quicker. You must break all the Commandments *well* in this Western country, and Shorty should have stayed in Brooklyn, for he will be a novice his livelong days" (p. 399).

In the Virginian's statement we notice the peculiar blending of the ideas of ability and of insight which we mentioned earlier. Shorty's inability to understand either himself or the nature of the world in which he moves is mirrored in his lack of ability to do things well. He is a perpetual "novice," that is, one bereft of ability to learn. In the symbolic environment of the Western such a man as Shorty must inevitably come to grief, for the basic fact of such life (at least as conceived in literary terms) is that it tests one's insight. There is no room in such a West for a perennial novice: he must either come to some understanding of Western values (as Wister does in the course of the novel); or he must go back East where his lack of insight will not be tested; or he must be worsted by the very nature of the Western environment in which he finds himself. There are no other alternatives.

That insight into the world which Wister sees as the most significant quality possessed by the Western hero is basic to the character of most other fictional Westerners, who are conceived ultimately as men of insight, and whose success depends upon their ability to see more deeply into the meaning of circumstances than their opponents. Nowhere is this aspect of the Western hero's character more evident than in those Westerns which closely resemble the typical detective story. There is a certain basic similarity between the traditional detective and the cowboy detective who, whether by accident or profession, must solve some crime or unravel some mystery. Like the traditional cowboy hero, the detective must be able to explain facts which apparently make no sense, and must be able to understand the cause of inexplicable or misleading circumstances. Finally, like the detective, the cowboy's success depends upon his superior powers of observation, whether of his fellow man (as Wister's Virginian was enabled to win at poker by his understanding of his opponents' probable behavior) or of the "clues" provided by the external world.

One of the more interesting of those Western novels which closely resemble the detective story is *Destry Rides Again* (1930) by Frederick Schiller Faust (Max Brand). In this novel Harrison Destry, the local ne'er-do-well of the town of Wham, is convicted by twelve good men and true and sent to prison for a crime he did not commit. He is convicted largely on the basis of his unsavory reputation rather than on the actual evidence; the jurymen tacitly assume that no one else in Wham is capable of committing the crime and convict Destry accordingly. When Destry gets out of prison he undertakes a vendetta against the men who have sent him to jail, determined to hunt down and kill each one. At first he is concerned only with avenging

himself upon those who have done him wrong, but the scope
of his revenge widens to include a search for the real culprit as
well as the punishment of the unfortunate jurymen. The real
criminal turns out to be his friend Chester Bent, the one man
in whom, throughout the novel, Destry had had complete trust.

The plot of *Destry Rides Again*, as should be clear from this
cursory summary, very closely resembles that of the conventional
whodunit. The story of the unjustly accused man who struggles
to clear himself, and in so doing of necessity discovers the
real perpetrator of whatever dastardly deed he has been convicted
of committing, is a perfectly familiar figure in detective literature. The great weakness of *Destry Rides Again* is also a weakness of much poor detective fiction. For Destry does not inevitably discover, on the basis of his own researches, the fact
that his best friend is in fact the villain whom he seeks; he is
told this by a boy whom he has befriended. The reader has the
uneasy suspicion that, left to his own devices, Destry would
continue to be Chester's dupe.

In sum, the real flaw in Faust's conception of Destry's character lies precisely in the fact that he does not present his
hero as insightful. Wister's Virginian (and more to the point
here, any good fictional detective) would have arrived at an
understanding of Chester's villainy without being told. But
Destry, despite Faust's intentions, generates little interest in
the reader. Like the Virginian, he has great abilities in the conventional fictional skills of the range. He is an expert horseman, a resourceful and daring desperado, and a man of great
skill in weaponry. But none of these skills adds up to anything;
they are not symbols of a deeper perception into the meaning
of things.

A more successful Western detective story than *Destry Rides
Again* is the recent novel *Station West* (1947) by Frederick D.
Glidden (Luke Short). The hero of this novel, an army lieutenant,
has to discover an answer to the bizarre and apparently unimportant mystery of who stole seventy uniforms from a government quartermaster train. The crime is seen to be more serious,
however, when we discover that the U. S. Army post near the
mining town of South Pass City, where the novel takes place, is
keeping gold for the residents of the town who cannot ship
it out for fear of its being stolen. The post is undermanned, and
someone is stirring up various rumors of trouble, each of which

the garrison must examine at the cost of a still further reduction in strength. Obviously the master criminal, whoever he may be, is biding his time until the garrison is scattered over the countryside on futile cavalry patrols, when he will dress his men in the stolen uniforms, swoop down on the weakened post, and steal the gold. No one has any idea of who the master criminal might be, and to complicate Lieutenant Haven's job further is the fact that time is running out. The expected robbery attempt is imminent.

The world of *Station West,* unlike that of *Destry Rides Again,* is obviously organized in terms of "outsiders" and "insiders." Lieutenant Haven, working incognito, must somehow discover who stole the uniforms and must penetrate into his councils. Haven goes about this task in a typical way. Understanding that it is impossible for him to find out anything by merely snooping around the outside of the criminal world of South Pass City, he beats up the local tough guy, thus establishing a reputation as a dangerous man, and is circumspectly approached as a result by the local town magnate, who offers him a job running his stage line. Haven manages to use this slender connection with the "inside" world of South Pass City as a means of worming himself more deeply into the councils of his employer and ultimately of discovering the whereabouts of the uniforms, which are then repossessed by the army.

Haven's ability to solve the mystery is, as is the typical detective's, due to his gift for penetrating beneath the surface of things. His more definitely Western qualities, however, set him off somewhat from the ordinary private eye. He shares the capability to outwit and outthink his opponent, the gift for interpreting clues, and general powers of observation with the more conventional detective, but he shows these capabilities in a different way; for the metaphors for his insight beneath the superficial appearances of the world are not specifically related to his profession as a detective. Though he is a good fighter, a good stage driver, and a good tracker, and though he understands animals and the nature of blackmail, and though it is true that all these attributes help him immeasurably in solving the mystery, none of them is a specific requirement of the detective's profession. In fact, Haven is not himself either a professional or an amateur detective by choice; he is an army officer on detached duty, which in the case of his assignment in *Station West* involves some detective work. The point of course is that where the traditional detective is seen as one whose profession requires of him the ability to discover the truth beneath enigmatic facts which others find completely baffling, the Western hero is conversely seen as one whose ability to understand the significance behind often confusing facts enables him, should occasion require, to assume successfully the role of detective.

The ability to assess facts in such a way as to understand their underlying significance is also at the heart of the many portrayals of Western heroes by Eugene Manlove Rhodes, without question one of the best writers in the Western tradition. Himself a cowboy, Rhodes is one of the few Western authors who is both qualified at first hand to write about the "West-that-was" and who has the literary ability to transcend the often pointless anecdotalism of such writing. He is the only Western author to have received the scholarly accolades of republication in two full-length reprints and of a careful and thorough bibliography.[3] Though his *aficionados* are often somewhat extravagant in their praise, their general point is well taken; for Rhodes's work is immeasurably superior to the generality of slick Western fiction, even though Rhodes himself was a writer for the slick magazines.

All this is not an attempt to explain away the manifest faults which spoil much of Rhodes's work. At times, when his adherence to the conventions of "slick" writing trips him up, he can be one of the most maddening of writers. His stories are marred by an annoying coincidental quality, in which someone invariably happens along just at the right moment to hear the villains plotting their crimes, which they do explicitly and at great length. On occasion his overexplicitness destroys an otherwise profoundly moving fictional moment; as in "Loved I Not Honor More," where the story—based on an incident of Rhodes's own biography—of a rancher who will not sell his spare horses to the British cavalry for remounts because he does not want to support the British war against the Boers is spoiled by a sentimental ending in which the rancher and the English major who has come to buy the horses first box with one another and afterwards shake hands to prove there are no hard feelings. Even his often beautifully conceived dialogue deteriorates far too much into the tedious smartness which passes for wit among the devotees of the slick magazines. When Rhodes is at his best, however, these faults are only those of detail, which may mar but do not destroy the real quality of his fiction.

Rhodes's greatest strength as a Western writer is to be found in his presentation of the Western hero, with the explication of whose character he concerns himself in most of his novels and stories. One of the more interesting, though certainly not the best, of these is *Good Men and True* (1910). This novel tells of a rancher, Jeff Bransford (who, like many of Rhodes's heroes, appears in several works), who is involved in a shooting scrape and is captured by a local politician and former State Senator named Judge Thorpe. Thorpe had engineered the assassination of one Captain Charles Tillotson of the Texas Rangers, which Bransford's coincidental arrival on the scene had frustrated. Thorpe, however, being a resourceful man, had kidnapped the wounded Bransford so that Tillotson would be accused of murder, one of the assassins having been killed in the gunfight and Bransford being the only witness. Thorpe's plan is to hold Bransford incommunicado until Tillotson is convicted of murder and duly executed, after which he will be released. Bransford, who before his kidnapping had been teaching himself to type, agrees to keep quiet in his captivity if Thorpe will get him a typewriter, and asks as well for permission to write to his wife. Thorpe agrees to both of these proposals, providing Bransford submit the letter to his censorship. Bransford accordingly writes a long and involved letter recounting his adventures in Old Mexico which passes Thorpe's censorship and is duly posted. The letter is mailed to Bransford's wife, but his friends get it, for Bransford is not married—a detail he had neglected to mention to Judge Thorpe. This clever ruse alerts Bransford's friends, who manage to deduce from the clues contained in the apparently innocuous letter that Bransford is held captive in a certain area of Juarez and on the basis of this deduction begin a search for him, letting him know their plans by means of enigmatic notices placed in the personal columns of the local newspaper with which Judge Thorpe has considerately provided Bransford. The rest of the novel tells of the progress of the search and ends with Bransford's rescue, after which Judge Thorpe is captured and turned over to justice and Captain Tillotson is vindicated.

As this summary should have emphasized, *Good Men and True* bears a very close resemblance to one typical kind of detective story, the tale of ratiocination in which the detective ponders the meaning behind some baffling clue. Most significant in terms of our discussion of the cowboy hero is the enigmatic letter which

Bransford sends to his friends and which they successfully decipher. Both Bransford and his friends are able to communicate by means of language which they understand but which their opponents do not, and in their correspondence they convey information by a language of allusion of which their adversaries are unaware. The metaphorical structure of the novel is summed up in the scene where Judge Thorpe reads the letter which Bransford has so carefully constructed. Thorpe can see nothing beneath the surface meaning of the letter and assumes that it has been written according to his instructions, while in fact the entire document is a cleverly reasoned exercise in code.

Rhodes's stories generally have a distinct detective-story flavor. Usually, however, as in this novel, Rhodes's preoccupations go beyond the mere discovery of the "truth" behind a particular event. Bransford's friends not only decipher the letter but act upon their information in order to set Bransford free. In this regard they are typical of another related aspect of the character of the Western hero, the fact that he is conceived as basically an *active* person. His insight beneath the surfaces of the world around him does not lead him to a position of philosophical despair. He sees what must be done and then does it, knowing that what he does is justifiable because he understands more of the facts than does anyone else.

The fact that the cowboy hero is both insightful and active gives him a certain distrust of the forms by which less gifted mortals operate; for he believes that he is better able to resolve problems on his own than by means of the conventional methods used by ordinary men. It is significant that none of Bransford's friends thinks of calling in the police, or for that matter any outsider. They would only gum things up. Bransford's friends, impatient of restrictions, work outside the law, and here is precisely the point; for if one knows, through a deeper perception into the heart of things, what the right course of action is, one should act on this knowledge despite the forms of legality or of conventional opinion. Destry is another convenient example of the same idea: he does not attempt to take legal action against the twelve good men and true who have unjustly convicted him, but trusts in his six-shooter and his knowledge of the truth. If one knows the truth, why bother with the conventional forms of proof?

The cowboy hero here reflects another preoccupation of American society at large, the idea that the individual must in certain instances be prepared to act on his own outside of conventional forms. More than that, the individual's conscience is what is ultimately to be followed, rather than any social consensus. Thoreau's eloquent argument defending civil disobedience is by no means unrelated to Harrison Destry's decision to solve problems by the effective if unconventional code of justice of Judge Colt, nor is the idea a particularly novel one in Western fiction. It will be recalled that in *The Pioneers* the sympathetic residents of Templeton connive in Natty Bumppo's escape from the prison to which Judge Temple had sentenced him.

An interesting corollary to this idea is the notion—not hard to find in either *Destry* or *Good Men and True*—that the respected citizen is not all he seems. In *Destry* this idea is not much more profound than the detective story convention of "the butler did it," that is, of making one's villain be the least likely suspect. In *Good Men and True,* however, the idea is more carefully developed, for here Rhodes's villain cynically uses the forms of respectability to cover his traces. In order to be a successful villain, Judge Thorpe must have about him the trappings of respectability. This in turn implies another intriguing notion, the fact that in one respect at least the villain sees almost as deeply beneath the surface appearances of things as the hero, and like the hero is capable of using his understanding to manipulate the world around him. The similarities between the hero and the villain in the Western often lead them to a kind of mutual respect —or if that is too strong a word, at least a mutual admiration— for each other's abilities. This is not true of Destry, who is clearly the dupe of his friend Chester Bent, but it is true of the relationship between Bransford and Judge Thorpe, both of whom are almost fulsome in each other's praise. It is also true of Lieutenant Haven, who openly admires the genius which can think up so clever a way to steal someone else's gold.[4] In a way it is rather refreshing to see a Western hero's admiration for his adversary's ability, however deplorable his moral sense may be.

Indeed, quite often in Western fiction it is not the great villains who are deplored but the lesser criminals, the petty chiselers, and the dupes. One thinks immediately of Shorty in *The Virginian,* a man without the capacity for outstanding good or overarching evil. In the world of the novel he is universally treated with contempt; there is little pity for the plight of the perpetual novice in the Western.

A clearer example may be found in the fortunes of a minor character in *Station West* named Mark Bristow. When the novel opens he is in debt for $12,000—significantly, he is a perpetual loser at the gambling table—to Saul Prince, the villain. Against the larger plot of Lieutenant Haven's attempt to discover the whereabouts of the stolen uniforms, Glidden plays off Bristow's frantic efforts to pay his debts. Bristow is a foil to Haven in much the same way that Shorty is one to the Virginian; his ineffectuality places him in contrast to the successful hero. Throughout *Station West* Bristow's attempts to lay his hands on the money, whether by honest or dishonest means, are inevitably frustrated. He tries without success to blackmail Prince, and finally, in desperation, promotes a prize-fight between Haven and the blacksmith at the local army post. He instructs Haven, who is the heavy favorite, to throw the fight, so that he, by placing bets on the blacksmith at favorable odds, can make a killing. Though the fight never comes off, Haven has no intention of throwing it, and when Prince gets wind of Bristow's plot he also places heavy bets on the blacksmith and, by reducing the odds, ruins Bristow's scheme. The Virginian's remark about Shorty, that "if you go to try a thing on in this Western country, you've got to do it *well*," might just as well apply to Bristow.

The notion that the most contemptible, though admittedly not the most evil, member of Western society is the dupe rather than the villain is one ramification of the theme of the dude, who is by definition unknowing and easily preyed upon by the unscrupulous. Owen Wister handles this theme brilliantly in one of his best short stories, a little-known masterpiece called "The Gift Horse." In this story Wister befriends a likable young man named McDonough. When McDonough is thrown from a horse and his leg broken, Wister offers to pay his hospital bills; in gratitude McDonough tells him that if he comes back West next year he "shall have the best horse on the river" (p. 171). Wister, who is trying to prove his ability as a Westerner by searching for a hidden valley called Still Hunt Spring, is delighted to take up McDonough's offer when he does return the following summer. McDonough, who for some reason Wister cannot understand is not held in much esteem by the other cowboys, makes good on his promise and presents Wister with a beautiful horse and the cryptic suggestion that he keep west of the mountains. Wister disregards this well-meant warning and sets off toward the east, eventually finding Still Hunt Spring, where he is almost lynched by a party of vigilantes. For the gift horse had been stolen by McDonough, who had been using Still Hunt Spring as the hideaway for his rustled horses.

In this story we again see the ubiquitous theme of the inability of the dude to see beneath the surface of things. Wister cannot understand why the cowboys do not share his admiration for McDonough, nor why they view anyone who is too interested in the whereabouts of Still Hunt Spring with some suspicion. He is not even warned by the gift horse, whose brand he does not recognize, nor are his apprehensions raised when he discovers that the horse knows the way to Still Hunt Spring. Furthermore, he will not take warning from the suspicions of those who presumably know better, the cowboys who have not been able to catch McDonough with any stolen horses in his possession, but are nevertheless thoroughly convinced that he is the rustler whom they seek.

More to our specific point is the fact that the story of "The Gift Horse" is a kind of ironic descant on the well-worn theme of the joke played on the tenderfoot by those in the know. McDonough's promise to give Wister "the best horse on the river" is really a pretty good joke in a grim sort of way, though it nearly has disastrous consequences when Wister is caught by the vigilantes while in possession of stolen goods. But the final moral to the story is given in unequivocal terms by Scipio LeMoyne, who rescues Wister from the lynching party. "You need a nurse!" he says contemptuously: "Any travelling you do should be in a baby coach" (p. 201).

The idea we have been exploring that the Western hero is to be praised for following his insight rather than relying upon legal and social forms has yet another dimension in Western fiction. For if the man with insight is defined by his ability to act outside the law, the man who stands within the law and acts according to established social codes may well be viewed somewhat suspiciously. The chances are, from the cowboy hero's point of view, that such a man will either be imperceptive and contemptible like the dude or the other dupes of Western fiction, or that he will be, like the respectable villain, a morally corrupt man who cynically manipulates the forms of legality for his own nefarious purposes.

In any event, the nature of legality in the Western is that it is a rather suspicious concept. Though the Western may well affirm the concepts of law and justice—there is very little Western literature of even a faintly nihilistic moral tone—it simultaneously points out that law and justice are no close relations to legalistic forms. At times the contempt for legalism is expressed through a particular character in a story. Bret Harte, for instance, is inordinately fond of the outcast from society who is in some way morally superior to those who remain within. His Mr. John Oakhurst, for example, though a professional gambler and hence beyond the pale of polite society, is in the habit of returning his winnings to those who cannot afford to lose or who are too green to make successful gamblers;[5] and Miggles, the prostitute-heroine of the story of the same name, is more virtuous than the conventionally "virtuous" members of the community at large.

In Harte's writing this convention tends to have little meaning and to reduce itself to a device for arousing a spurious sympathy for a misunderstood hero under whose predictably rough exterior beats an equally predictable heart of gold. Other writers are more explicit in their contempt for the forms of law. The reader may recall the two trials in *The Sea of Grass,* both of which make a mockery of the concept of justice. A more interesting example still is to be found in the common reliance of the Western hero upon various irregular forms of justice, notably vigilante law or appeal to the equalizer, Judge Colt.

The vigilante justice which so nearly unjustly executes Wister in "The Gift Horse" comes in for considerable praise in *The Virginian.* In this novel the Virginian and some of the other honest cattlemen take action against the rustlers who are plaguing the Wyoming countryside.[6] Molly Stark is deeply shocked by what she considers the breakdown of law and order which such vigilante justice implies. Judge Henry, the owner of the Sunk Creek Ranch and a political figure of some importance in the territory, defends Western lynch law, which he places in explicit contrast to an apparently similar folkway in the South. The lynching of a Negro in the South, he says, is a defiance of the law, for there the convicted criminal is taken away from the due forms of law by which justice would eventually be done. In contrast, Wyoming is a territory which is without effective formal law. Courts and juries are corrupt and habitually let rustlers go. In such a situation, Judge Henry concludes, "your ordinary citizen ... must take justice back into his own hands where it was once at the beginning of all things. Call this primitive, if you will. But so far from being a *defiance* of the law, it is an *assertion* of it" (p. 436).

Judge Henry here has eloquently expressed an idea with which, in some situations at least, almost everyone would agree. The difficulty lies in determining exactly when the law is in fact being ineptly or corruptly administered, and it should be added that the very nature of the cowboy hero quite often causes him to assume a larger degree of judicial boondoggling than a sober examination of the facts might warrant. The insight the cowboy hero possesses, which gives him the right to act according to his own code of action rather than that of society, and his concomitant belief that justice, at least in the West, is better administered directly than by means of corrupt or inefficient officials are both thoroughly taken to task in Walter Van Tilburg Clark's ironic study of frontier "justice," *The Ox-Bow Incident* (1940).

The story of *The Ox-Bow Incident* stands as an ironic footnote to the moral position Judge Henry so eloquently describes. Rustlers are active in the desolate town of Bridger's Wells, where the action of this novel takes place, as they were in the Wyoming of *The Virginian*. Likewise, the aggrieved stockmen have a suspicion that the law is not doing its duty. Consequently, when word is brought in that a stockman has been killed and his cattle stolen, the denizens of Bridger's Wells form a posse to bring the perpetrators of this crime to justice. They eventually capture three men who are driving the missing cattle for which they have no bill of sale, and one of the men, to make appearances even more incriminating, has in his possession a revolver belonging to the slain cattleman. The posse, which has no legal sanction, decides that the presumption of guilt is overwhelming and executes the three men rather than taking them back to stand trial. But on the way back to Bridger's Wells the returning vigilantes meet a party of riders which includes the sheriff and the supposedly murdered rancher who, it turns out, had in fact sold the cattle to the accused rustlers.

In his parable of the posse which, though acting from the highest motives nevertheless does the worst possible thing, Clark focuses upon two separate but related themes. The first of these, which from our point of view is the lesser in importance, is the study of the way in which a group of generally decent men can be turned into a bloodthirsty mob. The second is an equally tragic exploration of the problem of how appearances can be deceiving, even to those who think they understand the truth. Clark cleverly develops and presents the evidence by which the alleged rustlers are convicted in such a manner that the reader can have little doubt of their guilt. They have in their possession goods which are apparently stolen, and for the possession of which they can account only by a wildly improbable story. More important, they have the gun of the supposedly slain man, and an equally improbable story to account for that; their explanation that he had lost it is not very convincing on the surface, even though, as it develops, it happens to be true.

On the basis of the evidence it has in its possession the posse is certainly justified in entertaining grave suspicion of its three captives' guilt. Its error comes when it translates these suspicions into action for, says Clark, the facts the posse has at its disposal are faulty and hence, however rightly it thinks it is acting, it cannot act in accordance with justice. The supposed rustlers should have been taken into custody until the facts became clear, and the posse's assumption of superior knowledge has no justification in reality. In short, the cowboy "heroes" of *The Ox-Bow Incident* are just as prone to error as the ordinary men whom they look down upon, but their capacity to do evil is much greater, for they act on their own without the various formal limitations upon their actions which society puts upon those who act within the law.

The completely opposite "morals" to the stories of *The Virginian* and *The Ox-Bow Incident* serve to point up the paradoxical nature of the whole idea of civil disobedience, and to emphasize the American's own divided mind about the subject. For the American finds himself in theoretical defense of both sides of the issue: with Thoreau he believes that civil disobedience is at times the only possible moral action; yet at the same time he is aware that unlicensed disrespect for duly constituted authority may become a greater evil than the abuses which it attempts to rectify. Both Wister and Clark emphasize the paradoxical nature of civil disobedience by presenting their characters themselves with divided minds about the proper course of action. In *The Virginian* Molly Stark is silenced but not convinced by Judge Henry's eloquent argument, and the near miscarriage of vigilante "justice" in "The Gift Horse" presents another argument on Wister's part for at least the possibility of error by self-appointed legal authority. Similarly, in *The Ox-Bow Incident* not all the posse is willing to go along with the idea of hanging the captives, even though the presumption of their guilt seems overwhelming. A minority of the posse, though powerless to stay the execution, refuses to take active part in it.

The other common way in which the Western hero conventionally takes the administration of justice into his own hands is by means of an appeal directly to the "equalizer," Judge Colt. The man who, like Harrison Destry, goes "gunning" for someone is a stock figure in many Westerns, though his type is perhaps best seen in the figure of the professional gunfighter, the "hired gun."

It should be noted immediately that the professional gunfighter differs somewhat from the vigilante. Where the vigilante is almost by definition an expression of the community will (however misguided or reprehensible this will may on occasion be), the gunman is a man who works completely on his own. He not only lays aside the forms of legality, but he defines himself as standing outside the pale of society.

In the figure of the professional gunman we can immediately recognize the presence of the by now familiar man of "craft," the Western hero who does something well. This fact alone, in terms of the convention we have been discussing, gives him at least the presumption of moral insight, and the fact that he defines himself as a "loner" gives additional reason to assume his moral superiority to the corruption of society. But such a character's actions place him in what is often a profoundly paradoxical position.

In the typical story of the professional gunfighter, the protagonist sells his skill in weaponry to someone else for wages. Symbolically what he has done is to abnegate his right of moral choice, for when one hires out his gun for wages, one shoots whomever one is told to shoot, whatever one may think about the rights and wrongs of the case.[7] In consequence, the gunfighter has two large areas of choice within his own world. He may remain unattached to any party, true to some kind of personal vision of moral justice, or he may sell his gun for wages and by so doing either abnegate his moral responsibility or cynically use his abilities for immoral ends. Often the ideological conflict between these two areas of choice is shown in terms of two gunfighters, one of whom cynically hires his gun out for wages in contrast to the other who retains his freedom of moral action. The reader will recall countless Western films in which the conflict between good and evil is signalized by the villain's bringing in a horde of rowdy gunmen to enforce his will, who are opposed by the "good" gunfighter of equal proficiency and superior morality, who has agreed to help the other side.

One of the best of these films was *Shane,* based upon an interesting novel of the same title by Jack Schaefer (1949). In this novel Shane, the "good" gunfighter, rides into a little Western town and settles down with a family of homesteaders. The homesteaders and small ranchers are engaged in a range war with the great cattle baron of the valley, who is trying to run them out. The situation deteriorates as the novel progresses until finally Shane, who has tried to remain neutral, is forced to take the homesteaders' part. The cattle baron imports another gunman, and in the novel's climactic scene Shane kills both the gunman and the cattle baron in a gun duel and, his work done, rides out of town.

In many ways *Shane* is a heavily flawed novel, largely because Schaefer is unable to control the fictional world of his story. As a result, everything is a little too vivid and overdone, even for a story which must depend upon bloodshed and violence for its effect. Combined with this is the fact that Schaefer tells his story through the eyes of a small boy, to whom Shane is wont to impart bits of platitudinous wisdom which are totally gratuitous both in themselves and in the context of the novel. This habit of didacticism is not confined to Shane alone, for the other characters in the novel are forever explaining at great length just what is going on. A more annoying fault is that Schaefer himself seems uncertain at times of what Shane is meant to symbolize. Shane's outcast status is fine as a symbolic statement of the inevitable fate of a man such as he must be, but when Schaefer tries to breathe some life into his character the results are unfortunate. Shane is not only solitary but, it develops, is nursing some kind of Byronic sorrow brought about by his lawless life. It is strongly implied that this sorrow has something to do with his having been, in the past, a cynical gunman like his present opponents, and Schaefer unsuccessfully tries to use this idea to give more depth to the conflict between his hero and the various adversaries with whom he is thrown into conflict.

Even when all this is admitted, however, *Shane* has a number of strengths. The greatest of these is the fact that the novel is not conceived realistically, nor does it depend much upon suspense. Schaefer here avoids a trap which many lesser Western writers fall into; for he clearly understands that if one is given a figure who is without question "the fastest gun in the West" no legitimate interest can be added to the story by raising the question of who will or will not win the inevitable gun duel. There is no question but that Shane will win it, for in the world of the novel no one else can.[8] "No man need be ashamed of being beat by Shane" (p. 185) Shane himself once says, and indeed the point of the novel is that no man can escape being beat by him.

If our interest cannot be held by suspense, the only significance which such a novel can possibly contain lies in the explication of the meaning which inheres in the inevitable gun duel, the outcome of which is a foregone conclusion. As Schaefer develops the meaning of his parable, it becomes clear that the world of the Western town in which the story of Shane is unfolding is a symbolic one in which Schaefer can present a basically allegorical concern. For Shane is a walking figure of God's providence in the confusing world of flux. At the beginning of the novel the forces of good (the homesteaders) are at the mercy of those of evil (the cattle baron); the arrival of Shane changes the whole picture, not merely by giving another gun to the weaker side but by symbolically affirming the inevitability of its victory.

Put thus strongly the novel sounds rather pat, but this is a quality it shares with all allegorical fiction, none of which stands up very well under the scrutiny of plot summary. What gives the novel its power is Schaefer's presentation of the character of Shane, who is depicted as an unknowable figure emblematic at once of solitariness and power. One of the more effective touches in the story is the preoccupation the other characters have with finding out who Shane is. All they succeed in discovering are his attributes, most of which they had known from the first. That he is a good gunfighter is all the knowledge they have of him, and when he rides away at the end of the novel he is just as mysterious as when he rode in at its beginning. Though the townsmen may try to discover Shane's identity they are unsuccessful, as indeed anyone must be who attempts to discover what such an allegorical figure is. For in itself Providence is unknowable to man; it can only be known through its actions in the world. The ultimate mysteriousness of Shane is affirmed by the little boy who narrates the story when he tells, at its end, of the rumors of Shane's identity which from time to time penetrated the town. For he knows better than any of them who Shane really was: "He was the man who rode into our little valley out of the heart of the great shining West and when his work was done rode back whence he had come and he was Shane" (p. 214).

One other aspect of Shane's character ought briefly to be noted. This is his solitariness, a characteristic which he shares with many another Western hero, gunfighter or no. In this novel it should be clear that Shane's isolation is a function of his allegorical nature rather than, as is often assumed of the Western hero, some kind of inability to relate to society. Shane does not *relate* to society or for that matter to anything else; he *dominates* it. His ability as a gunfighter and his habit of solitude are both attributes of an allegorical figure who by definition is superior to, and hence stands aloof from, the weakness and hypocrisy of society.

Schaefer's presentation of the conflict between the two gunfighters by no means exhausts the possibilities of the theme of the hired gunman, though any fiction which deals with the conflict between two gunfighters must be presented in a way analogous to *Shane*. That is, the story, to have any significance, must be conceived in some kind of allegorical terms in which the two characters are presented as types of opposite moral positions. When, however, the attributes of the two gunmen are combined into one figure, a different kind of story develops, as in Eugene Manlove Rhodes's "Beyond the Desert" (1914).

"Beyond the Desert" is the story of a man named MacGregor who, at the beginning, has robbed a bank and is fleeing from a posse. After successfully eluding it, he meets a rancher named Clay Mundy, who agrees to shelter him in return for his aid in a range war in which Mundy is involved. As the story develops, MacGregor meets the daughter of one of Mundy's adversaries, who is in love with Mundy. MacGregor discovers that the two are secretly meeting, and he has hopes they will marry. Ironically, however, Mundy sets up a mock marriage with the girl, hoping that by dishonoring her he can hurt his adversaries more profoundly than they can ever hurt him. When MacGregor discovers the plot he confronts Mundy with the evidence; Mundy refuses to marry the girl and in the ensuing gunfight both men are killed.

The unfortunate death-or-worse quality of this story makes it sound, particularly in summary, rather silly. Its strength, however, has little to do with its plot, for the profundity of "Beyond the Desert" lies in Rhodes's ironic handling of some of the Western themes we have already discussed. The basic concern of the story is the presentation of the moral conflict faced by Mac-Gregor, the gunman who sells his gun but not his conscience. At the climax of the story he must choose between his personal debt to Mundy—who had saved his life and for whom he had agreed to work—and his duty to a higher moral code. The ironic force of the story does not, however, come primarily from the sentimental implications of the conflict between these divided loyalties in MacGregor's character, to which Rhodes devotes relatively little attention. For the irony in the story is deeper than this, residing in the fact that MacGregor must think through the implications of the conventional code to which he, as many another Western hero, subscribes.

Like the other Western heroes we have been discussing, Mac-Gregor stands outside the law and takes great pride in that fact. He assumes, as do so many of his brethren, that there is at least strong presumptive evidence that virtue may best be discovered among those who, like himself, are superior to and free of the trammels of society. Hence he assumes almost as an article of faith that Clay Mundy is a man of moral integrity, only to discover that in fact Mundy is nothing of the kind. To reinforce the irony is the concomitant fact of MacGregor's character that he is a "thinker," and that his skill as a gunman is due to his ability to see into the meaning of a situation rather than to merely mechanical skill with a revolver. His ability to think things through becomes the vehicle by which he comes to discover the limitations of his own moral code, for the "facts" which he must interpret reveal the inadequacies of his moral premises. His death is at once a device of slick fiction by which Rhodes can wind up his story without leaving any embarrassing loose ends and a more profound statement of the way in which Mac-Gregor's code has been found an inadequate explanation of the hard facts of life in the Western world.

A close relative of the professional gunman is another common

Western hero, the "bad man," or perhaps it would be more accurate to say that the bad man is a general type of which the professional gunman is one particular manifestation. Like the hired gunman, the professional bad man is conventionally assumed to stand outside the law, not just occasionally but as a matter of personal definition, and his comments upon society are usually trenchant observations about its hypocrisy and its various moral inadequacies.

The bad man-hero is not of course confined to Western fiction, either historically or in terms of contemporary usage. The outlaw tale has a long history in English literature, at least as ancient as Robin Hood and his merry men and likewise as modern as the gangster hero. In America, however, the outlaw hero was seen from a very early date to have at least a metaphorical affinity with the Western hero.

When the "West" was the Mississippi Valley one of its chroniclers, James Hall, attempted in *Harpe's Head* (1833) to cast the story of a once notorious band of outlaws into fictional form, an endeavor which had little success. Hall presents the story of the Harpe gang as merely a sensational historical event of Western history, to which he appends a tiresome love plot as well as a number of somewhat more interesting descriptions of local Western customs. He finds little more significance in his outlaw subjects than the relation of bizarre events in which they were involved. He does not attempt to justify the outlaws' conduct, and insofar as he explains their actions at all it is as more or less conventionally Gothic villains.

Many later chroniclers of historical bad men follow Hall's precedent in treating their subject. The anonymous chapbook chronicle of Jesse James (1886)[9] follows this format as does one of the better modern outlaw tales, H. H. Kroll's *Rogues' Company* (1943), a fictionalized life of another famous bandit of the Mississippi Valley, John Murrell. The advantage to the writer of this kind of presentation is clear, for he can inform the reader of the bizarre and/or titillating facts of his subject's life without having to justify his subject's moral character, which is, by all these writers, universally deplored. In all such tales the writer's moral stand is on the side of conventional value judgments. The subject is a monster—whether Gothic or Freudian really makes little difference—and all right-thinking people, though they may avidly read about his adventures, should deplore them.

Such a sensational presentation of the outlaw hero has proved unsatisfactory to many Western writers, most of whom are united basically in being unable to accept the implicit moral judgment in such tales that right and justice are only to be found within the confines of the social code. More congenial to the Western writer is precisely the opposite notion, that society is in the wrong and the outlaw hero in the right. At the very least such a man is more sinned against than sinning, but even such qualified acceptance of the bad man is rare. Usually his values are unhesitatingly affirmed, while those of society are equally inclusively condemned. In contrast to the 1886 biography of Jesse James may be placed the almost exactly contemporary ballad, which has had a much more durable reputation. According to the anonymous balladeer's way of telling the story, though it may be true that "the devil will be upon his knee," we must still remember that Jesse James, unlike "Robert Ford, that dirty little coward" who shot him, would never willingly "see a man suffer pain" and, more to the point, was a kind of Robin Hood character whose most notable characteristic was a laudable desire to equalize the distribution of wealth: "He stole from the rich and he gave to the poor,/He'd a hand and a heart and a brain," as our balladeer approvingly tells us. It goes without saying of course that this Jesse James bears little relation to the vicious killer whose band of cutthroats terrorized the middle western frontier after the close of the Civil War, but in justification, he is not really supposed to. His actions are not realistic, but represent rather a symbolic yearning on the part of the balladeer for a land where he need not sit by and watch injustice done.

At times the balladeer's world can become ethically rather confusing. Thus it is almost impossible to find "a better hearted fellow" than the cowboy's own favorite hero, "the Robin Hood of Texas," Sam Bass. Though it may be true that he had an unfortunate penchant for robbing stagecoaches, still he made up for this insignificant foible by helping old widows to pay off their mortgages and by paying tremendous sums for the getaway horses which his professional needs required. There is no doubt about it, either, at least to the balladeer's mind, that the man who betrayed Sam Bass has nothing at all to be said for him: "He'll get a scorching when Gabriel blows his horn" we are told, and that's that.[10] This is nothing, however, to the most improbable bad man of all, Pretty Boy Floyd, the gangster bank robber who has been assimilated as a typical cowboy folk hero in the Southwest. As Woody Guthrie, his biographer in song, tells the story, Floyd's troubles began when a deputy sheriff said something to him one day to which the inoffensive Pretty Boy was forced to take exception because he was accompanied by his wife, who was offended by the sheriff's gaucherie. As a result of the ensuing battle, which Floyd won, he had to depart rather hurriedly, and in his outcast state he developed those virtues of concomitant economic success and selflessness which he shares with most of his bandit colleagues. He was wont to beg a meal at a poor farm and in payment for it leave a hundred-dollar bill under his plate; similarly, one Christmas he bought a huge amount of groceries which he sent to unfortunate Oklahoma families on relief. Precisely here is the point of Guthrie's fable, for Pretty Boy's conduct is placed in explicit contrast to the malefactors of great wealth who steal with pen rather than revolver, and give nothing in return. Though both are robbers, the outlaw will only take your money, and the chances are good that if you need it more than he does he will give it back to you; such muscular Christianity does not rule in the breast of the financier, who picks up the mortgage on your homestead and drives you out into the cold.

The glorification of the real-life outlaw is by no means limited only to the world of folk ballads. Charles C. Park's *A Plaything of the Gods* (1912), a novel based upon the life of Joaquin Murieta, a famous California bandit, is a case in point. In this novel Murieta, an inoffensive man whose real emotional commitment is directed toward the Church, is forced by a series of outrages to take arms against the encroaching Yankee settlers of California. He is first convicted of a crime which he did not commit, then run off his mining claim and later his homestead, all of which he bears meekly. But when he discovers that his wife had been raped by the Americans who had run him off, and when his brother is lynched and his wife herself commits suicide, he vows revenge.[11] Park glosses over the actual details of Murieta's crimes, asking us to be content with his explanation that the outrages which Murieta had suffered extenuated his actions. His robber band consists of all those outcast Spaniards who had suffered wrongs and indignities at the hands of the Americans, and Joaquin himself keeps a ledger in which he meticulously records each outrage and its punishment. These punishments are by no means arbitrary, and when "justice" has finally been done the outlaws disband and Joaquin himself retires to a peaceful old age.

Even Gore Vidal's recent television play "The Death of Billy the Kid" (1955) depicts its outlaw hero as, if not a good man, at least a better man than his adversaries. Though Vidal's Billy is not conceived in the simplistic way of Park's Murieta, he is none-theless visualized as superior to those who oppose him. General Lew Wallace, who wants Billy to settle down and accept the general amnesty offered to the participants of the Lincoln County War,[12] is presented as a kind of Pontius Pilate who, though he recognizes and respects Billy's idealistic relationship to his "out-law" friends, nonetheless puts the value of civil order above that of moral right; Pat Garrett, the sheriff who finally kills Billy, is presented as a man driven by some inner compulsion to measure himself against "the fastest gun in the West"; and the man who betrays Billy to the law, like Robert Ford the "dirty little coward" who killed Jesse James, is a social pariah who chooses this bizarre way of proving his importance before the community. Conversely, there is an alliance between the townspeople and Billy against the forces of "law" (Pat Garrett and the territorial officials of New Mexico), which resembles the traditional re-lationship of *noblesse oblige* between the bandit hero and the helpless society he defends against the rapacities and injustices of constituted and corrupt authority.

This conception of the bad man-hero is by no means limited to descants upon the lives of historic outlaws, however; it is a convention in fictional outlawry as well. Roger Pocock's *Curly. A Tale of the Arizona Desert* (1905) may serve to make the point. The story of *Curly* depends upon the separation of the world of the novel into two opposing groups, both easily recog-nizable by now. On the one hand we have the cowboys, most of whom are peaceable honest citizens but who, when aroused, are accustomed to stand outside the law in order to see justice done. Opposed to them are society's minions, again easily recog-nizable as men of great apparent plausibility, under whose sur-face respectability lurks an infinite capacity for evil. Ryan, the leader of the apparently respectable citizens is, the narrator of the story tells us, "a cheery old soul, popular with the crowd, a power in local politics, well qualified on the outside of him for paradise, and in the innards of him for the other place" (p. 89).

In explicit contrast stands McCalmont, the leader of a band of robbers who unite with the virtuous party against Ryan; Curly, his daughter, says of him that "he only kills when he has to, and not for his own honour and glory," and more significantly, that "he won't rob a man unless he's got lots of wealth" (p. 175). Furthermore he believes "that robbery is a sign that the law is rotten, and a proof that the Government's too pore and weak to cast a proper shadow," and she tells us as well that he and his robber band were honest men, but "rich men came stealing our water-holes, fencing in our grass, driving our cattle away." He, for example, had been a mild and inoffensive farmer until a big cattle company "turned their cattle into his crops" and killed his son. Legal redress had proved vain, for the lawyers had charged exorbitant fees and the judge was a shareholder in the very cattle company which had tried to drive McCalmont off his land. After an appeal which the Supreme Court had decided in his favor, the cattle company had "set the grass on fire" and burned him out, destroying his house and killing his wife. As a result of this outrage "he went bad," as Curly says, and after taking personal revenge on the unjust judge "went all through Kansas and Colorado, gathering pore stockmen what had been robbed and ruined by the rich men's law" (pp. 177-78).

Though the villains and heroes of this piece are by now easily recognizable, Curly's tirade serves to make explicit something which we have only seen handled by implication up to this point. This is the value association of "wealth," "the law," and "the city," which are placed in explicit contrast to "poverty," "outlawry," and "the range." Ryan, the arch-villain, is not only a politician but has made a huge fortune in a manner very like the cattle company which had earlier stolen McCalmont's farm, and the reason the robbers come to the aid of the honest ranchmen in the novel is simply because Ryan had tried, through financial chicanery backed by force, to drive its rightful owners from a ranch which he coveted. This had made the honest outlaws—and honest citizens everywhere—see red, and the country-side had revolted against Ryan's empire of fraud.

None too subtly concealed in *Curly* is a program for action which we have already seen implicit in most of the other treatments of outlaws. The rhetoric of Curly's justification for her father closely parallels the angry speeches of agrarian protest from the Civil War to the 1930's, and it is no accident that the heroes and villains of the novel bear more than a passing resemblance to similar characters in Populist rhetoric. To throw the rascals out is the moral duty of the good men and true who make up the alliance of robbers and cowboys constituting the party of virtue, and the plot of the story as well is a sort of metaphorical footnote to Mary Ellen Lease's famous exhortation to more peaceable farmers that they "raise less corn and more hell."

This point should not be forgotten, for many commentators who have deplored the alleged American glorification of the bad man —be he cowboy, outlaw, gangster, or whatever—have seemed almost willfully blind to the real or fancied social grievances which are so often reflected in such literature. In *Curly* the real villain is not merely an individual who cynically hides behind the cloak of respectability, but a symbol for a social evil which from the agrarian-Populist point of view of the novel represents a clear and present danger. Ryan is a financier (one of that shadowy crew of international tricksters who manipulate honest men's currency for their own nefarious ends and who figure prominently in the demonology of the time) who steals the property of hard-working yeomen, who forecloses on mortgages and drives helpless women and children forth from their only shelter, who is both impervious to moral considerations and unrestrained by any legal sanctions.

It is important to note that the adversaries of such a man, though conventionally they are considered to be outlaws, do not in any respect represent the position of contempt for justice. They do not believe that might equals right, and they do not accept the morally nihilistic position that to the victor belong the spoils. They represent rather the confusion which must reign in any thinking man's mind when he believes that in a particular situation law and justice are not synonymous terms. For purposes of the parable, the outlaws are presented as those who have, given this dilemma, stood up for justice, while Ryan and his party are those who have chosen the law.

The world of *Curly* is not so far from Thoreau's civil disobedience as it at first appears, for in both worlds law is assumed to be a means by which the ends of justice may be served. When the law no longer serves these ends, the moral citizen's allegiance should unquestioningly lie on the side of justice. In *Curly* the point is made explicitly when the sheriff, by his position theoretically committed to upholding the law, connives with the outlaws who represent the party of justice. To the narrator of the story he says, at one point, "Put her thar . . . and you'll know that there's one official in this hull corrupt and filthy outfit who cares for justice more'n he cares for law" (p. 259).

It ought to be mentioned as well that the purpose of *Curly* is not to present in fictional form any examination of the practical difficulties of action based on the concept of responsible illegality. Unlike, say, *The Ox-Bow Incident*, which focuses on the dangers which result from the premise that man should on occasion work outside the law, *Curly* concentrates upon an examination of the premise itself, and in so doing uncovers an ambiguity of which Americans are uneasily conscious but which they do not like to admit, the ambiguity that law and justice are related terms but not always identical ones. In its examination of the ambiguous nature of conventionally accepted premises *Curly* is much more typical of Western fiction in general than *The Ox-Bow Incident;* for, as has been suggested throughout this study, the world of the Western is commonly the world of self-contradictory ideals, all of which the American is tempted to affirm at once.

At this point, before concluding, a brief summary might well be in order. We have seen that the Western hero moves within a set of stereotyped conventions, some but by no means all of which bear a reasonably close relation to the actual facts of life in the West. The most basic of these conceptions is that the Western hero is a man of "craft," that is, one who does something well. There is practically no limit to the possible things he can do well, except the limits implied by the demands of the fictional environment of the West. It is unlikely, for instance, that he be conceived as playing chess well, though skill at games, as in the case of the Virginian's ability at poker, may be used as an example of his craft. The Western hero's skill is seen as emblematic of his greater perception, and the contrast between his own abilities in the world around him and the ineptitude of a number of assorted foils, the most notable of which is the dude, becomes a metaphor for his superior perception into the meaning of events and often of life itself. This superior perception in turn leads to the Western hero's habit of acting on his own, either outside society or on occasion in direct opposition to conventional legal and social codes. Consequently, the Western hero is conventionally conceived as a "loner" and his symbolic role in Western fiction is often seen as an extension of this solitariness. He is often a vigilante, a gunman, or an outlaw, and even when he is not explicitly presented as some kind of social outcast he nonetheless possesses a penchant for acting on his own.

In contrast to this Western hero stands social man, whose attributes are almost exact opposites and who is conceived precisely as the Western hero is not, as a man who cannot do anything well. His lack of "craft" becomes an emblem of his lack of that moral perception the Western hero possesses; and from this follows his role in Western fiction as either an inferior being or, on occasion, as a moral hypocrite. The contrast between the solitary man of craft and the social man may have many dimensions: it may be representative of a metaphysical insight into the world, as it is in *The Virginian* and in many another story in which the cowboy hero is conceived as a symbolic detective; it may have a more specifically political dimension as it does in many outlaw tales; or it may be the basis, as it is in *Shane*, for a rigidly conceived allegorical world. The only constant preoccupation lies in the way in which this conventional contrast is itself conceived; for whatever contrasting points of view they may represent in any particular work of fiction, the Western hero and social man are invariably conceived as metaphorical opposites.

One more dimension of the cowboy hero remains to be discussed in conclusion. Like the many characters discussed in the last chapter, the cowboy hero does not exist entirely in a timeless world of moral allegory. The world is constantly changing around him. The Virginian successfully changes with his world, marrying and settling down on land which he had foreseen would be of future value; the irrepressible practical joker and implacable dispenser of frontier justice understands the way the country will develop and lays claim to presently worthless land from which, once the railroad reaches Wyoming, he mines and sells coal. Shane, once his work is done, rides away into the West, leaving behind him a land in which he will never again be needed. Even Destry eventually hangs up his gun, and the town of Wham which he so aptly symbolizes settles down to a life of comparative quiet. Though many authors do not choose to emphasize the way in which times change in the world of Western fiction, this theme is never far beneath the surface.

Perhaps the most successful combination of the typical cowboy hero with the ever present *ubi sunt* may be found in Eugene Manlove Rhodes's magnificent novelette *Pasó por Aquí* (1926).

This story tells of a man named Ross McEwen, who has robbed a store and made a successful getaway into the wilderness. He has only managed to make his escape, however, by abandoning his stolen money to the pursuing posse. When almost trapped, he had thrown the money away "lak a man to feed the hen een hees yard" (p. 10), as Monte, the Spanish-American narrator of part of the story puts it, and when the posse had dismounted to chase the blowing currency McEwen had successfully eluded them. His pursuers have no intention of giving up the chase because of this temporary setback; they know he must make a break for the Mexican border and they also know that they will catch him sooner or later if they merely stake out the water holes, to which he must come for water before making the long, dry trip across the desert. McEwen's attempts to elude the posse become consistently both more cunning and more desperate, and the conflict between the two parties turns into a battle of wits similar to those we have seen between the cowboy hero and his adversaries in other stories. McEwen has all the odds against him, and he loses his only great advantage when the posse declines to chase him but decides instead to wait at the water holes until he is driven out of the hills by thirst. McEwen must abandon his first horse, and he steals a second one, choosing an unshod mount which will be harder for the pursuit to track. This horse too fails him and as his next mount he takes a steer, which will leave no distinguishable tracks. Finally—afoot—he manages to arrive at a well which the posse has left unguarded, only to discover that the Mexican inhabitants of the little ranch for which this well supplies the water are all stricken with diphtheria. Though McEwen could now escape, he elects to stay and to nurse the Mexican family. "I am here to help you" (p. 28), he says.

So far the story of *Pasó por Aquí* is a reasonably conventional one of romantic peril and escape, but Rhodes is not content to leave it that way. When McEwen is finally run down, the leader of the pursuers is Pat Garrett, the sheriff who had killed Billy the Kid.[13] McEwen does not know him by sight, and Garrett preserves his incognito. After the Mexican family has been restored to health, Garrett and McEwen ride off to Tularosa, where McEwen, still unaware of Garrett's real identity, will take the train and get safely away.

In this story we see another approach to the theme of law and justice which we have examined throughout this chapter. Garrett, convinced that, as Monte says, McEwen "ees tek eshame for thees bad life" (p. 43), decides to take the law into his own hands and see justice done by turning McEwen loose rather than by turning him over to the legal machinery of New Mexico. As in many another Western story a dude is present who, until the course of action is explained, cannot understand it. She, a nurse from the East, remarks that Garrett could legally be impeached and thrown out of office for dereliction of duty; but, as Monte significantly says in the lines which conclude the story, "Who will tell? . . . We are all decent people" (p. 44).

It is obvious on the surface that one preoccupation of *Pasó por Aquí* is precisely this familiar discussion of how justice can best be done outside the law. McEwen has atoned for his misdeed of robbing the store by his later moral action of helping the stricken Mexican family; and since no harm has been done to anyone—the money had all been recovered when McEwen had scattered it in front of the posse and no one else had been injured by McEwen—Garrett feels that the whole incident is best forgotten.

Combined with this preoccupation is a completely different theme, however, a lament for the passing of the old order. McEwen and Garrett are both presented as the last men of their particular types. Garrett, the man who shot Billy the Kid, is the last of the old-time sheriffs, at home in Tularosa with the "old-timers," rather than in Alamogordo with the "new peoples." To Tularosa, where he is known, he takes McEwen who will be accepted at the train as one of Garrett's friends. Similarly McEwen is the last of the old-time bad men, and his renunciation of his free and easy ways at the end of the story symbolically represents the passing of the wild freedom of the old times.

On another level, then, the story is a lament for the old days, and this theme is beautifully developed in the world of the tale, in which the great symbolic fact of life is the fact that the world has changed. McEwen, who has not been in the country for many years, is no longer at home there, for the face of the country is different from the way it had been on his last visit. New Mexico is no longer the wilderness he had remembered, but is now filled with the windmills of the "new peoples" who prevent his escape. It is at one of these new ranches that he is finally symbolically "trapped" by civilization, when he stops to help the family crippled by diphtheria, a disease unknown to the older time. The same symbolic defeat by civilization which keeps him from successfully escaping his pursuers is reinforced by the moral change which he undergoes at the ranch. When he discovers that there is no longer any room for the old-style bad man his final escape becomes ironic; for though he is set free he is at the same time banished. There is no room for Ross McEwen in the new country.

The basic theme of the story, then, is mirrored in its title *Pasó por Aquí*—"passed by here"—and to the nurse whose Eastern perceptions represent the inability to understand what is happening beneath the surface of the world around her Monte explains the meaning of the story's action. His explanation is itself a metaphor from the history of New Mexico, for he tells her of the famous landmark, Inscription Rock. Long ago, he says, when his Spanish ancestors first settled the Southwest, they were in the habit of writing on this rock as they passed by it, *pasó por aquí*, with their names and the date. All of these men, as Monte tells the story, had thought to themselves "What lar-rge weelderness ees thees! And me, I go now eento thees beeg lonesome, and perhaps I shall not to r-return!" (p. 43), and had made for themselves a gravestone on Inscription Rock. McEwen is the last man to "pass by here," and at the end of the story the last sheriff and the last bad man ride away from the country of the new peoples, never to return.

Pasó por Aquí, which begins as a particular examination of the relationship between law and justice in a world of permanence, ends as a metaphor of the course of history in a world of change. The conflict between McEwen and Pat Garrett is strongly reminiscent of the similar conflict between Scratchy Wilson and Jack Potter in "The Bride Comes to Yellow Sky." In both stories the course of history renders the conflict itself irrelevant, and the bad man has ultimately no choice but that of laying aside his gun. He can no longer stand against the course of history, but must acquiesce in the passing of the wild and free world he had loved. The inscription he leaves behind him, carved into solid rock, ironically symbolizes only his own impermanence.

chapter five

The Vanishing American

The Indian has been a stock figure in American literature almost from its inception, and his literary representation reflects a number of often contradictory streams in American intellectual thought; for early in his literary career he became a focal point for the discussion of primitivism which plays so large a part in eighteenth-century intellectual history. Contemporaneously with his emergence as a not altogether congenial vehicle for philosophical controversy, he was also arriving at a less desirable pinnacle of eminence as the quintessence of bestiality in human form. In this latter guise he is familiar to much later fiction, notably the ubiquitous "captivity narrative" which served as escape literature in an age to which novels were morally suspect.[1] Throughout most of the early nineteenth century, the Indian in literature reflected the terms of the debate over the nature of primitivism in what was, in the last analysis, a historic way. For the Indian was supposed somehow to "prove" the desirability of that civilization which, it was alleged, he would accept with open arms. At first, European hopes had run high that the very diverse Indian and white cultures could be reconciled, once the Indians had been shown the superiority of white ways. This hope was early doomed to failure; though all apparently began well enough, it soon became evident that the Indians were not so convinced of the superiority of white civilization as the whites wished, and this resulted in a lamentable lack of motivation for accepting white cultural values on the Indians' part. The inevitable conflict which followed was interpreted by the whites as

141

a necessary, though unfortunate, working out of that providential historic order which decreed the replacement of savagery by civilization. "It is as unchangeable as the laws of nature, that savages should give place to civilized men, possessed of the strength, spirit and improvement of the social compact," wrote Timothy Flint in 1832,[2] and though his casuistry is not so subtle as that of other commentators, the spirit which informs it is identical. Most of the nineteenth-century discussion of the nature and the respective futures of white and Indian culture, though often insensitively argued and, at least in terms of twentieth-century knowledge, based on complete misinformation and almost total misunderstanding of Indian life, had, at least at one remove, some practical application. It was both the rationale for and the result of an ever-present historic problem. Whether conceived in moral, ethical, metaphysical, religious, or legal terms, the intellectual debate over the Indian had immediate practical consequences.

This can be seen immediately upon even a cursory examination of earlier nineteenth-century fiction dealing with Indians. Robert Montgomery Bird's *Nick of the Woods, or the Jibbenainosay* (1837)—a novel of considerable merit—is a convenient example. Onto the body of the novel—a blood-and-thunder tale of an Indian uprising—is grafted the moral earnestness of a Cato demanding the destruction of Carthage. The Indians are presented as brutal, debased, and incredibly cruel, and imbedded in the actions of the hero of the book is a none-too-carefully concealed program for action against them. Bird's hero, Nathan Slaughter (the name is not accidental), is a gentle Quaker whose peaceful exterior conceals an implacable hatred of all Indians. He, it turns out, is the fearful Jibbenainosay or "spirit-who-walks," dedicated to their destruction. How this mild-mannered and gentle man could have turned into a bloodthirsty murderer is one of the questions raised by the novel. The answer, needless to say, is not too difficult to find: Nathan, who had come west expecting evil from no man, had himself been scalped and had seen his wife and family slaughtered before his eyes, largely because his belief in the goodness of human nature had made him neglect to take sufficient precautions against the savages. These disasters had turned him into an implacable enemy of all Indians, dedicated to their extermination. Though the dashing and romantic young lover of the story—a dispossessed Virginia gentleman

named Roland Forrester—is at first somewhat doubtful of the
necessity for such extreme measures, when the facts of the case
are told him, and when his own cousin is carried off to suffer
death or worse (an eventuality fortunately frustrated by the
Jibbenainosay) he unqualifiedly accepts Nathan's point of view.
So, Bird clearly implies, would any reasonable man.

It requires no prolonged reflection to comprehend the significance of this little parable. The sentimentality of those who do
not understand the facts about the frontier, Bird says, is the main
obstacle to a peaceful and prosperous West. It is necessary that
the Indians be destroyed.

In case anyone had missed the point, Bird made it explicit in
a Preface, written in 1853, to a later edition of *Nick of the Woods.*
At the time when the book was written, he says, "the genius of
Chateaubriand and of our own Cooper ... had thrown a poetical
illusion over the Indian character; and the red men were presented ... as the embodiments of grand and tender sentiment—a
new style of the beau-ideal—brave, gentle, loving, refined, honorable, romantic personages—nature's nobles, the chivalry of the
forest." Such, however, is not the case; for the Indian "in his
natural barbaric state ... is a barbarian. ... ignorant, violent, debased, brutal" (pp. 7-8).

Even in the context of the earlier nineteenth century Bird's
Realpolitik is somewhat extreme; but other more humane writers
accepted at least the terms in which Bird stated his uncompromising history. James S. French's fictionalized account of Te-
cumseh's unsuccessful attempt to withstand white encroachments
Elkswatawa; or, The Prophet of the West (1836) is a good
example. French is by no means completely unsympathetic to the
Indians. The various Indian characters are compassionately if
ineptly drawn—*Elkswatawa* is by no means so good a novel as
Nick of the Woods—and almost extravagant praise is reserved for
Tecumseh, who symbolizes the best aspects of Indian character.
French's romantic hero, Richard Rolfe, who like Bird's Roland
Forrester is "a high-toned and chivalrous Virginian" (I, 39), is
unlike Forrester in his unequivocal rejection of the Indian-hating
point of view, represented in *Elkswatawa* by a semi-comic character named Earthquake, who is obviously modeled after similar
characters—notably Hurry Harry of *The Deerslayer*—in the
Leatherstocking Tales. Indeed, the whole discussion of the nature
of law and history in French's novel is clearly derivative from the

similar ones in the Leatherstocking Tales, three of which had appeared by 1836.

"How beautiful are these plains," said Rolfe. "Earth [quake], do you blame the Indians for not surrendering them?"

"No, I cannot say that I do: nor do I blame the whites for endeavouring to take them away."

"Why? are not the Indians the rightful owners, and have not their fathers owned them time out of mind?"

"Rolfe, it will not do to argue this matter: we have treated the Ingens so badly, that we cannot now live in peace, but are obliged to add insult to injury. You know I've a great many grudges agin 'em, and use them up on all occasions, for I well know they would have killed me long before this, if they had a good chance."

"And because you have treated them badly, you think you ought to kill them? Is that your argument?"

"No, I never argue about it; if one comes near me, and he gives me a cause, I'm very apt to kill him. Somehow or other it is bred in me, and I hate them; for you see they are always straggling along the frontiers, and committing murders."

"Yes, and you see our frontiers are always extending, so that the Indians are compelled either to move or else to be continually at war."

"The fact is," said Earth, "I believe I think as most of the whites do, and that is, that these lands are too good for them; they should be cultivated instead of lying waste for them to prowl over" (I, 93).

Unlike Bird's Forrester, Rolfe is not converted by Earthquake's arguments, nor indeed are the arguments themselves very convincing in French's presentation. In fact, Earthquake is partially converted to Rolfe's point of view upon meeting a good Indian, a figure not to be encountered in Bird's work. Nor, whatever the conclusion of the above argument suggests, does *Elkswatawa* advocate Bird's *Realpolitik* on the basis of enlightened self-interest rather that of self-defense.

However less artistically effective than Bird's, French's argument is philosophically more respectable. For as he tells the story of Tecumseh's battle with the whites he defines the conflict in such a way as to give the whites no choice but to make war against the Indians. The great weakness in Indian society as French sees it is that it has no legal sanctions other than the force of custom. Hence Tecumseh, in French's pages almost a caricature of those romantic Indian qualities to which Bird was to take exception, is thwarted by his brother Elkswatawa, "the prophet," the kind of dastardly Indian in whom Bird would wholeheartedly believe. The plot of *Elkswatawa* describes the unscrupulous methods by which Elkswatawa uses Tecumseh for his own nefarious ends, and the history of Tecumseh's conspiracy becomes a story of the way in which, in a society where personal influence has the force of law, the highest moral principles must inevitably be corrupted by the lure of self-aggrandizement. With such a society, French sadly concludes, treaties or legal agreements of any kind can have no meaning, since they do not represent the binding commitments of governments but the whims of individuals, to be honored or repudiated at will. Against the vagaries of such self-interest, unprotected by legal sanctions, the only law to which the whites can appeal is the force of arms.

French's view is much more typical than Bird's of moderate nineteenth-century opinion, and however much it may ignore or gloss over the unsavory facts of colonization it has a certain surface plausibility more easily acceptable to the squeamish. Timothy Flint, who is fictionally kinder to the Indians than his factual statements would seem to warrant, has much the same view of the inherent instability of Indian society. In *The Shoshonee Valley* (1830), he describes the precariousness of life in a society governed only by the force of custom. His hero, William Weldon, who goes to live among the Shoshonee under the influence of "the wild and pernicious sophism of Rousseau, that the savage is happier, than the social state" discovers too late the magnitude of his logical error. Though his wife Yensi, "a Chinese lady of a most interesting appearance, and the daughter of a Mandarin of considerable rank," hopes that God will "incline her husband's heart to remove from the Shoshonee to his country or hers; that they might spend their days in the security of law and order,"[3] he will not do so, and he reaps the rewards of his intellectual obstinacy when he and his wife are massacred by the Shoshonee. Though Flint does not present the Shoshonee themselves as villains—they are encouraged in their massacre of William Weldon and his family by a white man who gives them whiskey—he does insist on the necessity of law for social order. Hence, though the Indians are perhaps personally blameless for what happens, they are socially culpable. Whites, in dealing with them, had better keep in mind the instructive example of the unfortunate William Weldon.

These three novels, although different in particular focus, have in common a similar social philosophy about the Indians, a philosophy which at the time of their publication was so commonplace as to be thought scarcely worthy of comment. In its broadest terms this was the idea that, whatever the ultimate moral worth of the individual Indian character might be, the social value of the Indian way of life was quite another thing. And these three authors, who form a representative range of contemporary opinion, are unanimous in the opinion that the Indian as a political being must be summarily dealt with. In this attitude they of course reflect the constant opinion of all generations of American westerners who have had to face the Indian problem in practical rather than abstract terms. Such men wanted a workable pragmatic method of defense more than a philosophical disquisition on the theoretical rights and wrongs of the case, and writers like Bird, French, and Flint gave a certain respectability to an approach which, if not properly understood, might seem to smack rather too much of opportunism and expediency.

Precisely here lies the different emphasis placed on the literary Indian by the three writers just discussed and later writers of Westerns. For in the Western the debate over treatment of the Indian no longer has any practical application. The modern Western became identifiable as a genre distinct from earlier novels about the frontier only after the Indian question had been pragmatically settled. By the time of appearance of *The Virginian* in 1902 the frontier was twelve years dead. Its demise had been announced in the census of 1890; and it had been laid to rest by Frederick Jackson Turner in 1893. Geronimo, the last of the great Apache chieftains, had surrendered for the second time in 1886 and was contemplating various public appearances—in Pawnee Bill's Wild West Show, at the St. Louis, Buffalo, and Omaha expositions, and in Theodore Roosevelt's inaugural parade; Sitting Bull, the Sioux conqueror of Custer, had been killed in 1890; and the Ghost Dance, the last pitiful messianic hope of the Indians, had come to nothing in the same year. The prophetic words of Chief Joseph upon his surrender to General Miles—"I will fight no more forever"—had become an epitaph for Indian resistance.

In consequence, literary treatment of the Indian which, how-ever wrongly, had traditionally been considered to have at least a nodding acquaintance with the Indian problem, was trans-formed in the Western into a frame of reference which need answer only the artistic demands of a particular work of imagina-tion. Whatever the writer's concern might be, whether serious or trivial, he no longer had to make his Indians "true to life"—or perhaps it would be more accurate to say, true to what his white readers considered the facts of Indian life.

The effect on the subliterary character of the Indian was disastrous. Where earlier even unsympathetic writers like Bird had tried to understand Indian motives, if only through in-adequate frames of reference to concepts such as "civilization" and "barbarism" which failed to fit the facts, later writers felt no need at all even to give the pretense of plausibility to Indian character. As a result, the Indian was treated more and more like "the enemy" in the propaganda war movies. Particular Indians grew increasingly dastardly, and the Indian problem as reflected in such works became a more or less straightforward statement of how "our side" won. The Indian, in such works, plays the negative to positive American virtues which are un-hesitatingly affirmed.

Occasionally it is true that a particular Indian may be con-verted to white ways. In such a case the Indian plays an honor-able but subsidiary role; he is faithful, even though appearances may at times seem to be against him, and he obeys without question the orders given by his white companion. A certain touching wish-fulfillment in this figure is not too far to seek; for on a very simple-minded level this "good Indian" represents what the whites had always wished the Indian might become. He is not too different from the stock type of the faithful Negro servant who plays so large a part in the plantation mythology of the ante-bellum South.[4] The most familiar imaginative figures of this type are the well-known Lone Ranger and Tonto, whose relationship points up the inherently ludicrous quality of this pathetic mixture of *noblesse oblige* with fantasy. The Lone Ranger rides a magnificent white horse, Silver, who has almost mythical qualities: generations of boys of all ages have tensed to the magic incantation, "Out of the past come the thundering hoofbeats of the great horse Silver," even though the illusion was somewhat spoiled at one time in Silver's radio career by the fact that his hoofbeats were not above thundering the name of a breakfast food. Tonto, in contrast, rides a modest paint named Scout. In moments of stress, the Lone Ranger is wont to encourage the great horse Silver by exhorting "Hi-yo Silver, awa-a-a-a-a-ay!" At similar times Tonto rises to the occasion with a stolid "Git-em up, Scout." Tonto covets neither the Lone Ranger's reputation (a characteristic he may share with historic Indians) nor the great horse Silver (a characteristic which clearly places the relationship in the realm of fantasy); in short, he knows his place.[5]

The figures of the heroic white man and his faithful Indian companion are more familiar to movie-goers than to readers of all but the most abysmally bad Western fiction, but in both pairing is often combined with another concern. In this subsidiary theme, the Indian has for one reason or another become a convert to white ways, and is possessed not only with faithfulness but high moral purpose; for he realizes that to help his people he must bring about the defeat of the reactionary elements who would keep the old Indian way of life. Again, wish-fulfillment is not too hard to find, for implicit in such a theme is the cherished eighteenth-century notion of eventual conversion of the Indians.

When this theme is ineptly handled it is almost perfect as a vehicle for escape fiction. It has the one great requirement of all escape literature—that it tell an exciting story which raises no unsettling questions. Such a story typically recounts the adventures of a band of Indians who are misguidedly following the leadership of a persuasive but reactionary chief. This chief leads his followers in a series of attacks against the whites, during which enough (usually, as a matter of fact, too many) lurid outrages are committed to satisfy the reader's vicarious taste for blood. Finally, however, the good Indian manages to make his misguided brothers see the error of their ways and they are finally defeated in battle (though not necessarily in this order). The story ends happily with the death or conversion of the reactionary chief, after which the others retire to the reservation under the enlightened guidance of the good Indian who will, we are usually told, lead them along the difficult path to civilization.

The reader of this volume has undoubtedly come across a story much like this if he has ever been lured or trapped into watching a poor Western film. Such a story, he must agree, is unutterably silly. Yet when sensitively approached, this theme is capable of more profound treatment. Hamlin Garland's neglected studies of the American Indian may serve to make the point.

In many ways Hamlin Garland's Indian studies are a transition between traditional and modern literary treatments of the Indian. Both "The Silent Eaters"—a fictionalized biography of Sitting Bull—and the short stories which together make up *The Book of the American Indian* (1923) are written out of a feeling of indignation over unjust treatment of the Indian; and both as well have a very definite social reference which, in the weakest of the stories, deteriorates into a thinly disguised program of social action. Yet this program is significantly different from earlier fictional discussions of the Indian problem; for, as Garland sees, the problem itself has changed. No longer is it conceived in terms of how best to defeat the Indians; rather it has become the question of how best to rehabilitate a defeated enemy. "The Silent Eaters" and the stories in *The Book of the American Indian* are rather specifically concerned with providing answers to this problem, and the method of explication Garland uses is closely related to the idea of Indian conversion mentioned previously. Garland, however, sees that the question of whether the old ways are "good" or "bad" must be approached differently in order for it to have any relevance to the actual world. As a result, the standard plot of escape fiction, the story of the reactionary old chief who is replaced by the modern progressive young Indian is put in a different perspective. Where the escapist plot concerns itself primarily with the events leading to the subjugation of the Indian, after which he is converted, Garland focuses primarily upon the Indian's condition after his subjugation, and hence emphasizes the absolute necessity for his conversion; and where the escapist plot concerns itself primarily with the description of unmotivated event, Garland's primary concern is with the nature of the process of conversion.

This is most clearly seen in "The Silent Eaters," which in format most closely resembles the escapist plot. In this biographical account of the Sioux chief Sitting Bull, Garland presents an expanded metaphor for the decline of the Sioux nation, from its early proud self-sufficiency to its final utter dependence upon the whites. Garland tells his story with considerable skill, especially when he succeeds in generalizing the character of Sitting Bull from that of a conventional "bad" Indian into a sympathetic type of the Sioux nation in general. And just here is the focus of Garland's story; for "The Silent Eaters" universalizes the particular figure of Sitting Bull into a general statement of the nature of that historic process which has inevitably ended with the triumph of the whites and the subjugation of the Indians.

Such a focus enables Garland to establish a double point of view toward his material. While he can admire Sitting Bull's courage, resourcefulness, and so on, at the same time he may consistently condemn these qualities as out of place in the white world inevitably to come. Hence Sitting Bull can be personally admired, but at the same time the position for which he stands need not be affirmed. Garland establishes this double viewpoint by means of his narrator, a young Sioux Indian named Iapi. When Sitting Bull finally surrenders, Iapi is befriended by a Lieutenant Davies of the U. S. Army, who gives him the opportunity for education in the white man's ways, even sending him East to study. Lieutenant Davies has a great respect both for the Indians as a race and for education as a means to ameliorate their unhappy reservation conditions. "The plains Indian was a perfect adaptation of organism to environment," he once tells Iapi, who also tells us that "he looked upon each people as the product of its conditions" (p. 205). The moral is not far to seek, nor does it escape Iapi. Now that the environment is changed, the organism must change with it, and Iapi's role must be that of the educator of his people.

The creation of the character of Iapi is Garland's only major fictional tampering with the historic facts of the life of Sitting Bull. Such a character as Iapi, however, is admirably suited for telling Sitting Bull's story. He is first of all an Indian, and his white ways are only superimposed upon the virtues of what Lieutenant Davies calls "a wonderful race" (p. 205). Hence he can be sympathetic to Indian ways without appearing condescending, and at the same time need not pretend to be anything other than outraged over the excesses and outrages which various whites perpetrate upon his people. His white schooling, on the other hand, has given him another perspective on Indian history which enables him to interpret Sitting Bull not in a personal light but in a historic one. From this historic perspective Sitting Bull, however admirably he may appear as a character, is nevertheless the voice of the past. "He epitomized the epic, tragic story of my kind," Iapi sums up. "His life spanned the gulf between the days of our freedom and the death of every custom native to us.

He saw the invader come and he watched the buffalo disappear. Within the half century of his conscious life he witnessed greater changes and comprehended more of my tribe's tragic history than any other red man" (pp. 273-74). But this elegy for Sitting Bull and the heroic past is alloyed with optimism; for the future belongs to Iapi.

The present pessimism and future optimism which Garland notes as the process of Indian history in "The Silent Eaters" are by no means confined to this least fictional of his treatments of the Indian. The historic process of evolution described specifically (and by Lieutenant Davies, at least, in pseudo-scientific Social Darwinian terms) here is also clearly illustrated by the various stories in *The Book of the American Indian*.

The general philosophical burden of these various tales is that, like it or not, the Indian must change. This is emphasized by a recurrent image which is made explicit in a number of the stories, that the Indian's trial has ended, and that the white man's road is the only one left for the Indians to follow. Even when not explicit, this image is always close to the surface. For instance, "Wahiah—A Spartan Mother" tells of the necessity for Indian children to adopt the white man's ways. In this story Wahiah realizes that she must send her son Atokan to the Indian school, no matter how much the reactionary Indians may disapprove of it. When Atokan refuses to go, the schoolteacher gives him a whipping, and Wahiah, in a clearly symbolic gesture, breaks the boy's bow and arrows, his "symbols of freedom," and after saying only "Obey" (p. 12) leaves Atokan at the school.

The theme is most clearly stated in one of the best stories in the book, "Rising Wolf—Ghost Dancer." Rising Wolf, who tells the story of his life himself, recounts how as a young brave he had become a medicine man. He had an honorable position in the tribe before the white men came and, Garland makes clear, he was no cynical prestidigitator but one who sincerely believed in the value of his medicine. After the Indian defeat, Rising Wolf and the rest of his tribe had been sent to a reservation where all had heard of the Ghost Dance. To a medicine man and hence presumably something of an authority on the subject, the idea of the Ghost Dance seemed to make some sense, and he became a convert. The Ghost Dance, Rising Wolf and the other Indians believed, was to operate by magic. The Indians were to dance for four days, and on the fourth day the white men would disappear and the buffalo return, and all Indians, alive or dead, would be reunited on the rejuvenated earth.

The ending of the story describes, in a very sensitively handled tragicomic manner, the Dance itself. The whites, fearing that the gathering dancers represent a threat to civil order, send soldiers to watch lest the dance prove hostile in intent. Of course the Indians, confident of their "medicine," are peaceable in the extreme. For four days they dance, and when they have finished Rising Wolf retires to rest satisfied with a job well done and sure that when he wakes the following morning the whites will have vanished and the buffalo returned.

When he awakes the millennium has unaccountably been delayed; the whites are still there. Convinced by the visible proof that the Ghost Dance in particular and Indian medicine in general have both been in error, he renounces them and resolves to take up white ways. The conclusion of the story is worth examination in detail.

> "When I rose, it was morning. I flung off my blanket, and looked down on the valley where the tepees of the white soldiers stood. I heard their drums and their music. I had made up my mind. The white man's trail was wide and dusty by reason of many feet passing thereon, but it was long. The trail of my people was ended.
>
> "I said, 'I will follow the white man's trail. I will make him my friend, but I will not bend my neck to his burdens. I will be cunning as the coyote. I will ask him to help me to understand his ways, and then I will prepare the way for my children. Maybe they will outrun the white man in his own shoes. Anyhow, there are but two ways. One leads to hunger and death, the other leads where the poor white man lives. Beyond is the happy hunting ground, where the white man cannot go'" (pp. 62-63).

The general similarity between the conclusion of "Rising Wolf" and the more detailed interpretation of history in "The Silent Eaters" is obvious. What is perhaps not so obvious are the implications inherent in Garland's choice of Rising Wolf for his hero. In the character of Rising Wolf, Garland has combined the two points of view represented in "The Silent Eaters" by Sitting Bull and Iapi. By making Rising Wolf first a medicine man and then a believer in the Ghost Dance, Garland has made him symbolically stand for the most reactionary and unprogressive elements in the old order; his conversion to white ways, however anthropologically dubious and psychologically untenable it may seem, represents Garland's deeply held belief that the Indian can be made to accept these ways. Even the most reactionary Indian, when once he understands the hard facts of history, can adjust to the new life forced on him by its inevitable processes.

Garland's insistence upon the inevitability of change relieves him from the fictional necessity to choose sides and accept either white or red ways without qualification; he need not categorically defend or excuse either whites or Indians. Hence villains as well as heroes can be either white or red, and in fact there are many white villains in *The Book of the American Indian*. As a general rule, these white villains are missionaries, for whom Garland has little respect. The general tone of *The Book of the American Indian* is, if not exactly anti-religious, certainly anti-clerical and anti-missionary. One of the most poignant stories, "The Iron Kiva," clearly shows Garland's typical attitude; it tells of two Indian children who kill themselves rather than let the white missionary take them away to school in the East. Significantly, the children like the idea of the white man's school, but distrust and fear the missionaries.

Garland's white heroes are usually Indian agents and school-teachers, whose tolerance and kindliness stand in none too subtle contrast to missionary bigotry. The agents and schoolteachers are sympathetic to those Indian ways which are not immediately harmful and do not stand in the way of the Indians' education. They view the process of education as basically one of training the Indians in the use of unfamiliar skills which he will need to survive in the white man's world. The missionaries, in contrast, view the educational process as one of total ruthless eradication of Indian customs. Without sympathy for or understanding of the Indians, the missionaries are helpless either to convert them or to ameliorate their lot. To rehabilitate the Indian, Garland says, it is not necessary to turn him into a white man; Indian customs need not be entirely blotted out, as the missionaries would have it. The Indian desperately needs training in the general skills of civilized life, for in order to survive he must become literate and learn how to use the white man's agricultural tools. But further than this, education should not go; it is possible to assent to the truth of mathematics without swearing undying allegiance to the Apostles' Creed.

Ultimately Garland's point is that the Indian can and should be allowed to have the best of both white and red worlds. Like Iapi and Rising Wolf, the modern Indian can keep the cultural traditions of his fathers and combine them successfully with the demands of life in a world dominated by white values. Perhaps, as Rising Wolf suggests, if he is cunning enough he can outstrip the white man on his own grounds.

This is true of all the stories in *The Book of the American Indian* with the exception of the best one, "The Story of Howling Wolf." In this somber tale the often complacent "long view" of history which justifies particular present hardship is subjected to serious qualification. When the story opens Howling Wolf hates white men because his brother had been killed for sport by cowboys seven years before. He has never forgiven the whites and has taken a vow to kill the men responsible for his brother's death, but the Indian agent manages to talk him out of his lust for vengeance. Howling Wolf is strongly influenced by the example of the Indian agent, with whom he makes friends, and, renouncing his savage ways, determines to turn himself into the kind of Indian white men will respect. He even gets the agent to write him a paper which, he ingenuously thinks, "will tell [all men] that my heart is made good" (p. 141). This paper, which he carries with him as a sort of passport, says "I am Howling Wolf. Long I hated the white man. Now my heart is good and I want to make friends with all white men. I want to work with a plow and live in a house like the white man. These are my words. [Signed] Howling Wolf" (p. 140).

Armed with his passport, Howling Wolf does what a sober, industrious Indian should and gets a job hauling hides. But when he transports a wagonload of hides to town the whites laugh at him and spurn his offers of friendship. A cowboy picks a fight with him and fires a wild shot which hits another white man in the knee. The outraged citizenry assume that Howling Wolf has fired the shot, and are all for lynching him until he gives them the paper which, when they read it, cools their anger, and they compromise their earlier position by throwing Howling Wolf into jail on more or less general principles. The agent's efforts to have Howling Wolf released are futile. One day Howling Wolf, who has borne up patiently throughout the whole affair, is taken from jail by the sheriff, who wants to attend a baseball game and is afraid to leave the Indian unattended. Howling Wolf thinks he is being taken to his execution, so he tries to escape; but he is apprehended by a group of cowboys who lasso him and drag him behind their horses for amusement. A Catholic priest manages to make the cowboys stop, albeit only after Howling Wolf has apparently been dragged to death. Though he finally recovers, he is "so battered, so misshapen that his own wife did not know him" (p. 155). Howling Wolf's attempt to civilize himself has ended disastrously; he will speak only to the priest and the agent, and when he dies no white man knows where his grave is hidden.

In many ways "The Story of Howling Wolf" is an exact inversion of the other stories in *The Book of the American Indian.* Howling Wolf's story, like Iapi's and Rising Wolf's, is a description of education; but what he learns stands in direct opposition to the lesson the other progressive Indians have been taught. Howling Wolf's education is much like Sitting Bull's; that the whites are cruel, selfish, and not to be trusted.

The most sobering aspect of "The Story of Howling Wolf" and what sets it apart from the other stories is Garland's conception of the limited possibilities for goodness in the nature of man. In the brutal and savage "civilized" world to which Howling Wolf is introduced, there is little room for the optimism which Garland elsewhere shows. Evil in this story is not a product of the conflict between different social values, a conflict which, the other stories lead us to believe, can be smoothed away when one set of social values disappears; rather evil is understood as an expression of the bestiality in man, and social values are not its causes but the ways in which it is made manifest in the world. To such a view history cannot possibly appear optimistic; for all hopes of meliorating human life depend upon the assumption that man's character can be changed for the better. In "The Story of Howling Wolf" such is simply not the case. The parable of history in this story resembles that in the Leatherstocking Tales. Change is certain, but it does not represent progress; history records the frustration of hope.

Hamlin Garland's concern over the future of the Indian is interestingly, if ineptly, echoed in Zane Grey's *The Vanishing American* (1925). Grey writes with a polemic purpose which is not too different from Garland's; how to rehabilitate the Indian is the basic concern of *The Vanishing American.* Like Garland, Grey sees the most serious particular evil in white programs to modernize Indian life as the presence of missionaries. *The Vanishing American* is filled with dastardly men of God beside whom Garland's stern and puritanical ministers seem almost benign. In Grey's pages the ministers are not only misguided and bigoted but lecherous, greedy, and even traitorous. In contrast to these melodramatic stereotypes stand the good white traders and the better Indians. The best Indian of all is the chief Nophaie, *alias* Lo Blandy, who had been carried off as a youth and given the advantages of a white education. Like the narrator of "The Silent Eaters" Nophaie returns to the reservation, bringing with him a young white girl named Marian Warner who is in love with him and who has dedicated herself to working with him in order to uplift the reservation Indians. Their work, however, is doomed to failure by the machinations of the missionaries, who are in cahoots with the reservation superintendent, a German sympathizer who turns out to be not only disloyal to his charges but to the country as well. When the United States becomes involved in the first World War the Indians, for some obscure motivation Grey never bothers to clarify, rush to the colors, and honorably acquit themselves in various ways overseas. Nophaie wins a medal for valor, and another Indian distinguishes himself by standing motionless for several days—coated with whitewash to deceive the enemy into thinking he is a post. After the war the Indians' lot does not improve. Many die of influenza—including Nophaie—and the book ends on a note of sentimental pathos, with Marian "watching the Indians ride away into the sunset," and thinking of them "moving on, diminishing, fading, vanishing —vanishing" (p. 308).

A plot summary of *The Vanishing American* serves to emphasize Grey's similarity to Garland. Unfortunately, it also serves to disguise the real difference between them and hence make Grey's very limited fictional achievement seem greater than it is. What a plot summary ignores is the fact that Grey's real concern is not with Indians in particular or even society in general. Where Garland attempts a serious discussion of the Indian problem, and from this generalizes his fictional characters into a statement about the nature of history, Grey ignores both Indians and history. Garland's bitter, uncompromising, often misguided, and sometimes evil characters become in Grey's hands nothing more than stereotypes. Nowhere is this more evident than in Grey's discussion of attempts to Christianize the Indians, an aspect of white policy which both men understand is at the heart of the Indians' cultural future. Unlike Garland, Grey never faces the problem squarely. We discover early in the book that Nophaie has lost both his white and Indian religions, and in the face of this catastrophe minor problems such as white maltreatment of Indians, poor sanitary conditions on the reservations, inadequate medical care, and indeed the threatened extinction of the entire Indian race dwindle to matters of almost no importance. At the end of *The Vanishing American* Nophaie comes to the comforting realization that the God of the Indian and the God of the white man is the same. The rush of insight which opens his mind to this complacent universal truth also elevates him to a pinnacle of philosophical understanding where he can realize that "the tragic fate of the vanishing American . . . ceased to exist" (p. 302). Secure in this profound knowledge he can—and does—die happily, untortured by the doubts which have pursued him throughout the book.

The Vanishing American, then, becomes escape literature of the most insidious kind. Grey is interested in nothing other than the most complacent romanticizing. The fate of the Indian is exploited to lend to the book a dim melancholy quality and, hopefully, the illusion of profundity to a story which celebrates nothing more profound than a total retreat from life. The stereotyped characters—evil missionaries and nefarious agents on the one side and noble Indians and sympathetic traders on the other —serve only to reveal the utter conventionality of Grey's mind. In his hands a great and tragic theme is reduced to the most insipid bathos.

However dissimilar in quality the work of these two writers is, in their basic assumptions the two men are fairly close. The polemic concern of both authors is to explore the problem of how the values of white and Indian life can be reconciled. Both are closely bound to the appearances at least of the historic world at the time when the racial extinction of the Indian seemed almost a certainty. Both men begin with an implicit practical concern— how to rehabilitate the Indian in order that he may live in a world of white cultural values—though Grey quickly turns his back on his material in favor of a world of romantic fantasy while Garland transcends his particular practical concerns, transforming them into a statement of the course of history in general. For both men, as for anyone who had to deal with the rehabilitation of the Indian in practical terms, the solution to the vexing question of the Indian's future had to be found in some kind of viable combination of Indian and white ways of life. In his search for some way to combine the best of both Indian and white worlds, each author reflects a wider American concern, though Garland's compassionate understanding renders his understanding of the problem far more sensitive than the ordinary, while Grey's romantic escapism renders his discussion superficial and condescending.

However inferior to Garland's work in quality, in one way Grey's is much more modern. His very disinterest in and inability to find a realistic solution to the question of the Indian's future is a harbinger of subsequent literary treatment of Indian life, in which the realities of the Indian problem become constantly more remote. For this search to find some eclectic way of combining the conflicting values represented symbolically by Indian and white ways of life is not the only concern of books which focus primarily upon the vanishing American, and it becomes less important as the historic Indian problem becomes more distant. Indian and white ways come to be presented as not only mutually hostile but as mutually incompatible and, finally, as irreconcilable. Though this literary treatment of the difference between Indian and white ways of life has a long history in American writing, in the twentieth century it becomes much more important; moreover, in twentieth-century writing the traditional literary relationship of Indian values to white is at least partially inverted. Where nineteenth-century writers had generally taken the position that Indian ways, though possibly valuable in certain situations, were categorically inferior to white, the twentieth-century artist often uses Indian values— or what he conceives to be Indian values—as a method of castigating the imperfections of modern civilization. In such novels Indian values are often seen as categorically superior to white, and with such point of view the discussion of history must necessarily contain an inherent melancholy refutation of the idea of progress. Quite often the fictional form such a presentation assumes is that of an attack upon the possibility of any melding of Indian and white values. Where Garland—except in "The Story of Howling Wolf"—had hoped for the eclectic combination of the best ways of both cultures, much other more modern writing seeks explicitly to deny the possibility of this kind of synthesis.

White ways and red, in this view, are incompatible because they stand for two completely irreconcilable attitudes toward life.

A clear statement of this modern treatment of Indian life may be found in Conrad Richter's *The Light in the Forest* (1953). Though not strictly speaking a Western—the frontier in the book is the Western Pennsylvania frontier of the mid-eighteenth century—it gives a clear picture of the modern development of the character of the literary Indian. *The Light in the Forest* tells the simple story of a fifteen-year-old white boy who, when a child, had been carried off by the Indians and adopted. He had been given the name of True Son—a name which proves ironic—and had grown up as an Indian. When the book opens he, along with other captives, is being given up to the whites who have forced the Indians to surrender their prisoners. He is turned over to his former parents who attempt to civilize him. Their efforts are at first unavailing, but his resistance to white ways is gradually broken down, primarily because of his growing attachment to his younger brother Gordie. One day his Indian cousin Half Arrow comes and True Son runs away with him back to the Indians. The two boys stop off for a while on the way and live temporarily in a state of idyllic hedonism, catching fish for food, but eventually they have to go on to the Indian village. In this village live the relatives of Little Crane, another Indian friend of True Son's, who had been killed by whites; they have determined to avenge themselves. Because True Son's white uncle had been responsible for Little Crane's death, and because True Son wants to prove himself a loyal Indian, he goes along on this punitive expedition. The Indians decide to wait in ambush along the shores of a large river, and to use True Son as a decoy to lure passing boats to destruction. The first boat to come by is an emigrant flatboat which puts in to shore to rescue True Son, who is trying to entice it within range of the Indians. At the last moment, however, True Son sees a small boy on the boat who reminds him of his brother Gordie, and he cries "Take him back! It's an ambush!" (p. 168). The boat gets safely away, but the Indians drive True Son from the tribe, taking him as far as a white man's road and there abandoning him.

The concluding metaphor of the two roads in *The Light in the Forest* emphasizes Richter's metaphorical kinship with Garland for whom, as we noted earlier, the same image was a favorite symbolic device. The two men's respective use of this common symbol, however, emphasizes as well the great difference between them. For while Garland had used the image of the two roads as a metaphor for a philosophical position of qualified optimism to make the point that there was at least one road left for the Indian to follow, Richter uses the same image as a metaphor of despair. True Son cannot follow either road, and where Garland had held forth the possibility of acceptance Richter concludes his book with an image of rejection.

The same symbolic image of rejection is intensified by the name of the hero of the book, True Son. To be a true son, or indeed a son of any kind, implies a father, but by the end of the story True Son has in turn rejected and been rejected by both his fathers, each of whom symbolically represents the way of life of one of the two groups to which True Son supposedly "belongs." When Cuyloga, the boy's Indian father, ultimately rejects him, the image is made explicit. Upon arrival at the white man's road, True Son tries to bid farewell to Cuyloga. Cuyloga, however, will not accept the bond of affection which such a farewell expresses, and spurns the boy's entreaty.

> "My father. Do we say good-by to each other now?"
> "Enemies do not do so," Cuyloga told him harshly. "I am no longer your father, nor you my son."
> "Then who is my father?" the boy cried in despair and turned quickly to hide the blinding wetness in his eyes (p. 178).

In the symbolic structure of the story, Richter tells us in a brief foreword, the incompatibility of Indian and white life is a metaphor of the curtailment of individual freedom by civilization. Even "two hundred years ago," he writes, "when restrictions were comparatively few with us, our ideals and restrained manner of existence repelled the Indians." As a result, one of the purposes of the book "is to point out that in the pride of our American liberties, we're apt to forget that already we've lost a good many to civilization" (p. viii).

The irony in the name True Son is reinforced by the ironic nature of the concept of freedom, which is seen in a strangely ambiguous light in the book. Conventionally considered, True Son had been freed by his white parents from the Indian captivity, but, Richter suggests, in actuality he has been made captive by the whites and carried off from Indian freedom. The ambiguity inherent in the various definitions of freedom is again emphasized in a scene where True Son goes to visit a Negro basket-maker who had also at one time been captured by the Indians. In the person of this Negro the ambiguous nature of the concept of freedom is personified, for he is a slave, and his rescue from the Indians had again delivered him into bondage.

Richter's presentation of the paradoxical nature of freedom is reinforced by his discussion of an allied theme to which our attention is first called by the quotation from Wordsworth's *Intimations* ode which serves as the motto of the book and is echoed in its title:

> Shades of the prison-house begin to close
> Upon the growing Boy,
> But he beholds the light, and whence it flows,
> He sees it in his joy.

The novel, this clearly implies, will deal with the process of maturing. If we apply Wordsworth's quotation to the particular world of *The Light in the Forest*, the light is symbolically presented as emanating from the forest homes of the Indians to the prison-house of the whites. Such is certainly the case on the evidence of the novel's symbolic structure, where the values represented by the whites are portrayed in explicit images of imprisonment. The house in which True Son must live with his white parents is seen, on the basis of his Indian perceptions, as a trap. White man's clothes limit the freedom of motion he had enjoyed in his Indian garments, and shoes, as opposed to moccasins, represent the confinement and cramping imposed upon him by white ways. When True Son escapes from his white captivity he revels in the irresponsible freedom of the woods.

What Richter has done, it should by now be clear, is to combine the metaphors of freedom (represented by Indian life) and responsibility (represented by white) with two analogous metaphors of freedom (youth) and responsibility (maturity). Hence the dilemma of True Son, the Indian captive, is finally divorced from a purely historical context, and the ultimate purpose of the novel becomes that of showing, by means of a parable, the loss of freedom which is the inevitable price of maturity. The boy wishes he could remain young and an Indian forever; but the prison-house of maturity inexorably removes him from his Indian life.

For Richter as for Wordsworth the process of maturing is tragic, and this meaning too inheres in the symbol of the two roads which concludes the book. True Son can no longer be happy on either road. The remembrance of youth is the price of maturity.

True Son's final question—"Who is my father?"—emphasizes his role as a man between two societies, a role which has also been made apparent by his physical paternity in one culture and his emotional paternity in another. This theme of the "man between," though used for many different purposes, is never far to seek in modern literary treatment of the Indian. Such a conception is immediately evident in *The Vanishing American,* where Nophaie is also conceived as a man with a kind of dual allegiance, and in *The Book of the American Indian,* where Garland assumes that such a double paternity is the only course open for the Indian. All these, of course, are specific instances of a ubiquitous fictional plot, the story of a man caught between two disparate ways of life and searching for some way to reconcile them. This general theme has a long literary history in Indian story, but is most clearly seen in the various tales of the Indian captivity. Though many of the so-called "captivity narratives" follow a somewhat different convention—the story of an adult white captive who can report upon the excesses and barbarities of the Indian society to which he or she has been unwillingly subjected— a different convention describes the lot of prisoners who, like True Son, are not unwilling to remain among their Indian captors. Historically, such cases are numerous. One immediately recalls the story of Simon Girty and other white renegades, as well as of various lost children such as Lucy Keyes, whose name is still a commercial memory in central Massachusetts, and who aptly symbolizes the various white captives who grew up apparently quite happily among Indian foster-parents. The "Indianizing" of whites has been a constant theme in literature on the subject at least as far back as the story of Daniel Boone, who was adopted into an Indian tribe and who, his biographer worries, may have been more taken with Indian ways than he should have been.[6]

Fictionally, this theme goes back at least to Crèvecoeur's *Letters from an American Farmer* (1782). At the end of this volume, in a letter titled "Distresses of a Frontier Man," Crève- coeur's farmer, after reflecting upon the various cases of white men who have refused to be repatriated, decides that life with the Indians has something to be said for it, especially since the peaceable savages seem to offer a better alternative than the bellicose whites. Just how seriously this is to be taken as a personal expression of Crèvecoeur's own views is open to question; the letter is practically a caricature of the most ludicrous eighteenth-century conventions about the nature of the noble savage and the rewards of life among the primitive, and is almost certainly not to be accepted at face value, especially since the *Letters* taken as a whole make a completely different point. The "Distresses of a Frontier Man" nonetheless serves to indicate that the possibilities of such a theme for fictional treatment were early understood.

Among more recent novelists writing in a specifically Western context, Alan Le May, who has written two novels which deal specifically with the theme of Indian captivity, is the most intriguing. The first of these, *The Searchers* (1954), is a classic captivity narrative set in Texas rather than east of the Mississippi. It is the story of the capture of a ten-year-old child, Debbie Edwards, and her older sister, in an Indian raid in which her parents and the rest of her immediate family are killed. A rescue party is sent out but, when the searchers find the older girl dead and lose the trail of the raiding Indians, they turn back. Only the girl's uncle, Amos Edwards, and an adopted brother, Martin Pauley, whose own parents had been killed in an earlier massacre, continue the search. All reports of the captive Debbie prove illusory, and the search stretches out for six years as Amos and Martin criss-cross the plains running down one false rumor after another. During the six-year search Martin carries with him a miniature of Debbie, and can never be made to realize, though the image becomes faded and grimy, that she too will inevitably have changed from the way she was when she was captured. To him she remains the little ten-year-old girl she was when the Comanches abducted her. When the two searchers finally catch up with the Indian party with which Debbie is living, Martin discovers with horror not only that she has grown up but that the years of captivity have changed her into an Indian. The search has been in vain, for Debbie is no longer a white woman, nor does she wish to be repatriated.

So cursory a summary cannot do justice to the considerable esthetic achievement of *The Searchers*. Though marred by a conventional ending which features a cavalry charge in which the bad Indians are wiped out and an embarrassing love scene which unfortunately implies that Debbie's captivity and Martin's search are all parts of an inscrutable plan which tends in general toward good and in particular toward matrimony, on the whole the book is well visualized. In addition, Le May has a real gift for writing scenes of Gothic horror which brilliantly emphasize the novel's nightmare quality. The confrontation between Martin and Debbie mentioned above is a case in point, as is another scene where Martin, in conference with a solemn conclave of Indian dignitaries, notices a scalp which, he idly thinks, must have belonged to a beautiful white woman—only to discover later that it is his mother's. Such Gothic scenes are only one example of Le May's considerable ability for symbolic description. The slowly fading miniature of Debbie which Martin carries with him is a not so bizarre instance of the same skill.

Nevertheless, what gives *The Searchers* most of its force are the disturbing implications of the parable it tells. With all its apparent diffuseness, *The Searchers* is based on the contradictory implications inherent in two very simple but profound ironies. The first of these, briefly noted above, is the whole theme of the futile search which forms the plot of the novel. Martin and Amos discover, when they at last confront the long-captive Debbie, that she does not want to be rescued, and the supposedly terrible fate of Indian captivity is discovered not to be so awful after all, at least from her point of view. This final revelation is, to the two searchers, the most horrible of all.

The Searchers, it has probably already occurred to the reader, has a marked similarity to a rather unexpected analogue, the ghost story. Debbie, when Amos and Martin meet her, rather closely resembles the zombie (or werewolf, or vampire) in horror story, or his modern descendant in science fiction, the one-time human being who has somehow been changed into something terrible. The theme is at least as old as Homer's Lotus-eaters, and literary treatment of it almost inevitably requires that the demonic agents—those who offer the lotus or make the zombie or, in this case, change their captive into an Indian—not be handled sympathetically; for ultimately such demonic agents exchange man's precious humanity for something else, usually by trading his human sympathies for something unhuman. In *The Searchers* the terror, never far below the realistic surface of the story, is given added emphasis by Le May's symbolic handling of the Comanches, who come to stand for a type of sub-human, bestial, demonic life. The point is clearly emphasized in the scene when Martin meets Debbie, whom Le May describes in terms which emphasize how her humanity has been changed. "Debbie's face, delicately made, and now in the first bloom of maturity" has "all expression . . . locked away from it." She faces him "impassively, as an Indian faces a stranger," and Martin can no longer recognize the little girl whose miniature he has so faithfully carried for so long, since "behind the surface of this long-loved face was a Comanche squaw" (p. 236). From this description the pictorial resemblance between the Indianized Debbie and the dehumanized zombie is perfectly clear, and the kinship is further emphasized by Le May's admittedly unrealistic treatment of the Comanches, whose stoical, cunning, treacherous, war-like nature is also a symbol of their unhumanity.

The second irony is also demonic in quality and serves to emphasize the first. This irony resides in Le May's examination of the motives which lie behind the search and the price which such single-minded pursuit exacts from the searchers. In the characters of the two searchers Le May presents a serious travesty of a commonplace romantic theme, that of search for some kind of ideal. This theme is often presented in the sexual terms of the search for a beautiful woman and, as in *The Searchers,* the beautiful ideal is often discovered to have a more than casual resemblance to the demon lover. Whether the ideal be divine or satanic, however, its pursuit demands rigorous training on the part of the searcher who must, whether he follow the Grail or Satan, undertake a course of action in which he renounces all human ties. The difference between the searcher for God and the searcher for Satan lies only in the motives with which either undertakes his quest; both searchers' courses of action are identical.

In his development of the respective characters of the two searchers, Le May emphasizes the different motives which lie behind identical actions. Both men in the course of their six-year search symbolically renounce the world and all its gifts. Martin, always following the ideal represented by the miniature of Debbie which he carries with him, renounces the human love represented in the novel by his sweetheart, Laurie, who eventually marries another. In one striking symbolic scene which takes place during an interlude in the search when Martin and Amos have temporarily returned home, Laurie agrees to come to Martin at night. That night news of Debbie is brought to the ranch and the searchers start out again, Martin's love unconsummated. Like Martin, Amos too renounces earthly ties, but unlike Martin he follows an ideal not of love but of revenge. Not until late in the story do we discover Amos' motivation to be not the rescue of Debbie but the destruction of the Indians who have murdered his brother's wife, with whom he had been in love. Indeed, through a curiously inverted puritanism Amos decides to kill Debbie when he finds her. Not only does he believe that by the time she is rescued she will be nothing other than an Indian and hence not worth saving, but his warped mind assumes that she should be killed since her sexual purity has presumably been destroyed by the Comanches.

Martin's dual discovery that his search requires the renunciation of even the possibility of earthly happiness and that the motives which drive his fellow searcher are by no means either pure or admirable becomes a symbolic statement of the necessary loss of naive happiness which accompanies maturing. Like the fading miniature of Debbie which Martin carries with him, his ideals must be qualified to take account of reality.

When one compares the Comanches of *The Searchers* with the various Indians of *The Book of the American Indian* the great difference between modern and more traditional literary Indians becomes immediately evident. Unlike Garland, Le May makes no pretense at drawing true-to-life Indians nor, as I hope this discussion of *The Searchers* has made clear, is his concern for realism more than superficial. *The Searchers* is clearly intended as a parable, and the Indians in it partake of abstract quasi-allegorical qualities which are not intended to have more than a minimal similarity to the historic facts of Indian life.

That Le May's unsympathetic picture of Indian life is symbolic rather than realistic may be further shown by a brief glance at his other captivity narrative, *The Unforgiven* (1957). Not so successful a story as *The Searchers, The Unforgiven* is weak precisely where the earlier book is strong: Le May does not develop the implications of his parable so profoundly, and as a result his Gothic talent for nightmare deteriorates from an essential mode of apprehending his story into an often shallow sensationalism.

The Unforgiven is a captivity narrative in reverse. The captive in the story is a young girl, Rachel Zachary, who had been found as a baby by "Old Zack" Zachary, a redoubtable Indian fighter, on a punitive raid against the Kiowas. Old Zack had brought the infant home to his wife as a replacement for a baby girl of their own who had previously died. The child had been raised as a member of the family and her parentage concealed. What her parentage actually is never becomes clear; she may be either a white captive dropped by the Indians or a part-Indian child of a Kiowa brave and a white captive squaw.

The point of the story lies in the parentage which various characters in the novel attribute to her and of how this affects both their behavior toward her and, once she discovers the question of her birth, her own actions. The Kiowas assume (and the implication is that their assumption is correct, though we are never told in so many words) that she is an Indian child, and they try to recapture her and take her back. The whites also assume she is an Indian—a "red nigger" as they succinctly put it— and should be returned. More than that, they assume that the Zacharys' immunity from Indian raids is due not to their watchfulness and the fact that their house is so strongly built that it is almost impregnable, but to some unholy understanding they have with the Indians, guaranteeing their immunity to attack and symbolized by the Indian girl whom they have adopted. The Zacharys, at the beginning of the novel, believe just as strongly that Rachel is white and a member of the family, and hence that they owe her protection.

The question of Rachel's parentage, in sum, is interpreted by everyone in the book as determining to which society she "belongs." Everyone—Kiowas, Zacharys, other whites—is agreed that if the fact of her parentage could once be positively determined, the question of what to do with her might finally be settled. She is, in short, either "red" or "white" and hence belongs with "her own people," whichever color they may turn out to be. The preoccupation of *The Unforgiven* is the education of Ben Zachary, Rachel's oldest "brother," to the realization that such a distinction is spurious, and that she, as any person, must be considered as an individual rather than as a type. After a pitched battle with the Indians—*The Unforgiven,* like *The Searchers,* concludes with an unfortunate conventional battle scene which rather spoils the story—Ben comes into possession of a paper, sent him by

Striking Horse, an Indian medicine man, which will once and for all resolve the question of Rachel's birth. Rather than find out he burns the paper, for the question of whether she is red or white is, he says, a "mean-minded question" (p. 245).

Our discussion of *The Unforgiven* brings up another aspect of the relation between Indian and white ways, the theme of miscegenation. It has probably occurred to the reader that in some of the books already mentioned the possibility of white marriage to an Indian is at least a peripheral concern. In *The Vanishing American* the marriage is agreed upon but Nophaie's untimely death frustrates its consummation; in *The Searchers,* though Martin is to marry a white girl, she is at least symbolically partially Indian; but in *The Unforgiven* the implication is that Rachel really is an Indian and, more than that, whether she is or no, the question is beside the point.

In terms of Western literature as a whole the miscegenation theme is not so important as one would expect, especially if one looks for an analogy between the Indian in literature about the West and the Negro in literature about the South. Only comparatively rarely, as in *The Unforgiven,* is the problem of race made explicit. Usually the romantic plot is symbolic of some other concern, and marriage, when it takes place, becomes an emblem of the hero's decision to cast his lot with one or the other of two different cultures. *The Big Sky* may be cited as a convenient example; in that novel, it will be recalled, Boone's marriage to the Blackfoot Teal Eye is symbolic of his decision to identify himself with Indian rather than white values.

Occasionally, however, the theme of interracial marriage is used in the Western in a manner very like its treatment in Southern literature. One of the earliest writers about the West, William Joseph Snelling, in his story "The Bois Brulé" (1830), handles the theme in a way which has scarcely changed since. The *"bois brulé"* of the story (the term is a French-Canadian one for a man of mixed European and Indian parentage) is one William Gordon. He is in love with Flora Cameron, the daughter of a poor but proud Scot who has no objection at all to Gordon except the classic one that he wouldn't want him to marry his daughter. Not until the end of the story does the father relent and on his deathbed confess that he had "listened to the voice of pride and vain glory rather than to natural affection" (p. 142), and consent to the marriage. Even in Snelling's treatment of the miscegenation theme, however, one startling difference between the literary Indian and the literary Negro is clearly apparent. This difference is to be found in the conventionally assumed nobility of the Indian which reflects in the even greater nobility of the *bois brulé*. "The halfbreeds of the North-west," Snelling tells us, "are physically a fine race of men. The mixture of blood seems an improvement on the Indian and white. By it, the muscular strength of the one, and the easy grace, and power of endurance of the other, are blended" (p. 78). Snelling's praise which, he implies, is the honest appraisal of any reasonable man, forms a remarkable contrast to the inferior status which society conventionally assigns to the literary Negro. Where the *bois brulé* is a noble character to whom no purely racial stigma is attached except by a few misguided souls, the mulatto is inevitably consigned to an unending battle against the racial prejudice of an entire society. The difference is not so much one of kind as of degree, but it is clearly reflected in the greater ease with which the Indian or *bois brulé* can receive white acceptance.

Helen Hunt Jackson's once famous novel *Ramona* (1884) gives a longer treatment of the miscegenation theme which, though written without knowledge of *Tales of the Northwest* and laid in Spanish California rather than the Louisiana Purchase, is still conceived in essentially the same terms as "The Bois Brulé." Ramona, the story's heroine, is the daughter of a Scotchman and an Indian and, like William Gordon, combines the best qualities of both races. She falls in love with Alessandro, a cultivated and educated Indian, whom she eventually marries against the wishes of her guardian. She is disinherited and after numerous harrowing adventures too pathetic to relate at length is finally married to her first love, Felipe, after Alessandro dies.

The overly sentimental love story sadly dates *Ramona* for the modern reader, but underneath the coy and often saccharine detailing of Ramona's and Alessandro's courtship is a more serious theme. This is the theme of irrational pride which will not accept a man for his individual worth but insists upon considering him only as a representative of some racial type which is arbitrarily conceived as superior or inferior to all others. Ramona's proud Spanish guardian, Señora Moreno, will not consent to the marriage of Ramona and Alessandro, since Alessandro is an Indian and, as Señora Moreno says to her son Felipe, "would you be willing that your own sister should marry Alessandro?" (p. 193). She wants Ramona to marry "well," that is, to marry an aristocratic Spanish Californian, and she hopes to accomplish this by judiciously remaining silent about Ramona's Indian parentage and at the same time pointing out her ample dowry to prospective suitors. Her ambition that Ramona marry well does not extend so far as to include Felipe among possible mates, nor does she reflect that her own sister's marriage to a fine Spanish gentleman had resulted disastrously.

Señora Moreno's hostility to Alessandro reappears in the novel in the prejudices the various California racial groups hold against each other. The proud Catholic Spaniards hate the new plebeian Protestant Americans. (Señora Moreno even puts crosses up around her property in hopes of converting Protestant passers by, but without success.) The Americans cordially detest the Spanish, whose racial pride and religion they interpret respectively as arrogance and superstition. Both groups unite in hostility toward the hapless Indians. The Americans take their lands away and the Spanish accept them in their place. As long as they don't want to marry your sister the Indians are fine people.

But somehow none of this adds up to an indictment of racial prejudice, and its failure to do so is the novel's major weakness. Mrs. Jackson is unable to relate her criticism of California society to Señora Moreno's personal hatred for Ramona. While she rightly presents the social and political power struggle going on in California as a result of greed abetted by racial and religious prejudice, she falters when she has to make her views specific. As a result, the reader always remains at a loss to understand how anyone could possibly treat Ramona badly. She is so sweet, so good, so noble, and Señora Moreno so arbitrary and unconvincing that the personal conflict between the two women never seems real, nor, more to the point, is it a particular example of a general social evil. That it is not is largely the fault of Mrs. Jackson's hereditary literary attitude toward Indians, which conflicts with what is ostensibly going on in California society. As individuals, Alessandro and Ramona are generally treated kindly; only Señora Moreno does them specific ill, and her malicious attitude is clearly shown to be not only unreasonable but atypical. It is only when "the Yankees" are confronting "the Indians" that evil is done, and Mrs. Jackson is unable to portray convincingly the mixture of general social malevolence with personal kindliness.

Though the theme of miscegenation is comparatively rare in literature of the West, when it does appear it emphasizes one conventional fact of life about both real and literary Indians— their difference from whites. That this difference does not necessarily imply inferiority—though it may be made to do so—probably explains the relative rarity of the theme. White and Indian marriage in the Western is generally handled much more like American marriages to Europeans in novels with an international flavor, or like marriages in America between various socially equal but distinct ethnic groups, than it is like white and Negro marriages in novels about the South. Such treatment in terms of cultural differences rather than racial inferiority implies that the conflict symbolized by the marriage will not be so much that of social ostracism in society at large as that of the education of an individual into the understanding of the different values symbolized by another way of life.

This difference of the Indian from the white has been at the basis of treatment of the Indian in fiction since he first appeared as a noble savage in eighteenth-century primitivistic writing. One other aspect of it should be noted in conclusion, which has become constantly more important as the historic "Indian problem" has become more remote. In our discussion of *The Searchers* we examined the way in which Le May turned the Comanches into almost allegorical figures, based upon reality it is true, but far more responsible to the thematic demands of his story than to the facts of Indian life. In the work of modern writers of frankly parabolic intent, this treatment of the Indian has become even more noticeable. Quite often, as in *The Searchers*, the uncanny (at least to the whites) qualities of the Indian—his stoical reserve, his apparent lack of feeling, his woodsmanship—transform him into an almost supernatural being. The Indian's attributes, in other words, place him very obviously in a different category from the white man, and his deeper perception into the facts of primitive life may be used as an emblem of his deeper perception into the meaning of life itself. Such an allegorically handled Indian resembles quite closely the typical cowboy hero discussed in the preceding chapter.

The uncanny cunning of the literary Indian is by no means a new theme. It is clearly implied, for instance, in the character of

Cooper's Chingachgook and in the various bad Indians who skulk ominously through the Leatherstocking Tales. Indeed, in one of the Tales, *The Last of the Mohicans,* the theme nearly becomes explicit. The battle of wits between Uncas, Chingachgook, and to a lesser extent Natty Bumppo on the one hand and the evil Indian "Le Renard Subtil" (the name is intentionally symbolic) on the other is conceived in almost magical terms. The story—a plot of wilderness rescue of two beautiful captives—is almost a type of the fairy-tale theme of the rescue of the beautiful princess from the hands of an evil enchanter. The various devices Natty, Chingachgook, and Uncas use to effect the recapture of the two girls held captive by the Indians and the countermeasures taken by Le Renard Subtil are not so far as one might at first think from the magical spells of white and black magic. The unreality of the world of *The Last of the Mohicans* is emphasized by the total inability of Duncan Heyward (the young white romantic hero who is a clear prefiguration of the later stock figure of the dude) to understand what is going on once the story moves into the forest, and by the progressive unreality of the devices themselves. In every case Chingachgook's party is able to outsmart Le Renard Subtil by thinking of something he had overlooked (in which ability they closely resemble Bransford's later cowboy friends of *Good Men and True*), and their superior woodcraft is almost magical. The reader will recall that the rescue of one of the maidens which caps this battle of wits is made by Natty, who infiltrates the camp of Le Renard Subtil disguised as a bear. On closer examination, however, he turns out not to have disguised himself as a bear, but as a Mingo shaman who uses bear robes for making magic. The symbolism is certainly obvious; Natty has overcome Le Renard Subtil by turning his own magic against him (and again we may draw a parallel to the cowboy hero, this time to the Virginian's victory in tall story over Trampas).

These remarks have purposely exaggerated the magical and supernatural elements in *The Last of the Mohicans* in order to emphasize how near the surface of Indian story they lie. Even though in Cooper's work the magical qualities of his Indians are subordinated to other concerns, they are still easily found; they are even easier to find in later Western stories by writers whose concern is more frankly allegorical or fabular.

Walter Van Tilburg Clark's *The Track of the Cat* (1949) gives a clear example. This book is superficially a hunting story which concerns itself with the attempts of three brothers—Arthur, Curt, and Harold Bridges—to track down and kill a mountain lion which has killed some of their livestock. The first brother, Arthur, is an amiable dreamer who is fascinated by the Bridges' old and eccentric Indian ranch hand, Joe Sam. Joe Sam is obsessed with the image of a black panther, a "private, stalking god he had invented to mean the end of things" (p. 5) and Arthur, a clever wood-carver, every year whittles him a small wooden panther which he carries as a charm. Joe Sam's family had long ago been killed by a black panther which he is convinced was not a flesh-and-blood panther but some kind of supernatural agent. Arthur differs from Joe Sam in that he believes in the black panther-god only metaphorically. He is fond of abstract metaphysical speculation which has little to do with the workaday world. For Joe Sam the panther-god is real; he has seen it and it has killed his family.

The second brother, Curt, is almost exactly Arthur's opposite. He is matter-of-fact, prides himself on being realistic, and delights in taunting Joe Sam, whose obsession with the black panther he finds ridiculous. The character of the youngest brother, Harold, is amorphous at the beginning of the novel. He likes Arthur but admires Curt. When Arthur and Curt set out to track down the panther, Arthur, who significantly is daydreaming rather than paying attention to his surroundings, is almost immediately killed by the cat. After his death Curt sets out to "get" the panther, but when the chase goes on longer than he had anticipated and when he, a mighty hunter, gets lost, hunger and fear cause him to imagine the cat as Joe Sam's supernatural black panther. He panics and runs away from the vision in his mind and plunges over a cliff to his death. Ultimately Harold, with the aid of Joe Sam whom in the course of the book he has come to love and respect, kills the panther.

Added to this hunting story is a subsidiary—and for our purposes more important—plot. During the course of the novel's action Harold's betrothed is visiting the Bridges' ranch, the object of Arthur's kindly respect and Curt's lecherous advances. Their mother does not approve of the match, however, and does her best to discourage it. On another level, then, *The Track of the Cat* becomes a record of Harold's maturing, which is complete by the end of the novel and which enables him at once to kill the panther and to stand up for his own desires in opposition to his mother. His ability finally to kill the panther serves as a metaphor of his symbolic arrival in the adult world.

Though *The Track of the Cat* is rich in complexities, its basic concern is to discover a definition of the nature of the panther which plagues the Bridges' ranch. Arthur is willing speculatively to accept the panther as an admirable metaphor for the metaphysical fact of evil, a metaphor without much practical application to the world of affairs. While meditating on the poetic beauty of Joe Sam's concept he is caught unaware by the panther and killed. Curt, in contrast, has no sympathy at all for either Joe Sam's black panther or Arthur's metaphysical speculations upon its nature. To him the panther is just another wildcat with nothing, either real or metaphorical, to do with Joe Sam's foolish idea of a panther-god. After all, as he soon discovers, the raiding panther isn't even black. Unlike Arthur, Curt is not killed by the particular panther; rather he is killed by Joe Sam's panther-god, from whom he is desperately running when he plunges to his death.

Arthur and Curt represent two mutually exclusive and incomplete methods of coping with evil. Arthur, though aware of evil as a metaphysical principle, is unfortunately too prone to deny the reality of its particular manifestations; Curt in contrast can handle a flesh-and-blood panther, but his mind cannot cope with the idea of a metaphysical evil principle, and when such a principle is inadvertently forced upon him he goes mad. Harold's problem, then, is to combine these two incomplete conceptions and to arrive at an understanding of how evil in general relates to evil in particular. In terms of the symbolism of the story, Harold must arrive at the understanding possessed by Joe Sam, who believes in the general evil principle represented by his black panther-god but is also aware of how this evil principle is manifested in the world. Joe Sam, then, plays a role in this novel very like that of the cowboy hero in many another Western —the symbolic educator of a dude to understanding of the deeper meaning of the facts of life in the West.

In the course of the novel Harold penetrates through the superficial appearance of things to such an understanding of their significance, which is symbolized by his decision, when it comes his turn to hunt the panther, to take Joe Sam with him. With Joe Sam's aid Harold manages to track the panther down, and bullets from *both their guns* kill it. Standing over the panther's body Joe Sam says, "Not black painter." "No. I guess we'll never get that one," Harold answers. "Not get," Joe Sam agrees (p. 403).

The clearly allegorical structure of *The Track of the Cat* is even more noticeable when we become conscious of the startling similarity between the novel's plot and one of the most common themes of fairy tale. For all its particular setting on a Nevada ranch at about the turn of the century, *The Track of the Cat* is as timeless as the tale it so closely imitates, the story of the three princes who are sent on a quest, the successful completion of which will give one of them the hand of the beautiful princess. Invariably in this story the two older brothers lose out, and almost always the youngest brother wins the hand of the beautiful princess through the aid of a supernatural agent. This supernatural agent is usually unprepossessing in appearance, and the advice he gives is apparently so foolish that the older brothers treat it with contempt. Sometimes the supernatural agent is, like Joe Sam, himself a prince from another country who has been bewitched by an evil magician and can tell the truth he knows only in riddles.

Acceptance of the truth at which Joe Sam hints in *The Track of the Cat* is achieved only by Harold, and is the necessary price of his maturity. The knowledge which gives the young prince the right to the hand of the beautiful princess also destroys the enjoyment of that right, for to the returning knight errant home can never be the same. The knowledge of evil is bought at the price of naive youthful belief in the power of good, as the haunting image which concludes the book makes explicit. Riding home with Joe Sam, the dead Curt on a sled between them, Harold looks ahead to "the ranch, still tiny with distance, and already in the shadow of the mountain. Once in a while it showed clearly, so he could see even the smoke lining out from the chimney of the house, but more often it grew faint or even disappeared behind the running snow" (p. 404).

In the character of Joe Sam are summed up most of the traits of his Indian forebears in Western story. The knowledge he possesses sets him off from the other characters in *The Track of the Cat*, and his philosophical distance from them is emphasized by his racial difference. His racial attributes serve still more to reinforce this role as an outsider. He is a better woodsman than Curt and a better metaphysician than Arthur, and his apparent craziness both conceals and reveals a deeper knowledge than that possessed by the whites. The last of a vanishing race, he understands better than anyone else that evil is best understood through the symbol of death, and that the result of evil in the world is the fact of human loneliness. His habitual manner of speech is the *ubi sunt*, an elegy for the time before the black panther had come upon him. "All time much snow," he once tells Harold, early in the story. "Have much brother one time. All go now. Have much friend. They go now. My woman go, my boy, my girl. All go now. Much old" (p. 133).

chapter six

Growing Up with the Country

It is at least logically possible to distinguish two distinct methods for fictional treatment of Western themes. The first of these, most successfully pioneered by James Fenimore Cooper, is one which we have been analyzing thus far in our study: in it the author focuses his attention primarily upon a frontiersman and upon his reaction to the wild, uncivilized environment of the Great West. Such a novel chronicles man's impact upon the frontier, paying relatively little heed to the civilization which must follow upon the frontiersman's heels. The second method, which we will briefly examine in this chapter, is the converse of this: in it the author focuses his attention primarily upon a given area of land, which he then watches develop from the pioneer state through the various stages of civilization which follow.

It is of course impossible to separate novels about the West into these two categories in such a way as to avoid overlapping. Even in Cooper's chronicles of the frontier civilization is always present, if only by implication, and the same is true of most other novelists who write about the impact of the white frontiersman upon a wild environment; for the very existence of a frontier implies a more social, settled, "civilized" society which stands in some kind of symbolic opposition to it. Nevertheless, a viable distinction can be made between those works which, in the presentation of the conflict between civilization and the frontier center primarily upon the frontier, and those which center primarily upon the society which will succeed the frontier. In the first group the values of civilization, though ever present in the story, are usually handled by implication; in the latter, quite the reverse is true, the frontier virtues being handled more indirectly. The first group tends to identify itself, at least from the standpoint of fictional point of view, with the values of the frontier, often as seen through the eyes of a particular frontiersman; the second, conversely, adopts the values of some social order which follows the primitive frontier state.

Of the novels which take as their point of departure some social order succeeding the frontier state, the first important category consists of what someone has called "granger novels"; that is, novels which concern themselves primarily with agrarian America. Though these novels differ in particular detail, taken together they provide a broad social picture of remarkably consistent American attitudes toward the rural life. We notice immediately one great similarity which the granger novels have to the novels of the frontier—both groups are dissatisfied with the course of history. However much the granger novelist rhetorically likes to pay lip service to the glories of the agrarian utopia and to himself and his heroes as nature's noblemen, granger literature in general turns into a casebook against the agrarian utopia and the society of noblemen in which the novelist finds himself.

One of the first (and best) granger novels, Edgar Watson Howe's *The Story of a Country Town* (1883), sets the tone for much later granger fiction. In this story, the idealism which motivates the agrarian hero is seen to be an inadequate method for coping with the hard facts of life of the rural environment. Howe's narrator begins his story of his country town with the sardonic statement of an often positively presented platitude: "Ours was the prairie district, out West, where we had gone to grow up with the country." The rest of the novel rings changes on this initial sarcasm, for the actual process of "growing up with the country" has little in common with the high hopes of this optimistic idea. Throughout the novel the facts of country life militate against the ideal of agrarian progress. The harshness of the external environment not only makes happiness impossible in the country town, but brings out the worst qualities of character in its inhabitants. Jo Erring's unfounded jealousy and the Reverend John Westlock's uncontrollable sexual desire, which causes him to desert his wife for another woman, stand in ironic juxtaposition to the implicit optimism of the ideal of growing up with the country.

Equally important with the novel's polemical purpose is Howe's method of handling his ironic examination of the agrarian ideal.

Howe presents his story by giving, first of all, a statement of the ideal of the agrarian utopia. The rest of the novel holds this ideal up to the actual facts of rural life, and as the novel progresses the ideal is shown to be at variance with these facts and hence unreal and unattainable. This method of exposing the cruel ironies of the agrarian ideal through presenting a picture of how it does not conform to the facts of rural American life becomes a commonplace in later granger fiction, most of which details the inevitable frustration of individuals who have tried to apply the agrarian ideal to the harsh facts of rural life, or whose gullible optimistic belief in progress is seen to be hopelessly at odds with the actual world around them.

The particular "case" against the rural life made by most granger novelists is that the agrarian utopia is somehow privative. The deprivations of loneliness and hard work which bring out the evil sides of Jo Erring's and the Reverend John Westlock's respective characters are echoed again and again in granger literature. Though the particular grievances may vary—hard work, loneliness, primitive living conditions, lack of cultural opportunities, poverty are only a few of the many obstacles to happiness in the rural utopia—all render life there a life of privation.

Brief mention here of the work of Herbert Quick, a once highly touted regional novelist, may make the point more specific. In his best work, *Vandemark's Folly* (1922), Quick tells the story of the early history of "Vandemark Township, Monterey County, State of Iowa" (p. [i]), of which his hero-narrator, Jacobus Teunis Vandemark, was the first settler. In this novel Quick presents a fairly conventional "official" history of the process of pioneering. Vandemark, whose land claim in what is later Vandemark Township turns out to lie almost entirely in a marsh called "Hell Slew" or alternatively "Vandemark's Folly," manages by patience and hard work to turn this unprofitable claim into a rich farm. The ingredients of hard work and patience, Quick explicitly tells us, bring the almost certain result of eventual comfort and wealth.

In his next novel, *The Hawkeye* (1923), however, Quick drastically modifies this position. *The Hawkeye* is the story of one Fremont McConkey, the son of a family of poor farmers, who grows up with the country to become first a politician and then a successful small-town journalist. From the standpoint of that material success which Quick had unhesitatingly affirmed in *Vandemark's Folly,* McConkey is a reasonably successful man, but his good fortune, unlike Vandemark's, has a marked ironic quality. First of all, the virtues of hard work and patience are no longer seen as guarantees of success. The elder McConkeys, try as they will, never manage like Vandemark to make much of a living out of farming, and Fremont himself succeeds in getting ahead only by abandoning the farm for local politics. Quick is specific in his view that the choice of politics over farming, however much more sense it makes economically, represents a significant moral decline on the part of his hero, and Fremont's own eventual disgust with the corruption of politics drives him out of public life. In *The Hawkeye,* then, is an ironic dimension which is absent from *Vandemark's Folly,* the position that worldly success and moral virtue are opposed. When McConkey abandons politics for journalism he regains his moral respectability, but even his "success" as a journalist is a qualified one, for he had not wanted to be a journalist but an author. Just as in Vandemark County idealism inevitably turns into political corruption, so does the intellectual life degenerate into hack journalism. Occasional citizens such as Vandemark may manage to make a killing, and for them, says McConkey, "Iowa has been a wonderful place." But for "her dreamers, her poets, her children with the divine fire in their souls" (p. 476), Iowa has been by no means a wonderful place. Such people have found Iowa a place of deprivation, and the compromises which the rural environment has forced them to make with their ideals have rendered their lives tragically ironic.

Probably the most interesting granger novelist is Hamlin Garland, the bitterness of whose work recalls the pessimism of Howe's view of the rural utopia rather than the often bland critique of Herbert Quick. Garland's appraisal is overwhelmingly negative, though the bases for his negativism are not completely consistent. As many critics have pointed out, Garland's social philosophy consists more of a series of reactions to particular evils than of a carefully reasoned and self-consistent body of philosophical beliefs. The inconsistency in his views may clearly be seen by comparing two of his admittedly best short stories, "Under the Lion's Paw" and "Up the Coulé," both of which appeared in *Main-Travelled Roads* (1891). In the first of these stories Garland's view of the rural utopia is at least implicitly optimistic. Evil in this tale does not inhere within the rural utopia itself but in the unjust economic system which has been foisted upon it from without. The story, as a recent critic mentions, "is a dramatized sermon on Henry George's single tax and the evils of unearned increment,"[1] and implicit in it is the notion that reformation of the unjust economic system under which the farmer suffers will render the rural life in fact a utopia. The concluding image of the story makes the point perfectly clear. Butler, the rascally landowner, confronts the farmer Haskins in the midst of his plenty and informs him that the price of the land Haskins had wanted to buy from him has gone up because of the improvements Haskins himself has made on it. Ironically, the hard work which Haskins has put into the farm will go only to enrich Butler. But Garland voices no doubt that the improved farm itself is desirable; the only evil is the injustice of the law which can make one man's toil profit someone else. Our final view of Haskins finds him sitting dejectedly amidst his ample harvest, surrounded by material plenty; if it were—as it should be—his own rather than another's, what more could a man ask?

The bitter answer to this implicit rhetorical question is found in "Up the Coulé," where the values of the rural world are seen as quite different indeed. In this story misfortune is not applied onto the agrarian society by a simplistically conceived economic system (though the injustice of the farmer's economic plight is presented as one of the evils under which he must suffer), but is seen to inhere unavoidably in the very nature of rural life. Moreover, the "good life" which is supposed to inhere in the agrarian utopia is presented in the story as nothing more than a projection onto the rural community of the non-farmer's romantic ideas. Such ideas, Garland none too subtly implies, are completely at variance with the facts.

The story of "Up the Coulé" develops through a series of ironic scenes in which the idyllic perceptions into the nature of country life of Howard, the man who has gone to the city and made at least a material success of himself, are shown to be absolutely false. The first scene establishes the continuing pattern in the story of the ironic contrast between Howard's romantic views of the rural life and the way this life actually is. Howard is first discovered on the train, riding toward his old home. From a distance, significantly, the countryside looks beautiful, and Howard indulges himself in romantic ruminations about the charms of the western landscape. When, however, he dismounts from the train and sees the western landscape close to, his perspective changes. The town at which he disembarks, with its "unpaved street" and "drab-colored, miserable, rotting wooden buildings," seems "poor and dull and sleepy and squalid" (p. 77). The same variance between the distant view and the close-up is again remarked when Howard arrives at the family farm, with its ramshackle barn and muddy yard. This contrast between Howard's romantic expectations and the actual facts is repeated over and over in various other scenes in the story, and finally reaches its culmination when Howard realizes the falsity of his own romantic view of the charms of the rural life. As he watches the hired man "racing around the filthy yard after one of the young heifers that had kicked over the pail in her agony with the flies and was unwilling to stand still and be eaten alive," he finally comes to understand that "the poet who writes of milking the cows does it from the hammock, looking on" (p. 115).

Clearly the hardship of such an existence cannot miraculously be eradicated by the Single Tax, for it inheres in the very nature of the rural life. However much the economic ills which distress the farmer can be alleviated, his lot will still of necessity be hard and his life one of deprivation. Garland's clearest statement of what this deprivation consists may be found in his Populist novel *A Spoil of Office* (1897). This book tells the story of Bradley Talcott, a western farmer who becomes active in the Grange, the Farmers' Alliance, and finally the People's party. His enthusiasm for agrarian crusades is strengthened by his affection for Ida Wilbur, a young woman with whom he falls in love after hearing her speak at a Grange picnic. While Bradley's idea of the hardship of the farmer's lot is implicitly economic and political, Ida's is social. In her speech to the Grange she makes perfectly clear what she considers the real drawbacks to life in the rural utopia. Though she admits that "the farmer is a free citizen of a great republic," still "he is a *Solitary* free citizen. He lives alone too much. He meets his fellow-men too little. His dull life, his hard work, make it almost impossible to keep his better nature uppermost." Her remedy for this situation is perfectly clear as well. She prophesies "a time when the farmer will not need to live in a cabin on a lonely farm," a time when farmers will come together in groups, when they will have "time to read, and time to visit with their fellows." When this time comes "the farmer will no longer be a drudge and his wife a bond slave" (pp. 13-15).

Added to this explicit statement of the drawbacks of the solitary life (which Ida Wilbur, in common with E. W. Howe, sees as bringing out the worst aspects of the farmer's character) are a constant series of scenes in which the myth of the rural utopia, inhabited by a happy yeomanry, is held up as not only at variance with the facts, but as being an outsider's myth to which no farmer himself would subscribe. The most effective of these is the scene which concludes *A Spoil of Office* and which closely resembles similar scenes in "Up the Coulé" where Grant's idealization of the rural utopia was similarly shown to be in complete opposition to the actual facts of agrarian life. In this scene Bradley and Ida attend a romantic play in a Washington theater. The scene is set in an idealized Sherwood Forest, "and there, in the land of Robin Hood, where snow never falls, where rains never slant through the shuddering leaves, the jocund foresters met to sing and drink October ale. . . . Fadeless and untarnished was each magnificent cloak and doublet, . . . straight and fair and supple was every back and limb. No marks of toil anywhere, no lines of care, no hopeless hunger, no threatening task; nothing to do but to sing and dance and drink after the hunt among the delightfully dry and commodious forest wilds—a glorious, free life!" Even as they watch this bland pageant, however, Ida reflects that it has little to do with reality. "That world of carefree, changeless youth, that world of love and comradeship, threw into painful relief the actual world from which she came. It brought up with terrible force the low cottage in the moaning pine forest of Wisconsin, or the equally lonely cabin on the Kansas plain" (pp. 371-72).

Garland's critique of the way the myth of agrarian happiness is at odds with the facts of rural life combines, in this scene, two distinct ideas. The first is that the rural life is one of hard work rather than of carefree play; the second, that it is lonely. The life of loneliness and toil is explicitly contrasted with the life of comradeship and play so as to make very clear Garland's idea that solitude is the greatest of the many deprivations of rural life.

This perception is at the heart of Garland's best extended treatment of the theme of "pioneering," *The Moccasin Ranch* (1909),[2] a story which relates the decay of high hopes based upon a false view of the actual facts of rural life. This story of a disastrous experiment in growing up with the country is presented in terms of a related twofold penetration through the rhetoric of the rural mystique to the actual facts of rural life. The first of these ironic perceptions entails a true discovery of the basic hostility of nature to man, however friendly it may at first appear. The novelette's action takes place over the course of a long half-year, beginning in March and concluding in December. In the spring nature conceals the harsh Dakota landscape from the eyes of the pioneers, but as the summer wears on, this landscape grows progressively more forbidding and more ominous. By June the idyllic quality of the landscape is gone; by August drought threatens; by November the plains are sere and the first year's harvest has been a disaster; and the novelette ends in the depths of winter, against the background of a bitter Dakota blizzard.

Combined with the theme of nature's hostility to man is the theme of loneliness. That happiness in the *solitude à deux* which Willard Burke and his wife Blanche had looked forward to on their claim proves as delusory as the apparent beneficence of nature itself. Just as the idyllic quality of spring inevitably turns into the droughts of summer and the storms of winter, so does the romantic idyll of life on their claim turn into a nightmare of solitude and monotony. When Blanche's few friends move back East in order to escape the horrors of a Dakota winter, the themes of the hostility of nature and the loneliness of the pioneer life are symbolically combined. Blanche cannot face life alone in the winter, and she leaves her husband for another man who, at the end of the story, takes her back East where she will have society, and where the symbolic "nature" which surrounds her will be more beneficent.

In *The Moccasin Ranch* the hostility of the external world combines with man's longing for society to militate against the possibility of happiness. Unreal ideals based upon a delusory view of life must give way before the actual facts, which in themselves render happiness impossible. Garland has taken exception here to the cherished—and too often unexamined—ideal of the "new start" which causes man to wish to go West and grow up with the country. It is possible, he suggests, to grow up with the country, but only at the cost of sacrificing the unreal ideals which first drove one to undertake the experiment. A "new start" and "the good life" are contradictions in terms. One can be attained only at the expense of the other.

This bitterly ironic view that the hope for a better life in the West is in its nature self-contradictory is by no means limited, among granger novelists, to Garland. Vardis Fisher's *Toilers of the Hills* (1928) furnishes an interesting though by no means unique analogue. In plot very similar to *The Moccasin Ranch*, this novel tells of the frustration and disillusion of Dock Hunter and his wife Opal, who attempt to dry-farm the high lands of Idaho. Dock is almost a caricature of the believer in the agrarian myth. Merely because he wants to make a success of dry-farming he is thoroughly convinced that nothing can stand in his way. As a result, the novel chronicles in a sardonically comic fashion his ineptitude in the face of fact. He is undaunted, for instance, by the unsettling discovery that his claim is completely covered with sagebrush. "Watch me take them brush out liken they was only pigweed," he says confidently to Opal before he sets out to begin his plowing. Two hours later he has made no headway except for breaking his doubletree, and Opal finds him trying to untangle his plow from a clump of brush, his optimism somewhat chastened. "Mother of Christ!" he says: "Who in the jumped-up Jesus could plow such land as that-air land is!" (pp. 23-24).

A little later Dock decides to construct a cistern in order to trap rainwater. He builds it badly and it becomes only a trap for drowned animals whose carcasses pollute the water so that it cannot be used. The only thing he will not give up is his belief in the propaganda of the agrarian myth; no amount of fact is sufficient to convince him that he cannot grow wheat in the unsuitable environment of the Idaho hills. He is perennially almost on the threshold of discovery of the secret, only to be inevitably frustrated.

Fisher's analysis of the necessary defeat of optimism in the face of fact does not only stop at this grimly comic appraisal. Dock may be a buffoon, but from Opal's point of view the joke loses some of its humor. For Dock is also boorish, cruel, and superstitious—all qualities which, Fisher suggests, serve to tie him to his futile task of trying to grow wheat where it can never grow. His invincible ignorance before the facts of life keeps him from seeing the truth, for he views reality through a haze of misinformation and superstition. Just as he believes that wheat must be planted at the time of the full moon or it will not grow, so does he believe the story one of his neighbors tells him about a man who shot the moon full of holes with a high-powered rifle. After all, his neighbor says, "I set right there and seen him do it" (p. 76). Who could doubt such unimpeachable testimony?

More frightening, however, is the fact that Dock's inability to understand the world about him leads him to react violently against it. Though a coward, he is subject to bullying rages in which he harms those too weak to fight back. Among other peccadilloes, he shoots a cow which crashes through his fence, and kills a puppy he had given to Opal to punish him for eating the family supper. In some way both these actions are supposed to affirm an abstract ideal of discipline and justice, but as is the case with Dock's futile attempts to farm, which should somehow "prove" the agrarian ideals to which he subscribes, the relationship between his particular actions and the ideal they are meant to uphold is difficult to discern. Nor is his brutality confined to animals. At one point in the novel, in order to teach his son a lesson, he hangs him from a tree, from which Opal barely manages to cut the boy down alive.

The harshness of the agrarian life which brings out the worst in Dock's character is seen as at least partially due to the loneliness under which the toilers must suffer. After Dock kills Opal's puppy, her solitude becomes so unbearable that in desperation she traps a toad from their dry well, and keeps it for a pet. For years Opal knows only the names of her neighbors, most of whom she has never met. Nor is the loneliness of the toiler's life limited to Dock and Opal; the solitude and hardship make all the toilers eccentric, and as the years go by the various solitary farmers grow more rather than less strange.

Fisher's view of the causes of sorrow in the agrarian utopia, like Garland's, is twofold. First is the fact that the external world is hostile to man, and in order to live at all on the frontier man must make heroic sacrifices and compromises with any ideas of luxury, or even of comfort, which he may have previously had. The second is that solitude which the pioneer must inevitably suffer, and which erodes his character from within as the hostility of nature erodes it from without. The pioneers' inevitable defeat is made more poignant because of the little they ask of the nature which breaks them; but the world of the granger novel allows little scope for wishes, however modest.

The idea—almost an axiom in granger fiction—that solitude and deprivation are interrelated concepts is antithetical to the contrary notion in conventional Western fiction that the solitary life is beneficial to man. This latter notion, to recall for a moment our previous discussion of the Western hero, is in origin a romantic one which exalts the life of the individual in a state of nature at the expense of that of the deprived denizen of cities, untouched by nature's gentle and beneficent hand. In the traditional Western novel nature must almost by definition be presented as less inimical to man than it is in granger writing. Again it should be mentioned, however, that the assumption of a beneficent nature which fills much conventional Western writing was long recognized in America at least to be a literary convention having little to do with the actual facts of frontier life. The hostile and inimical nature which fills the granger novel, then, is not only a late-nineteenth-century naturalistic convention. Timothy Flint, to take only one of many possible earlier examples, in his two histories of the Mississippi Valley (published respectively in 1828 and 1832), is firm in his opinion that the nascent Mississippi Valley grows in desirability as it leaves a state of nature behind and approaches a state of civilization. Flint even anticipates the later notion that solitude is itself one of the greatest horrors of life on the frontier. In his biography of Daniel Boone, Flint is explicit in his opinion that months spent entirely alone would suit only people of a very particular psychic make-up; and in his novel *The Life and Adventures of Arthur Clenning* (1828) he takes specific exception to the romantic notion that life on a desert island would be one of unalloyed pleasure.

Flint's attitude that life in society is superior to life in a state of nature is part of a tradition a good bit more venerable than the contrary romantic belief, and is itself often incorporated, if only by implication, in traditional Western fiction. The reader will recall the Western novels mentioned earlier which contrast masculine with feminine opinions of frontier life. Almost without exception such novels identify feminine perceptions with society, and at least from the point of view of the feminine characters in such novels social life is without question superior to life in the wild frontier state. In both the granger novel and the traditional Western, then, the question of whether life is "better" in society or on the frontier is often presented as a question to which there is no simple answer, precisely because "society" on the one hand and "nature" on the other are concepts which appeal to two opposed ideals, both of which a given individual often affirms at once. In the granger novel the ideal of going west to grow up with the country is rarely disparaged; misfortune in the granger novel comes rather from the fact that this ideal cannot be translated into practice on the frontier. Hence the granger novel develops through an ironic polarization of "ideals" and "facts." A man can return east and have the "facts" of material comfort and social companionship (as did Howard in Garland's "Up the Coulé") only by sacrificing the cherished ideal of going west to grow up with the country; or, contrariwise, he can follow his "ideals" and go west. In no symbolic location, however, can he have both the "ideal" of growing up with the country and the "facts" which such optimistic idealism implies.

The granger novel, then, is not quite so different from the conventional Western as at first appears. Both tend to be parables which develop in terms of symbolic places, broadly speaking the "East" and the "West," each of which is in some respects desirable, yet also in a profound sense unsatisfying and incomplete. The inability to combine the virtues of both places is at the root of the symbolic conflict of granger and Western novel alike. In both groups of novels the conflict is seen as arising out of a deeper perception of the nature of that choice faced by the characters in the story, who begin by assuming that the virtues of both "East" and "West" can be found in one symbolic place, but end with the discovery that they cannot.

The traditional Western novel and the granger novel are similar in another related way, for in both of them happiness is generally supposed to adhere in some kind of external (or at least externalized) good life. Consequently, in both, misfortune is due to the real world's not conforming to some kind of impossible ideal. The Western hero is almost always presented as being trapped in a battle to preserve his primitive way of life against the onrushing forces of civilization. The ideal of the good life which he cherishes cannot hold out against the inexorable progress of civilization. Like Boone Caudill in *The Big Sky*, the typical Western hero affirms an ideal of permanence which is impossible in a world of change. The hero of the typical granger novel pursues an equally unreal ideal of the good life which he as well cannot hope to find in the real world; for the facts of life which his ideal implies are in fact simply unattainable in the real world in which he finds himself.

Both the typical granger novel and the typical Western novel, then, tend to be pessimistic in tone, for they focus upon the self-contradictions inherent in the lives of those who on the one hand go west to grow up with the country or on the other go west to escape the process. Both the granger hero and the Western hero find their ideals of the good life unattainable in fact. It is possible, however, for one to take an optimistic view toward the course of settlement if he is committed to the historic *process* itself rather than to some particular stage of it. If one identifies himself with the process of history, the end result of which is assumed to be beneficent, misfortune and evil may well be understood as parts of a general design which works for good.

Such an attitude, though by no means as common as the typical one of pessimism which informs most literature of the West, is not difficult to discover. Among granger novelists, the best example of such optimism may be found in the work of Willa Cather. Unlike that of most granger fiction, Cather's world is one of hope based on an optimistic faith in the future. Her optimism, it should be mentioned, does not depend upon the fact that she is unable to see misfortune; indeed, her fictional world is always one of particular tragedy. In *O Pioneers!* (1913) the bitterness in the Linstrum family, the disastrous love affair between Emil Bergson and Marie Shabata which leads to both of their deaths, and the death of Emil's friend Amedee from appendicitis, and in *My Antonia* (1918) the suicide of Mr. Shimerda and Antonia's own unfortunate love affair could add up to a tremendous indictment of frontier life, but in fact they do not. The reason, of course, is that Cather's faith in the ultimate triumph of a benevolent historic process enables her to explain away the particular evils of present society. Of the heroine of *O Pioneers!*, Alexandra Bergson, she says approvingly: "A pioneer should have imagination, should be able to enjoy the idea of things more than the things themselves"' (p. 42), and this statement might well serve as a summary in brief of her own attitude toward pioneering. Very often in Willa Cather's novels of the West misfortune is expressed as inhering in an attitude of mind rather than in the external world. Though it is true that fortune strikes adversely in many cases—the unforeseeable death of Amedee in *O Pioneers!* is a clear example—in the overwhelming majority of cases misfortune is avoidable, or at least its results may be mitigated by understanding it properly. Even in the case of Amedee the implication is strong that his death was caused by his own foolishness in not calling the doctor immediately when he became ill.

This characteristic attitude of Willa Cather's may best be seen by comparing briefly the respective bad and good fortunes of Mr. Shimerda and Antonia in *My Antonia*. Mr. Shimerda, it is clear, commits suicide because his enjoyment of "the idea of things" is not strong enough to overcome his depression at the way "the things themselves" actually are. Put in another way, he does not have a sufficiently strong vision of the future to enable him to endure the deprivations of the present. In almost complete contrast stands Antonia, whose faith in the future is strong enough to enable her to overcome much greater particular misfortune than Mr. Shimerda is ever called upon to face. Where Mr. Shimerda's characteristic utterance in the novel is a lament for the good old days in Bohemia, Antonia is always talking of the good days to come. Cather's point is that both these attitudes tend to be self-proving. If one believes with Mr. Shimerda that all the good in life lies irrevocably lost in the past, the misfortunes of the present become overwhelming. If, on the other side, one believes with Antonia that good will inevitably come in the future, one can put up with whatever bad fortune one is asked to bear in the present.

Willa Cather's clearest statement of the qualities necessary to the successful pioneer may be found in *Death Comes for the Archbishop* (1926). Though not in subject matter a granger novel—the archbishop hero bears in fact a much closer resemblance to the typical Western hero than he does to the typical agrarian hero of the granger novel—the novel is nonetheless a story of pioneering and a novel in which the pioneer hero very clearly grows up with the country.[3] For the Archbishop identifies himself with the future, and hence is not prey to the tragic vision of the characteristic Western hero, lamenting the loss of some vanished or vanishing way of life. The same identification makes him accept present deprivation (unlike the typical granger heroes) in hopes of future good. Like Alexandra Bergson he has "imagination," shown in the novel through his progressively realized vision of the archdiocese of the future, and he enjoys "the idea of things more than the things themselves." Indeed, he and Father Vaillant are distinguished in the novel through their "vision," that is, their trust in the inevitable beneficent working out of the historic process. They are sustained in the present by their hopes for the future, and as old men their happiness comes from their contemplation of the partial realization of these hopes, and the sure faith that their final realization must inevitably come to pass. "We have done the things we used to plan to do, long ago," Father Vaillant tells the Archbishop near the end of the novel: "To fulfil the dreams of one's youth; that is the best that can happen to a man" (p. 303).

The two priests' personal identification with the future is emphasized in the novel by their devotion to making things. They are indefatigable gardeners and inveterate planters of trees; they are also tireless workers in the Garden of the Lord, establishing missions, founding schools and, symbolic of the whole, projecting a magnificent cathedral for Santa Fe, far too grand for the present needs of a frontier diocese, but admirably designed for the future.

In *Death Comes for the Archbishop* Willa Cather has also manipulated the traditional *ubi sunt* of the Western hero in a way to militate against the aura of tragedy which surrounds so many Westerns. Though any novel which deals, as this novel does, with the aging and eventual death of a sympathetic hero must of necessity have a certain melancholy aspect, yet it need not be tragic nor even particularly pathetic. For though the Archbishop must himself inevitably die, his principles are ultimately affirmed, and the reader identifies with the general eventual triumph of these principles rather than with the particular loss of the Archbishop. The situation is quite different in the typical Western novel built on the pattern of the Leatherstocking Tales, where the mood is much more tragic, for in such novels not only does the sympathetic hero die, but his death symbolizes as well the death of his beliefs.

Though an overwhelming majority of serious novels follow the pattern of the Leatherstocking Tales and from the perspective of the frontier criticize the advent of civilization, not all do so. Some, though they may well take their perspective from the frontier point of view, do not necessarily identify with frontier virtues as opposed to civilized vices.

The work of George Pattullo, another one-time cowboy turned author, is a case in point. Though many of his stories concern themselves primarily with the impact of civilization upon the frontier, they do not by any means unqualifiedly endorse the point of view of the frontiersman in opposition to the settlers who come after him. The figure of Hi Garrett, the West Texas pioneer cattleman who appears in a number of Pattullo's stories, is a good example. When we first see Garrett, in a story called "Pioneer," he is at the pinnacle of his worldly success, the owner of a huge and prosperous ranch. Placed in opposition to him is Ben Strusky, a Jewish immigrant pedlar who has come west to make his fortune. Though a rascally nester steals all his goods and his two pack burros, and though Strusky must walk thirty miles to the nearest town with only a canteen of water, still "he was there and going to stay" (p. 36). In a later story, "Survival," Hi Garrett, who does not understand the new world of encroaching nesters and financial speculations, loses his money and his ranch and, at the end of the story, must go to work for Strusky, now a prosperous merchant.

Though the story of the relationship between Garrett and Strusky is by no means particularly unusual, Pattullo's attitude toward his material is. For neither the cattle baron nor the itinerant pedlar is held up as some kind of moral paragon on whom the effect of the outside world is disastrous. Pattullo's implicit social philosophy is that the pioneer life consists of a series of reactions to challenges, and that success paradoxically brings with it the inability to react successfully. Hence the future in Pattullo's fiction lies with the immigrants such as Ben Strusky, and by extension with the other "have nots," who want something badly enough to work hard for it. Success—for Pattullo always an unquestioned virtue—then is a matter of reaction to the stimulus of want; when the stimulus disappears, so does the capacity for success.

The real villains of Pattullo's social philosophy are those of all classes who do not try to seize opportunity. On the evidence of his fiction, the presumption is that though such people are statistically more likely to be found among the idle rich, they are by no means limited to any social stratum. In "Unspanked Third" Pattullo sourly examines the degenerate children and grandchildren of Jake Raines, a pioneer banker and stockman. In juxtaposition to his own pampered and effete offspring stands the hustling newsboy of the story who has saved up "forty dollars and eighty cents" and represents the wave of the future. In "The More Abundant Life," however, the villain is the expected conventional one of Western fiction, the nester. Again the story contrasts the old Jake Raines with a man whom he hires, though he does not really need him, to do odd jobs. The nester, down-and-out and needing money, has appealed to old Jake to give him any kind of job, but when he is put to work digging a backhouse he considers the work degrading and strikes for higher wages.

It is evident that this social philosophy is implicitly progressive, for it depends upon the notion that positive values tend to be represented constantly by those at the bottom of the social ladder who are struggling to better themselves. Though for Pattullo this does not imply the view present in proletarian fiction that those at the top are necessarily morally corrupt, yet the inference is very strong that they are less able to cope with the demands which life makes upon them than are those at the bottom. That this notion is overly simplistic goes without saying; Pattullo has neither real understanding of or sympathy for the idea that any force is stronger than a sufficiently resolute individual. Yet however inadequate Pattullo's ideas may be as social philosophy, as literary attitudes they are often quite effective. His best short story, "Off the Trail," a jaundiced view of the perennial no-good, may be used as example.

"Off the Trail" is scarcely more than a vignette, but it is one of the most arresting pictures of the ne'er-do-well in Western fiction. It tells of one Ed Banty, a nester who appears at a ranch looking for a job. There is no work to be had, but the ranchers grubstake him to some food, and he sets off again with a sick wife, a wretched wagon, and a horse with the blind staggers, hoping to cross the desert to California. The ranchhands give them explicit directions to avoid losing their way, coupled with dire warnings of the dangers of getting off the trail in the midst of the desert, but the Bantys, either through carelessness or an ill-advised notion to try a short cut, leave the trail, and die.

The Bantys are representatives of a kind of shiftless pioneer whom Willa Cather might well recognize, those who are unable to make a living at farming and use their dreams of success as an excuse to keep from the necessity of facing facts. Just as the unsuccessful farmers in Cather's fiction blame "hard times" for their own inabilities and want to leave for some place where the land is better or the climate more suitable, so do the Bantys. But ironically "on their heels comes the plodding farmer, who goes patiently to work to wrest a living out of the claims they have abandoned, and wakes, some morning, to find that civilization is knocking at his door and he is rich" (518).

Even Eugene Manlove Rhodes on occasion writes stories in

which the course of history is interpreted in positive terms. Although, as was suggested above, Rhodes habitually imputes virtue and happiness to an older society which is gradually being replaced, he now and again affirms the course of history itself rather than any particular stage within it. Such a story is "No Mean City" (1919), in plot a melodramatic spy thriller about a World War I German attempt to blow up the strategic Engle Dam, near Engle, New Mexico. The story's interest, however, does not inhere in the plot, which is predictable and common-place; inevitably the German saboteurs are frustrated and the good men and true of Engle come out victorious. The interest in the story lies rather in Rhodes's brilliant development of the theme of the community, presented through the little town of Engle and its townsmen, which he develops so that it comes to stand as a metaphor for America. The men who frustrate the saboteurs are an old settler, Teagardner, the last survivor of the original band which had surveyed the site of Engle for the Santa Fe Railroad, and a younger one, Cady, the first boy born in Engle. The plot of the story takes Teagardner and Cady on a series of nostalgic pilgrimages into the community's past. Tea-gardner, starting from the town of Engle, goes first to the mine where he had prospected when he was young; then to another mine, now almost forgotten, where he and his best friend, now dead, had worked together many years before; and finally, in the best scene in the story, he and Cady together row a boat over the old Gonzales ranch, which they can see beneath them under one hundred feet of water, and where both had worked before the dam was built.

This nostalgic pilgrimage does not add up, however—as it does in *Pasó por Aquí*—to a lament for the old times. The historical process in "No Mean City" is seen not as a disaster but as an explanation of the loyal affection which the inhabitants of Engle feel for even such an unpromising place as this desolate New Mexican town. It is, as the title says, "no mean city," and it stands at once for the particular love of man for a place where he has roots and for the general love of Americans for their country. The love of man for his home is not limited in the story to one group of people—be they cattlemen, nesters, pioneers, or whoever—who allegedly have more understanding of and hence affection for their home than others. Rather this love is presented as a universal fact of history; the implication is clear that as long as Engle exists someone will love it enough to fight for it, and even if it is abandoned to progress as was the old Gonzales ranch, there will still be those who remember it.

In "No Mean City" Rhodes affirms a deeply held ideal which he often presents in a more peripheral way, the idea of "community."[4] As Rhodes usually defines the idea of community, it refers to a particular social group, isolated in time, who band together against hostile outsiders. The league of sympathy between Pat Garrett and McEwen against the "new peoples" in *Pasó por Aquí* comes to mind, as does the union of cattlemen against intruders in many of his other stories. Occasionally, however, as in "No Mean City," Rhodes perceives that a community may be defined in terms of continuity through time as well as in terms of identity of present interests. In such cases, the bond of communal relations must be that of similar perceptions into the significance of history. Those to whom Engle is dear are not limited to one time or to one social group, for to them the community is a symbol not of a particular time but of hope in the historic process.

On occasion the focus of stories dealing with the historic process is upon the conversion of some character from belief in the past to acceptance of the future. George Pattullo's Jake Raines is an example of such treatment. In "Unspanked Third" he changes from a belief that, because the third generation of his own family is effete and degenerate the country at large must be, to an affirmation of other characters such as the newsboy who will inevitably take the place of the older pioneers. The resolution of the story condemns those who worry about the fate of the country on the basis of the apparent degeneracy of their own families. "The country ain't going to the dogs because our own stock peters out," he says. "There's others just as good who'll come up to take our places and do the work" (p. 263).

A more expanded treatment of this theme is found in Arthur Miller's published screenplay of *The Misfits* (1961). This story tells of a cowboy, Gay, who stands in solitary defiance of the modern world. He insists upon keeping his independence, especially against the demands of conformity and regularity which the modern world makes. He will not work, as he constantly repeats, for "wages." To him, the concept of "wages" stands for all the demands of the twentieth century, which he hopes to avoid. The story of *The Misfits* details the necessity of Gay's coming to terms with "wages" and with the demands of life in the present. The plot describes his last desperate attempt to avoid "wages," during which he, together with a neurotic pilot friend and a cowboy whom they have picked up at a rodeo, go into the mountains to hunt for mustangs. "Mustanging" is the last survival of the Old West in present-day Nevada, and becomes the symbol for Gay's ultimate refusal to work for "wages." The development of the mustanging plot proves highly ironic, however. Instead of the herds of hundreds of horses of former days, there are now only six runty mustangs left. Nor do the mustangers catch them in the heroic ways of old; rather than running them down on horseback the mustang hunters chase them with airplane and truck. Finally, the mustangs themselves are, as Gay says, "misfit horses" (p. 101), and no longer of any real importance. Where in the old times mustangs had been used for riding and agricultural work—"They couldn't have settled here without somebody caught mustangs for them" (p. 93), Gay observes—now they will simply be slaughtered and processed into dog food.

It is clear, then, that Gay is enmeshed in an ironic endeavor, the true pointlessness of which he does not at first see. He is dedicated to an ideal of conduct which in the modern world has become a complete anachronism. The point is emphasized primarily through the "mustanging" which, though the same in end result as it always was, must now be considered in light of a completely different set of social values. Mustangs are no longer important. The mustanger, consequently, once a heroic figure, is now reduced to the half pathetic, half comic role of a purveyor of dog food. The irony inherent in living according to a code which no longer has any relevance is reinforced by the other great scene in the screenplay, the rodeo at which Gay and Pilot pick up their third hand. Like "mustanging," the rodeo itself is an anachronism from the old times which no longer has any meaning. Once an essential expression of Western culture, it is now only a senseless and cruel blood-sport in which men and animals are injured to no real purpose.

The point of all this, of course, is that a code of action cannot be divorced from its historic and social context. Like so many other Western heroes, Gay assumes that he lives in a world which is essentially changeless, a world where there will always be cowboys and mustangs and rodeos and in which working for "wages" must always be degrading. He has identified his values with a past state, and the story of *The Misfits* unfolds his coming to terms with the present. In the screenplay this moment comes when the three men have actually caught the six mustangs. With them on the expedition Gay has brought a girl, who represents the point of view of modern society. She is disconcerted when she finds out that the captured horses will be used for dog food, just as earlier she had been appalled at the senseless brutality of the rodeo. Her perspective into the values of the past world which Gay has always unthinkingly affirmed affects his own perceptions into their real nature, and he comes to understand at the end of the story that times change, and that the values of the past no longer necessarily represent the same things to the present. Eventually he realizes that "wages" are the only possible choice, and that they are not to be condemned out of hand on the basis of an arbitrary application of an anachronistic system of values. He symbolically renounces his old life for the life of "wages" by turning the horses loose, and accepts in its stead the new world represented by the girl Roslyn. Gay's renunciation of the horses in favor of the girl is an effective descant on one of the most common clichés of Western film; in *The Misfits* it represents his final renunciation of old ways for the new life of "wages."

As this scene actually works out in *The Misfits* it appears somewhat meretricious. One gets the uneasy feeling that Miller is suggesting that if one finally "gets the girl" all turns out to be right with the world, and the irony of human endeavor somehow disappears. This is a fault in execution, however, perhaps unavoidable in a story in which horses and a woman are placed in this kind of symbolic contrast. In conception, Miller's story is intended to make quite another point, the necessity for man to come to terms with the fact of change.

The Westerns we have discussed so far in this chapter focus primarily upon the plight of some individual caught between the past and the future, or upon the attitudes of some person toward the historic process. One final group of Westerns ought to be briefly mentioned in conclusion, those which, like the typical granger novels, concern themselves directly with the "fact" of progress itself, rather than with the attitudes of a single person toward it. Like the granger novel, such a Western typically focuses upon a given area of land—a town, a territory, or whatever—and watches it change. An examination of two recent

Westerns, Oakley Hall's *Warlock* (1958) and Tom Lea's *The Wonderful Country* (1952) may serve to show how this theme develops in typical Western fiction.

Warlock tells the story of the development of the town of that name from a lawless frontier community into a respectable city. Its basic theme, in common with so many other Westerns, is the coming of law—an emblem of civilized values—to the Wild West. Hall's sympathies are clearly on the side of law, and his villains are those who, from whatever walk of life, wish to substitute some kind of extra-legal "justice" for the due process of legality. These villains range from the obvious "bad men" of the local cowboy gang, through the robber baron mine owners who are engaged in a labor struggle with the local miners, to the well-meaning solid citizenry who hire a gunman to clean up the town. Hall's point is that all of these groups, however much they may talk about "law" and "justice," really mean something quite different.

The cowboy gang which terrorizes Warlock at the beginning of the novel stands for the principle of blind loyalty to "kin" and to one's own class of people. The members of this gang all believe in mutual solidarity against every outsider. In any conflict whatever, they have no interest in discovering the rights or wrongs of the case. Whoever opposes the cowboys must, to their mind, by definition be in the wrong. Consequently they have neither sympathy for nor understanding of John Gannon, a one-time cowboy who becomes a deputy sheriff in Warlock. Gannon is allied to the cowboy faction both by class identification and personal loyalty—he had been a cowboy and had once worked for Abe McQuown, the leader of the gang—and by the ties of kinship as well, since his brother Billy is still one of McQuown's riders. Gannon's assertion of his independence of choice, represented by his decision to become a deputy sheriff, produces only contempt from the cowboy faction.

The cowboys' essential belief that whatever favors their cause is justice is echoed in the book by the miners of Warlock who believe much the same thing. Though they have a just grievance against the mining companies which have cut their wages, their real interest, it develops, is not in justice but in getting even with the mine owners. When they go out on strike there is considerable sentiment on the miners' part for burning some of the mines in order to force the owners to settle the dispute—on the miners' terms. Though no mines are actually burnt, the situation in Warlock grows so grave that the owners hire a force of vigilantes to keep the peace. These "regulators" are themselves a lawless crew, and interpret their job as a mandate to coerce, intimidate, and on occasion even kill whichever miners refuse to work on the mine owners' terms. Neither the striking miners nor the owners have any conception of abstract justice. The miners, like the cowboys, view anyone who is not on their "side" as an enemy, and assume that justice means the complete realization of all their wishes. The mine owners are just as self-interested as the strikers. They refuse to give in to the reasonable demand that they restore the cut in the miners' wages, and justify the presence of their terrorist regulators in Warlock as necessary to preserve order and to protect the rights of private property.

Caught in the middle of all this are the respectable citizens of the town, oppressed by various kinds of mob rule—lawless cowboys, rioting miners, and murdering regulators. They decide that they must have their own law, and hire a gunman to impose it upon the town. The respectable citizens, though well-meaning, are unaware of the irony of their solution to the problem, for like the other contending parties they do not want justice but rather a victory for their side. In consequence, the gunman they hire becomes not a representative of law but of their own wishes which, as Hall presents them, are just as self-interested, albeit perhaps not so crudely expressed, as the wishes of the other groups.

All the various factions in Warlock, then, hold one fundamental assumption in common, the notion that justice is equatable with their own interests. Some of the factions express this idea more blatantly or crudely than others, but all agree on its essential validity. No group, in sum, is really interested in justice at all, but only in its own success. To add to the irony, however, few of the characters in the novel are aware of the way in which their ideals and their motives are in conflict. Most sincerely believe themselves to be disinterested citizens upholding a moral principle.

As the novel develops, the four-way conflict between cowboys, miners, mine owners, and respectable citizens over what the law ought to do develops into a series of vendettas which lead only to a never-ending train of killings. The law which each group tries to impose upon the community of Warlock is unacceptable to the other groups, and hence each attempt at "law and order" inevitably results in further chaos.

The only person who manages to rise above this identification of justice with the triumph of one's own personal wishes is John Gannon, the cowboy-turned-deputy hero of the novel. As *Warlock* progresses he comes to the realization that the reason for the lawlessness in the town is not, as the others think, due to the wrong party's being in control, but to the fact that none of the contending factions really believes in justice. His affirmation of justice against the various selfish group interests which pass by the same name in Warlock succeeds in alienating him from all the various parties. Gradually, however, the realization dawns on the more thoughtful members of the community that there may be something to Gannon's point and, in the climax of the novel, community opinion turns from self-interest to disinterested justice. Blaisedell, the gunman whom the respectable citizens had hired to clean up Warlock has, in pursuit of his own idea of personal justice, burned down one of the town's saloons, and Gannon goes to arrest him. Blaisedell, much the superior gunfighter, gets the drop on Gannon, but when Gannon holds his fire Blaisedell does not shoot and, conscious that Gannon represents a new community awareness of the futility of the various kinds of vendettas which have passed by the name of justice, quietly leaves town. His departure represents a symbolic reversal of his own first action as town marshal, when he had posted McQuown's cowboy gang out of Warlock as undesirables dangerous to the peace of the community. This symbolic triumph of law is made clear in the final pages of *Warlock* where we discover that Gannon himself had later been murdered by his own most bitter personal enemy in McQuown's gang. His assassin had been legally tried for murder, convicted, and executed according to the forms of law. This scene too represents a symbolic reversal of an earlier one, for at the start of the novel no jury would convict a cowboy murderer.

In many respects *Warlock* is almost a compendium of commonplace Western conventions. It is filled with shootings and the other melodramatic trappings of the Western tradition; moreover, the novel's plot is the familiar one of the gunman who is hired to clean up a lawless town. What sets *Warlock* apart from the generality of melodramatic Westerns is the different value which Hall applies to the conventions of his story. In all the

contending factions there is not one of which we can wholeheartedly approve, nor is his gunman-marshal Blaisedell a particularly admirable character. The whole situation in Warlock,
as Hall presents it, is emblematic of the barbarity of the frontier
state; however colorful the history of the town may be, Hall
clearly implies, we must not sentimentalize it by giving it an
aura of romance which it did not possess. It was a picturesque
time, to be sure, but its passing gives us no real cause for regret.

The most serious esthetic failing in *Warlock* lies in Hall's
inability to endow either his villains or his heroes with much
complexity. The cowboys are a gang of ruffians of whom we
are convinced that Warlock will be well rid; the miners and mine
owners are similarly a rapacious lot; and the respectable citizenry
are smug, pompous, and unbelievably self-righteous and self-
deluded. This may well make a good rational point, but it unfortunately results in our not caring much about what actually
happens in the novel. As a result, *Warlock* becomes too much a
fictionalized presentation of a philosophical argument, and too
little a work of imagination. Our sympathies are never aroused,
and as a result the novel, though a fine rational *tour de force*,
leaves us strangely unmoved.

Such is not the case with Tom Lea's *The Wonderful Country*,
one of the very best of recent Westerns. This novel tells the story
of one Martin Brady, an American who had had to flee the
United States as a youth and had grown up in Mexico, where
he had become a hired gunman for the Castro brothers, two
Mexican landlord-politician-bandits. Brady's double allegiance,
implicit in his life as an American exile in Mexico, is emphasized
by his double name—in Texas he is known as Martin Brady, in
Mexico as Martín Bredi—and by the plot of the novel, which
sends him constantly back and forth across the Texas-Mexico
border. One of the basic symbolic patterns of the novel, then,
becomes Brady's search for a home on one side of the border or
the other. As he himself says upon his arrival in Texas near
the beginning of the book, "I wish I was plain one thing. I wish
in my mind I was not the stranger everywhere, like nothing
was my own" (p. 59).

Throughout the novel, then, Brady searches for one country in
which he will not be a stranger, coming to a gradual realization
that he cannot live on both sides of the border. As Lea defines
Texas and Mexico, each becomes symbolic of a different set of

values. Mexico, where Brady had spent his youth, is a symbol for the wild, free, irresponsible life of childhood. It becomes identified with youthfulness itself, and the life there becomes in turn an image of the values of youth. Ultimately Mexico stands as an emblem of all the inchoate and often self-contradictory longings of the human soul for a land of youth and beauty. Its symbol in *The Wonderful Country* is Brady's magnificent horse, a black stallion given him by Cipriano Castro and ironically named Lágrimas.

In contrast to Mexico stands Texas, plain and unromantic. Representative of the world as it is, Texas is explicitly contrasted with the romanticism and youthfulness of Mexico. Its symbol is Louisa Rucker, the girl with whom Brady falls in love.

The story of *The Wonderful Country* explores the impossibility of living on both sides of the border. Specifically it concerns the joint attempts of the Mexican and Texas governments to destroy a band of Apaches which raids indiscriminately in both countries. The ultimate annihilation of the Apaches demonstrates that it is impossible to live on both sides of the Rio Grande, a bittersweet fact of life which Brady learns to his own sorrow; for he had hoped somehow to escape this general rule and to have the best of both worlds, living in Texas with the benefits of visiting Mexico. This proves impossible, however, and at the end of the novel Brady discovers that he cannot have the best of both worlds, but must choose either one world or the other. When he casts his lot with Texas he is successively stripped of each of his Mexican privileges: first, he must leave his Mexican home, Valdepeñas; next he loses his job with the Castros; then he is ordered out of Mexico; and finally Lágrimas, the emblem of all he had dearly loved in the land of his youth, is killed.

Combined with the story of Brady's own necessary choice between Texas and Mexico is a subsidiary plot concerned with the coming of civilization to Texas. The advent of civilization is typified by the ever-approaching railroad, which at the end of the story finally reaches Puerto, the Texas border town which is the focus of the novel's action. The coming of the railroad to Puerto is symbolically combined with the destruction of the Apaches to signify the end of the old order. With the Apaches wiped out and the railroad in Puerto, Texas "will be a different country" (p. 384), a country in which there will no longer be any place for the cavalry and the Texas Rangers and the colorful banditti of the old times. On balance the new world is a better one, but its price is high; Texas must be paid for with Mexico.

It is clear on the basis of this brief summary of *The Wonderful Country* how similar this novel is in both meaning and structure to many of the works discussed above in Chapter III. Its elegiac tone, its theme of the passing of an older, freer, frontier civilization, and its symbolism of the new order through the conventional figure of a woman and the familiar institution of marriage are only a few of the obvious structural similarities. There is, however, one significant difference in emphasis, for where most of the works discussed earlier view the course of history as at best a necessary evil and at worst an absolute disaster, *The Wonderful Country* gives positive, if qualified, approval to the historic process. Though to a superficial view Mexico appears romantically attractive and even profoundly desirable, nevertheless Texas, prosaic as it is, is the better choice. The real nature of the land of his youth is not truly indicated in Brady's nostalgic thoughts; it is a valley of sorrows (val de peñas) whose symbol is tears (lágrimas).

It is well to close our discussion of the Western with *The Wonderful Country*, since this novel is in many ways typical of commonplace Western themes, situations, and incidents, and yet is clearly superior to run-of-the-mill Western fiction. Even the symbolic contrast between the woman Louisa Rucker and the horse Lágrimas—potentially one of the most hackneyed of all Western clichés—is sensitively handled, and becomes in Lea's fable a profound statement of the different attractiveness of two opposed ideals. This is partly due to Lea's evocative presentation of his hero's attachment to his horse, for in common with Eugene Manlove Rhodes, and in contrast to almost all other Western writers, Lea can convincingly present the love of a horseman for his mount without lapsing into sentimentality. More important than this, however, is Lea's understanding of the implication of his two symbols; he realizes that in his parable Louisa Rucker and Lágrimas must be understood as representative of two opposed ideals which are both attractive. Whichever Brady chooses, his choice must be made at the price of renouncing something very dear to him. Nevertheless, he *must* choose, and the choice he faces is that which must be faced by the characters in almost all serious Western fiction who, like Brady, would like to be able to live on both sides of the frontier.

afterword

Westward the Course of Empire

To conclude this brief survey of the Western let us return to Bishop Berkeley's poetic justification of the subject, which has served as a running epigraph throughout this study; for it is fair to say that Bishop Berkeley was one of those who understood most clearly the implications of Western story. He realized first of all that its nature is not primarily realistic. It is not about frontiersmen, or about cowboys and Indians, nor is it about the facts of Western history in any specific historical sense. Rather it concerns itself with the presentation of the meaning which underlies the superficial facts of history, a meaning equally far from the recitation of events and the evocation of striking historical personalities. It celebrates not history but the themes of history; it sings "another golden age," a story about history but not of it, and the explanation it gives of history is an explanation in terms of myth.

The myth which Bishop Berkeley sees as informing literature about the West is not, however, solely the static presentation of the facts of life in the golden age. The Western will not sing of a past state, but of a state which is constantly becoming, "the *rise* of empire and of arts." The history which the Western explores, then, is not a static, immobile past but a constantly unfolding historic perspective. Such a history of course must best be apprehended in developmental terms, and Bishop Berkeley accurately foresees the most effective presentation of its course in terms of two related, though not necessarily logically connected, metaphorical series in which the development of society seen through the images of successive historical ages is combined with the related metaphor of the maturation of the individual. The "golden age" of which the Western will sing is specifically defined as being "not such as Europe breeds in her decay" but, in explicit contrast, "such as she bred when fresh and young." The "distant lands" and "happy climes" of this golden age are conceived as youthful lands—lands freed from the manifold tyrannies of civilization, where "the pedantry of courts and schools" is not imposed upon the guide of nature and the rule of virtue.

The combined metaphors of society's golden age and of individual youth imply that the rise of empire may best be presented as somehow analogous to the theme of coming of age, and about the ultimate value of this process Bishop Berkeley, in common with so many later writers about the American West, is ambiguous. Against the decay of Europe stands the metaphorical youth of America, an emblem reinforced by the historic metaphor of the European age of brass which stands in implicit contrast to the age of gold to be reborn in the New World. The poet's ambiguity toward the historic process lies in his preception that the desirable age of gold must inevitably pass, and that in consequence, though the specific theme of the Western may be to memorialize "the wisest heads and noblest hearts," its ultimate general theme, in ironic contrast, must be that of decay. For to sing the rise of empire is to imply a later "age and clime, barren of every glorious theme."

The perennial fascination of the Western is due precisely to the charm of this combined theme of both social and personal coming of age, and later Western literature almost always specifically develops Bishop Berkeley's metaphorical comparison. Its world, the world of the frontier, is one of youthful potential, a new world waiting to be born. Its spirit is the spirit of youth—optimistic, hopeful, trusting infinitely in its own potentialities. Combined with this youthful frontier world, however, is the contrary world of age, represented in the Western by the values of that society which stands behind and inevitably succeeds it. Maturation, whether social or personal, leads only to the frustration of youthful hopes. Inherent in the youthful world of the golden age is its own eventual destruction.

The emotive power of Western literature, then, is almost entirely attributable to the ironies and ambiguities inherent in the very presentation of these two related but contrary symbols. If, as

Bishop Berkeley implies, youth is desirable in itself rather than in any potentiality it may possess for maturity, the course of human life must be tragic, and by metaphorical extension so must the course of history. Yet the joys of youth are none the less real because they must inevitably pass. Perhaps indeed their very impermanence makes them the more dear, and explains our own longing for a golden age which, in the Western, takes the form of our at least partial identification with the values of the frontier. In any case, the theme of the civilizing of the Great West and of the passing of the frontier, metaphorically identified in Western literature with the passing of youth, becomes a vehicle for the exploration of the ironies inherent in human endeavor. Of all these ironies, the greatest is the cherished human notion of the possibility of a new start, of another golden age more closely modeled on the land of heart's desire. But every beginning implies an end, and here is the tragic vision of the literature of the Great West; for a golden age seems precious only after it has been lost, and the beauty of youth may only be understood from the perspective of age.

Notes and References

Chapter One

1. See, for example, David D. Davis' excellent study of the cowboy hero, "Ten-Gallon Hero," *American Quarterly*, VI (Summer, 1954), 111-25.

2. *Recollections of the Last Ten Years* (Boston, 1826), p. 67.

3. Isaac Appleton Jewett, "Themes for Western Fiction," *Western Monthly Magazine*, I (December, 1833), 575, 586.

4. *The Complete Works of Nathaniel Hawthorne* (Boston, 1899), III, 13.

5. *The Complete Works of Nathaniel Hawthorne*, V, 57; Charles Ryskamp, "The New England Sources of *The Scarlet Letter*," *American Literature*, XXXI (November, 1959), 257-72.

6. Commentators on the Western, however, often mention the book, usually as an example of what the Western should be but isn't. See, for example, one of the most recent commentaries on the cowboy, Joe B. Frantz and Julian Ernest Choate, Jr., *The American Cowboy, the Myth & the Reality* (Norman, Oklahoma, 1955), p. 165. See also J. Frank Dobie's "A Salute to Gene Rhodes" in *The Best Novels and Stories of Eugene Manlove Rhodes* (Boston, 1949), pp. xii-xiii, and his "Andy Adams, Cowboy Chronicler," *Southwest Review*, XI (January, 1926), 95. In the latter work Dobie makes the comparison between *Moby-Dick* and *Two Years before the Mast*, though in a somewhat different context from my own.

7. E. Douglas Branch, *The Cowboy and his Interpreters* (New York, 1926), p. 198.

8. This essay is reprinted in *Errand into the Wilderness* (Cambridge, Mass., 1956), pp. 1-15.

Chapter Two

1. *The Letters and Journals of James Fenimore Cooper*, ed. James Franklin Beard (Cambridge, Mass., 1960), of which two volumes have appeared so far; *The Leatherstocking Saga*, ed. Allan Nevins (New York, 1954); Henry Nash Smith, *Virgin Land: The American West as Symbol and Myth* (Cambridge, Mass., 1950), pp. 51-120.

2. The best comprehensive modern study of Cooper is Donald A. Ringe's *James Fenimore Cooper* (New York, 1962). See also the various essays in *James Fenimore Cooper, a Re-Appraisal*, ed. M. E. Cunningham (Cooperstown, 1954).

3. *The Complete Works of James Fenimore Cooper* (New York:

G. P. Putnam's Sons, n.d.), I, 1. All further references to the Leather-stocking Tales will be to this edition and included in the text.

4. *The History and Geography of the Mississippi Valley* (Boston, 1833), I, 133-34.

5. In order of publication, it will be recalled, the chronology of the Leatherstocking Tales is: *The Pioneers* (1823); *The Last of the Mohicans* (1826); *The Prairie* (1827); *The Pathfinder* (1840); *The Deerslayer* (1841). In terms of the chronology of Natty Bumppo's own life, however, *The Deerslayer* comes first, followed in order by *The Last of the Mohicans*, *The Pathfinder*, *The Pioneers*, and *The Prairie*.

6. This is supposedly a lament made by Mike Fink, the last of the riverboatmen, from Thomas Bangs Thorpe's 1842 account of him, "The Disgraced Scalp-Lock, or Incidents on the Western Waters." See Walter Blair and Franklin J. Meine (eds.), *Half Horse Half Alligator. The Growth of the Mike Fink Legend* (Chicago, 1956), p. 71.

7. Will James, *Cowboys North and South* (New York, 1929), pp. 70, 51; Tom Lea, *The Wonderful Country* (Boston, 1952), motto.

8. Roy Harvey Pearce has brilliantly analyzed this debate in *The Savages of America. A Study of the Indian and the Idea of Civilization* (Baltimore, 1953), pp. 196-236.

9. In this discussion of Indian history I am heavily indebted to Allan Nevins' admirable Introduction to *The Leatherstocking Saga*, pp. 25-34.

10. *Indian Wars of the West* (Cincinnati, 1833), pp. 36-37.

11. For the record, it should be pointed out that the literary conflict between cattle and sheep interests does not necessarily represent objective truth. Sheep if improperly grazed can destroy range, but it is not inevitable that they will. The responsibility for destruction of the range must fall alike on cattlemen and sheepmen, who before modern conservation regulations (and, it is alleged in some quarters, even since then) consistently overgrazed the range. A novel which clearly states the quarrel between the cattle and sheep interests is Dane Coolidge's *Hidden Water* (Chicago, 1910).

12. Even in *The Pioneers* the wildcat which threatens Elizabeth's life is clearly a type of wilderness peril.

13. *The Discovery, Settlement and Present State of Kentucke*, in Willard Rouse Judson (ed.), *Filson's Kentucke* (Louisville, 1930), p. 49. For a further explication of Filson and Flint, see my own *Timothy Flint* (New York, 1965), pp. 87-104.

Chapter Three

1. The best analysis of the debate over the "Great American Desert" is to be found in Henry Nash Smith, *Virgin Land*, pp. 123-210. Hoxie Neale Fairchild's *The Noble Savage, A Study in Romantic*

Naturalism (New York, 1928) is still the best analysis of the argument which has periodically convulsed Western Europe about whether the "good life" might best be realized within society or outside of it.

2. *Boswell's Life of Johnson*, ed. G. B. Hill, rev. L. F. Powell (Oxford: The Clarendon Press, 1934), II, 228.

3. A similar inability to make a closely analogous character believable flaws Louis Bromfield's *Colorado* (New York, 1947). Marguerite Eyssen's *Go-Devil* (Garden City, N. Y., 1947), though not strictly a Western—its subject is the Pennsylvania oil boom—is another interesting, and to my mind more successful analogue. The hero of this novel has not only the predictable mistress and other external status symbols but a great closet full of boots, all of which are too large for him. As a poor boy his boots had always been cheap and too small, and his idea of luxury had been to possess a pair which didn't hurt his feet. George Pattullo occasionally writes more specifically Western stories about the Oklahoma oil boom. These are usually anecdotes about some kind of elaborate swindle, and not in my opinion among his best. See his "Drycheck Charlie" and "Barrel-House Ben" in *A Good Rooster Crows Everywhere* (New York, 1939), pp. 143-58, 161-78.

4. It should be pointed out in passing that both these novels, along with many others concerned with the search for gold, were published during the Great Depression when to many writers the American experience seemed like a gigantic wild-goose chase. It takes no great imagination to read *The Golden Lady* in particular as a depression parable, but such a reading is rather too limited; the novel is more universal in application.

5. The story of the handcart migrations is not generally known to non-Mormons, and those who come upon it for the first time in *The Proselyte* may get a false impression. For dramatic purposes Susan Ertz focuses upon the ill-fated fourth and fifth companies, who were victims of a late start and an early winter which caught them on the plains short of Salt Lake City. Of the 1,076 persons in these two companies more than 200 died en route. Their experience was not typical; the handcart migrations were an astonishing success by and large, providing safe and inexpensive transportation from Iowa City to Salt Lake City. Of the nearly 1,900 persons on the other eight expeditions, less than fifty died en route. For the most complete account of the handcart migrations see LeRoy R. and Ann W. Hafen, *Handcarts to Zion, the Story of a Unique Western Migration, 1856-1860* (Glendale, California, 1960).

6. Whatever travelers might publicly say about the beauties of life in the wilds, many of them privately held that a little more comfort might prove a welcome leaven to nature in the rough. See Robert G. Athearn's *Westward the Briton* (New York, 1953) for privately confided reservations about Western life. See also Fanny Kemble Wister's

edition of Owen Wister's journals, *Owen Wister Out West. His Journals and Letters* (Chicago, 1958), for his private opinions about the West, often in startling contrast to his fictional views.

7. The notion put in Brice Chamberlain's mouth that "rain follows the plow" is one of the strangest beliefs of nineteenth-century scholarly folklore. See Henry Nash Smith, *Virgin Land,* pp. 174-83, for a thorough discussion. Richter's disillusionment with the idea may well have come as a result of the dust bowl of the 1930's which proved dramatically that God does not necessarily choose "sides" in such a situation.

Chapter Four

1. Albert Keiser's *The Indian in American Literature* (New York, 1933) is a useful survey work about the literary Indian, though much of it has been superseded by Roy Harvey Pearce's *The Savages of America.* The most thought-provoking study of the cowboy hero is David B. Davis' "Ten-Gallon Hero," though E. Douglas Branch in *The Cowboy and his Interpreters* and Joe B. Frantz and Julian Ernest Choate, Jr. in *The American Cowboy, the Myth & the Reality* add interesting documentation if little critical insight. The best factual account of cowboy life is still Philip Ashton Rollins' *The Cowboy: His Characteristics, His Equipment, and His Part in the Development of the West* (New York, 1922).

2. Harte had been attempting to foil a pursuing posse by riding a steer, whose tracks would be more difficult to follow than a horse's; the same ruse is used, much more successfully, in Eugene Manlove Rhodes's *Pasó por Aquí.*

3. Much of Rhodes's best work is easily accessible in *The Best Novels and Stories of Eugene Manlove Rhodes,* ed. Frank V. Dearing (Boston, 1949) and *The Rhodes Reader. Stories of Virgins, Villains, and Varmints,* ed. W. H. Hutchinson (Norman, Oklahoma, 1957), the foreword of which should be read by every student of Western story. Hutchinson has also compiled *A Bar Cross Liar. Bibliography of Eugene Manlove Rhodes Who Loved the West-That-Was When He Was Young* (Stillwater, Oklahoma, 1959), an invaluable work to the student of Rhodes, and has published as well an excellent biography, *The Life & Personal Writings of Eugene Manlove Rhodes. A Bar Cross Man* (Norman, Oklahoma, 1956).

4. The same admiration of the hero for the villain may often be found in detective story. Sherlock Holmes's respect for the arch-criminal Professor Moriarty comes immediately to mind.

5. Oakhurst is so fond of returning his winnings that one wonders how he ever manages to make a living. See "The Outcasts of Poker Flat" and "A Passage in the Life of Mr. John Oakhurst."

6. This incident in *The Virginian* is remotely based upon the so-called "Johnson County War." Wister's bias is pro-cattleman; for an

opposite point of view see Asa Shinn Mercer's famous polemical attack upon the cattle interests, *The Banditti of the Plains or the Cattlemen's Invasion of Wyoming in 1892, [The Crowning Infamy of the Ages]* ([Cheyenne, Wyoming: A. S. Mercer, 1894]). A good brief factual account of the struggle is to be found in Ernest Staples Osgood, *The Day of the Cattleman* (Minneapolis, 1929), pp. 237-55.

7. Television addicts may recall that this symbolic abnegation of moral choice was the basis of the conflict in two of the better Western serials, "Have Gun, Will Travel" and "Wanted: Dead or Alive." In the former, Richard Boone, as a professional gunman, was often faced with the unpleasant fact that the person he was supposed to kill was in fact either innocent or morally superior to Boone's employer. In the latter, Steve McQueen, a "bounty hunter" (one who brings in wanted men for the reward money), often discovered that the wanted man was in fact innocent and that to turn him in for the reward, though a legally justifiable action, was an immoral one.

8. Precisely here is where so many television Westerns go wrong. In a serial in which the hero is defined as unbeatable in a gun battle, little interest can be generated by raising the spurious question of whether he will or will not win. Besides, the viewer knows, and should the excitement become unbearable may solace himself with the knowledge, that no harm can come to the just man who has commitments to next week's program.

9. *Jesse James: The Life and Daring Adventures of This Bold Highwayman and Bank Robber* ... (1886); reprinted (Cliffside Park, New Jersey: W. F. Kelleher, 1951).

10. Both these ballads have been quoted from *A Treasury of American Folklore. Stories, Ballads, and Traditions of the People*, ed. B. A. Botkin (New York, 1944), pp. 107-8, 118-22.

11. The theme of outrages perpetrated upon the innocent native Californians by the encroaching Americans is a constant preoccupation of literature which concerns itself with the settlement of California. See, for another example, the discussion of Helen Hunt Jackson's *Ramona* (below, pp. 169-71).

12. The confused story of the Lincoln County War is summarized briefly in Dee Brown and Martin F. Schmitt, *Trail Driving Days* (New York, 1952), pp. 161-78. This account, though brief, is accompanied by a number of rare and interesting pictures, including the only known portrait of the Kid. Those interested in a longer study of Billy the Kid should obtain Walter Noble Burns, *The Saga of Billy the Kid* (Garden City, N. Y., 1925), the best survey of the Kid's biography and legend.

13. Rhodes was a great admirer of Pat Garrett, a man whom most other commentators have rather sentimentally condemned for shooting the Kid. See his "In Defense of Pat Garrett" in *The Rhodes Reader*, pp. 305-16.

Chapter Five

1. See Roy Harvey Pearce, "The Significances of the Captivity Narrative," *AL*, XIX (March, 1947), 1-20. My own summation in this chapter of American attitudes toward the Indians draws heavily upon his *The Savages of America*. To this excellent work I refer the reader interested in a more thorough study of the Indian as he figures in eighteenth- and nineteenth-century American thought.

2. *The History and Geography of the Mississippi Valley*, I, 112.

3. *The Shoshonee Valley: a Romance* (Cincinnati, 1830), 2 vols., I, 36-37, 41, 80. For a more thorough analysis of this novel see my own *Timothy Flint*, pp. 136-45.

4. The similarity of the Western to the "golden myth of the antebellum South" has been explored by David B. Davis, though not exactly in this connection, in "Ten-Gallon Hero," pp. 112 ff.

5. We should notice at this point how much the relationship of the Lone Ranger and Tonto has changed from its ultimate source, the friendship between Natty Bumppo and Chingachgook. In Cooper's work, the relative social status of the Indian and the white is reversed; for Chingachgook is a chieftain, albeit of a scattered people, and Natty is proud to be considered as one of the Delaware nation. This contrast is reflected in the personal relationship between the two men, for while Tonto is clearly the Lone Ranger's inferior, Chingachgook is Natty's equal. The relationship between Natty and Chingachgook is one of friendship and mutual respect; that of the Lone Ranger and Tonto is clearly one of master to servant.

6. See Timothy Flint, *Indian Wars of the West*, p. 54.

Chapter Six

1. Thomas A. Bledsoe, in his Introduction to *Main-Travelled Roads* (New York: Rinehart & Co., Inc., 1954), p. xxvi. Further citations to the text of *Main-Travelled Roads* are to the first edition (Boston: Arena Publishing Company, 1891).

2. *The Moccasin Ranch* was first published as "The Land of the Straddle-Bug" in 1894-95.

3. *Death Comes for the Archbishop* closely follows the history of the life and work of Bishop John Baptist Lamy (1814-1888), and of his friend Joseph Prospectus Machebeuf (1812-1889), the models respectively for Archbishop Jean Marie Latour and Father Joseph Vaillant of the novel.

4. For a provocative study of this idea in American literature see Norman Holmes Pearson, "The American Writer and the Feeling for Community," *English Studies*, XLIII (October, 1962), 1-10. W. H. Hutchinson has mentioned Rhodes's particular commitment to this ideal in numerous places in *The Rhodes Reader*.

Bibliography

The following bibliography makes no pretense at being a complete listing either of Westerns or of secondary materials about them. I have included only those Westerns which I have discussed in the body of this study, and only such secondary materials as have been especially germane to my purposes. Bibliographies of Westerns abound, and the student of Western story will find himself embarrassed by a multitude of riches rather than plagued by a dearth of information. I found Jens Christian Bay's three short bibliographies *A Handful of Western Books* (Cedar Rapids, Iowa, 1935), *A Second Handful of Western Books* (Cedar Rapids, Iowa, 1936), and *A Third Handful of Western Books* (Cedar Rapids, Iowa, 1937) to be a useful starting point. More complete bibliographies are Ramon F. Adams' *The Rampaging Herd; A Bibliography of Books and Pamphlets on Men and Events in the Cattle Industry* (Norman, Oklahoma: University of Oklahoma Press, [1959]), and his *Six-Guns and Saddle Leather; A Bibliography of Books and Pamphlets on Western Outlaws and Gunmen* (Norman, Oklahoma: University of Oklahoma Press, [1954]), both of which are indispensable to the student of Western history and literature. Levette Jay Davidson's *Rocky Mountain Life in Literature; A Descriptive Bibliography* ([Denver:] The University of Denver Book Store, 1936), is a useful—though incomplete—compilation of titles about one area of the West which is often overlooked by those who unthinkingly equate the West with the Plains States. J. Frank Dobie's *Guide to Life and Literature of the Southwest, Revised and Enlarged in Both Knowledge and Wisdom* (Dallas, Texas: Southern Methodist University Press, 1952) is probably the most useful single bibliography of Western Americana. Oscar Osburn Winther's *A Classified Bibliography of the Periodical Literature of the Trans-Mississippi West, 1811-1957* (Bloomington, Indiana: Indiana University Press, 1961) is a thorough and well-done guide to the fugitive periodical literature about the West. While bibliographies of the trans-Mississippi West abound, it is perhaps no surprise that the older "West" of the Mississippi Valley is still the Last Frontier of the bibliographical explorer. Dorothy Anne Dondore's *The Prairie and the Making of Middle America. Four Centuries of Description* (Cedar Rapids, Iowa: The Torch Press, 1926) and Ralph Leslie Rusk's *The Literature of the*

213

Middle Western Frontier, 2 vols. (New York: Columbia University Press, 1925) are still the best bibliographical studies of this area.

ADAMS, ANDY. *The Log of a Cowboy; A Narrative of the Old Trail Days.* Boston: Houghton Mifflin Company, 1903.

ALLEN, JOHN HOUGHTON. *Southwest.* Philadelphia: Lippincott, 1952.

ATHEARN, ROBERT G. *Westward the Briton: The Far West, 1865-1900, As Seen by British Sportsmen and Capitalists, Ranchers and Homesteaders, Lords and Ladies.* New York: Charles Scribner's Sons, 1953.

BEARD, JAMES FRANKLIN (ed.). *The Letters and Journals of James Fenimore Cooper.* 2 vols. Cambridge, Mass.: Harvard University Press, 1960.

BENNET, ROBERT AMES. *Branded.* New York: A. L. Burt Company, 1924.

BIRD, ROBERT MONTGOMERY. *Nick of the Woods, or the Jibbenainosay. A Tale of Kentucky.* New York: American Book Company, 1939.

BLAIR, WALTER, and MEINE, FRANKLIN J. (eds.). *Half Horse Half Alligator. The Growth of the Mike Fink Legend.* Chicago: University of Chicago Press, 1956.

BLEDSOE, THOMAS A. "Introduction" to *Main-Travelled Roads. Six Mississippi Valley Stories.* New York: Rinehart & Co., Inc., 1954, pp. ix-xl.

BOTKIN, B. A. (ed.). *A Treasury of American Folklore. Stories, Ballads, and Traditions of the People.* New York: Crown Publishers, 1944.

BRANCH, E. DOUGLAS. *The Cowboy and his Interpreters.* New York: D. Appleton and Co., 1926.

BROMFIELD, LOUIS. *Colorado.* New York: Harper & Brothers, 1947.

BROWN, DEE, and SCHMITT, MARTIN F. *Trail Driving Days.* New York: Charles Scribner's Sons, 1952.

BURNS, WALTER NOBLE. *The Saga of Billy the Kid.* Garden City, New York: Doubleday, Page & Co., 1925.

CATHER, WILLA. *Death Comes for the Archbishop.* Boston: Houghton Mifflin Company, 1938. Volume 9 of *The Novels and Stories of Willa Cather.*

————. *My Antonia.* Boston: Houghton Mifflin Company, 1937. Volume 4 of *The Novels and Stories of Willa Cather.*

————. *O Pioneers!* Boston: Houghton Mifflin Company, 1937. Volume 1 of *The Novels and Stories of Willa Cather.*

CLARK, WALTER VAN TILBURG. *The Ox-Bow Incident.* New York: Random House, 1940.

————. *The Track of the Cat.* New York: Random House, 1949.

COOLIDGE, DANE. *Hidden Water.* Chicago: A. C. McClurg and Co., 1910.

COOPER, JAMES FENIMORE. *The Deerslayer, or The First War-Path.*

New York: G. P. Putnam's Sons, n.d. Volume I of *The Complete Works of James Fenimore Cooper*. The Leather-Stocking Edition.

—————. *The Last of the Mohicans, or, A Narrative of 1757.* New York: G. P. Putnam's Sons, n.d. Volume II of *The Complete Works of James Fenimore Cooper*. The Leather-Stocking Edition.

—————. *The Pathfinder, or, The Inland Sea.* New York: G. P. Putnam's Sons, n.d. Volume III of *The Complete Works of James Fenimore Cooper*. The Leather-Stocking Edition.

—————. *The Pioneers, or, The Sources of the Susquehanna.* New York: G. P. Putnam's Sons, n.d. Volume IV of *The Complete Works of James Fenimore Cooper*. The Leather-Stocking Edition.

—————. *The Prairie.* New York: G. P. Putnam's Sons, n.d. Volume V of *The Complete Works of James Fenimore Cooper*. The Leather-Stocking Edition.

CRANE, STEPHEN. "The Bride Comes to Yellow Sky," in *Stephen Crane: Stories and Tales,* ed., ROBERT WOOSTER STALLMAN. New York: Alfred A. Knopf, 1952, pp. 273-85.

CREVECOEUR, J. HECTOR ST. JOHN DE. *Letters from an American Farmer.* New York: Fox, Duffield & Company, 1904.

CUNNINGHAM, M. S. (ed.). *James Fenimore Cooper: A Re-Appraisal.* Cooperstown, New York: New York Historical Association, 1954.

DAVIS, DAVID B. "Ten-Gallon Hero," *American Quarterly,* VI (Summer, 1954), 111-25.

DEARING, FRANK V. (ed.). *The Best Novels and Stories of Eugene Manlove Rhodes.* Boston: Houghton Mifflin Company, 1949.

DOBIE, J. FRANK. "Andy Adams, Cowboy Chronicler," *Southwest Review,* XI (January, 1926), 92-101.

—————. "A Salute to Gene Rhodes," in *The Best Novels and Stories of Eugene Manlove Rhodes,* (ed.) FRANK V. DEARING, pp. xi-xxii.

ERTZ, SUSAN. *The Proselyte.* New York: D. Appleton-Century Co., 1933.

EYSSEN, MARGUERITE. *Go-Devil.* Garden City, New York: Doubleday & Co., 1947.

FAIRCHILD, HOXIE NEALE. *The Noble Savage, A Study in Romantic Naturalism.* New York: Columbia University Press, 1928.

FAUST, FREDERICK SCHILLER [Max Brand]. *Destry Rides Again.* New York: Dodd, Mead & Company, 1930.

FERBER, EDNA. *Cimarron.* Garden City, New York: Doubleday, Doran and Company, 1930.

FILSON, JOHN. *The Discovery, Settlement and Present State of Kentucke: . . .* in *Filson's Kentucky,* ed. WILLARD ROUSE JUDSON. Louisville, Kentucky: John P. Morton & Company, 1930.

FISHER, VARDIS. *Toilers of the Hills.* Boston: Houghton Mifflin Company, 1928.

FISHWICK, MARSHALL W. "The Cowboy: America's Contribution to the World's Mythology," *Western Folklore*, XI (April, 1952), 77-92.

FLINT, TIMOTHY. *Biographical Memoir of Daniel Boone, the First Settler of Kentucky. Interspersed with Incidents in the Early Annals of the Country*. Cincinnati: N. & G. Guilford, 1833.

————. *The History and Geography of the Mississippi Valley*. Boston: Carter, Hendee, and Co., 1833.

————. *Indian Wars of the West*. Cincinnati: E. H. Flint, 1833.

————. *The Life and Adventures of Arthur Clenning*. 2 vols. Philadelphia: Towar & Hogan, 1828.

————. *Recollections of the Last Ten Years, Passed in Occasional Residences and Journeyings in the Valley of the Mississippi* ... Boston: Cummings, Hilliard, and Company, 1826.

————. *The Shoshonee Valley; A Romance*. 2 vols. Cincinnati: E. H. Flint, 1830.

FOLSOM, JAMES K. *Timothy Flint*. New York: Twayne Publishers, 1965.

FRANTZ, JOE B., and CHOATE, JULIAN ERNEST, JR. *The American Cowboy, the Myth & the Reality*. Norman, Oklahoma: University of Oklahoma Press, 1955.

[FRENCH, JAMES S.] *Elkswatawa; or, The Prophet of the West. A Tale of the Frontier*. 2 vols. New York: Harper & Brothers, 1836.

GANN, WALTER. *The Trail Boss*. Boston: Houghton Mifflin Co., 1937.

GARDINER, DOROTHY. *The Golden Lady*. New York: The Literary Guild, 1936.

GARLAND, HAMLIN. *The Book of the American Indian*. New York: Harper & Brothers, 1923.

————. *Main-Travelled Roads: Six Mississippi Valley Stories*. Boston: Arena Publishing Company, 1891.

————. *The Moccasin Ranch. A Story of Dakota*. New York: Harper & Brothers, 1909.

————. "Outlaw," *Harper's Weekly*, XLVII (June 13-20, 1903), 972-73; 1036-38.

————. *A Spoil of Office. A Story of the Modern West*. New York: D. Appleton and Company, 1897.

GLIDDEN, FREDERICK D. [Luke Short]. *Station West*. Boston: Houghton Mifflin Company, 1947.

GREY, ZANE. *The U. P. Trail*. New York: Harper & Brothers, 1918.

————. *The Vanishing American*. New York: Grosset & Dunlap, 1925.

GUTHRIE, A. B., JR. *The Big Sky*. New York: William Sloane Associates, 1947.

————. *These Thousand Hills*. Boston: Houghton Mifflin Company, 1956.

————. *The Way West*. New York: William Sloane Associates, 1949.

HAFEN, LEROY R., and ANN W. *Handcarts to Zion, The Story of a Unique Western Migration, 1856-1860.* Glendale, California: The Arthur H. Clark Company, 1960.

HALL, JAMES. *Legends of the West: Sketches Illustrative of the Habits, Occupations, Privations, Adventures and Sports of the Pioneers of the West.* Cincinnati: Robert Clarke & Co., 1874.

————. *The Romance of Western History; or, Sketches of History, Life, and Manners in the West.* Cincinnati: Robert Clarke & Co., 1885.

HALL, OAKLEY. *Warlock.* New York: The Viking Press, 1958.

HARTE, FRANCIS BRET. "The Luck of Roaring Camp," in *The Luck of Roaring Camp and Other Tales.* Boston: Houghton, Mifflin and Company, n.d., pp. 1-13. Volume I of *The Writings of Bret Harte.*

————. "Miggles," in *The Luck of Roaring Camp and Other Tales.* Boston: Houghton, Mifflin and Company, n.d., pp. 27-40. Volume I of *The Writings of Bret Harte.*

————. "The Outcasts of Poker Flat," in *The Luck of Roaring Camp and Other Tales.* Boston: Houghton, Mifflin and Company, n.d., pp. 14-26. Volume I of *The Writings of Bret Harte.*

————. "A Passage in the Life of Mr. John Oakhurst," in *Tales of the Argonauts.* Boston: Houghton, Mifflin and Company, n.d., pp. 171-96. Volume II of *The Writings of Bret Harte.*

HAWTHORNE, NATHANIEL. *The House of the Seven Gables.* Boston: Houghton, Mifflin and Co., 1883. *The Complete Works of Nathaniel Hawthorne,* III, 13-378. The Riverside Edition.

————. *The Marble Faun.* Boston: Houghton, Mifflin and Co., 1883. Volume VI of *The Complete Works of Nathaniel Hawthorne.* The Riverside Edition.

————. *The Scarlet Letter.* Boston: Houghton, Mifflin and Co., 1883. *The Complete Works of Nathaniel Hawthorne,* V, 15-312. The Riverside Edition.

HAZARD, MRS. LUCY LOCKWOOD. *The Frontier in American Literature.* New York: Thomas Y. Crowell Co., [1927].

HOWE, EDGAR WATSON. *The Story of a Country Town.* New York: Twayne Publishers, 1962.

HUTCHINSON, W. H. *A Bar Cross Liar. Bibliography of Eugene Manlove Rhodes Who Loved the West-That-Was When He Was Young.* Stillwater, Oklahoma: Redlands Press, 1959.

————. *The Life & Personal Writings of Eugene Manlove Rhodes. A Bar Cross Man.* Norman, Oklahoma: University of Oklahoma Press, 1956.

————. (ed.). *The Rhodes Reader. Stories of Virgins, Villains, and Varmints.* Norman, Oklahoma: University of Oklahoma Press, 1957.

————. "The 'Western Story' as Literature," *Western Humanities Review*, III (January, 1949), 33-37.

JACKSON, HELEN HUNT. *Ramona. A Story.* Boston: Roberts Brothers, 1884.

JAMES, WILLIAM RODERICK. *Cowboys North and South.* New York: Charles Scribner's Sons, 1929.

Jesse James: The Life and Daring Adventures of This Bold Highwayman and Bank Robber.... Cliffside Park, N. J.: W. F. Kelleher, 1951.

JEWETT, ISAAC APPLETON. "Themes for Western Fiction," *The Western Monthly Magazine*, I (December, 1833), 574-88.

KEISER, ALBERT. *The Indian in American Literature.* New York: Oxford University Press, 1933.

KROLL, HARRY HARRISON. *Rogues' Company. A Novel of John Murrell.* Indianapolis: Bobbs-Merrill, 1943.

LEA, TOM. *The Wonderful Country.* Boston: Little, Brown, and Company, 1952.

LE MAY, ALAN. *The Searchers.* New York: Harper & Brothers, 1954.
————. *The Unforgiven.* New York: Harper & Brothers, 1957.

MERCER, ASA SHINN. *The Banditti of the Plains or the Cattlemen's Invasion of Wyoming in 1892 [The Crowning Infamy of the Ages].* [Cheyenne, Wyoming: A. S. Mercer, 1894].

MILLER, ARTHUR. *The Misfits.* New York: The Viking Press, 1961.

MILLER, PERRY. *Errand into the Wilderness.* Cambridge, Mass.: Harvard University Press, 1956.

NEVINS, ALLAN (ed.). *The Leatherstocking Saga.* New York: Pantheon Books, 1954.

OSGOOD, ERNEST STAPLES. *The Day of the Cattleman.* Minneapolis: University of Minnesota Press, 1929.

PARK, CHARLES CALDWELL [Carl Gray]. *A Plaything of the Gods. A Tale of Old California.* Boston: Sherman, French & Co., 1912.

PATTULLO, GEORGE. "Barrel-House Ben," in *A Good Rooster Crows Everywhere.* New York: Privately printed, 1939, pp. 161-78.
————. "Drycheck Charlie," in *A Good Rooster Crows Everywhere.* New York: Privately printed, 1939, pp. 143-58.
————. "The More Abundant Life," in *A Good Rooster Crows Everywhere.* New York: Privately printed, 1939, pp. 281-86.
————. "Off the Trail. A Story," *McClure's Magazine*, XXXVIII (March, 1912), 515-22.
————. "Pioneer," in *A Good Rooster Crows Everywhere.* New York: Privately printed, 1939, pp. 29-36.
————. "Survival," in *A Good Rooster Crows Everywhere.* New York: Privately printed, 1939, pp. 267-77.
————. "Unspanked Third," in *A Good Rooster Crows Everywhere.* New York: Privately printed, 1939, pp. 241-63.

PAUL, ELLIOT. *A Ghost Town on the Yellowstone.* New York: Random House, [1948].

PEARCE, ROY HARVEY. *The Savages of America. A Study of the Indian and the Idea of Civilization.* Baltimore: The Johns Hopkins Press, 1953.

————. "The Significances of the Captivity Narrative," *American Literature,* XIX (March, 1947), 1-20.

PEARSON, NORMAN HOLMES. "The American Writer and the Feeling for Community," *English Studies,* XLIII (October, 1962), 1-10.

POCOCK, ROGER. *Curly. A Tale of the Arizona Desert.* Boston: Little, Brown, and Company, 1920.

QUICK, HERBERT. *The Hawkeye.* Indianapolis: The Bobbs-Merrill Company, 1923.

————. *Vandemark's Folly.* Indianapolis: The Bobbs-Merrill Company, 1922.

RHODES, EUGENE MANLOVE. "Beyond the Desert," in *The Best Novels and Stories of Eugene Manlove Rhodes,* ed., FRANK V. DEARING. Boston: Houghton Mifflin Company, 1949, pp. 451-76.

————. *Good Men and True,* in *The Best Novels and Stories,* pp. 45-104.

————. "In Defense of Pat Garrett," in *The Rhodes Reader,* ed. W. H. Hutchinson. Norman, Oklahoma: University of Oklahoma Press, 1957, pp. 305-16.

————. "Loved I Not Honor More," in *The Rhodes Reader,* pp. 3-13.

————. "No Mean City," in *The Rhodes Reader,* pp. 200-64.

————. *Pasó por Aquí,* in *The Best Novels and Stories,* pp. 1-44.

RICHTER, CONRAD. *The Light in the Forest.* New York: Alfred A. Knopf, 1953.

————. *The Sea of Grass.* New York: Alfred A. Knopf, 1937.

RINGE, DONALD A. *James Fenimore Cooper.* New York: Twayne Publishers, 1962.

ROLLINS, PHILIP ASHTON. *The Cowboy: His Characteristics, His Equipment, and His Part in the Development of the West.* New York: Charles Scribner's Sons, 1922.

RYSKAMP, CHARLES. "The New England Sources of *The Scarlet Letter,*" *American Literature,* XXXI (November, 1959), 257-72.

[SCARBOROUGH, DOROTHY]. *The Wind.* New York: Harper & Brothers, 1925.

SCHAEFER, JACK. *Shane.* Boston: Houghton Mifflin Company, 1949.

SIMMS, WILLIAM GILMORE. *The Yemassee.* New York: Twayne Publishers, 1964.

SMITH, HENRY NASH. *Virgin Land; The American West as Symbol and Myth.* Cambridge, Mass.: Harvard University Press, 1950.

SNELLING, WILLIAM JOSEPH. *Tales of the Northwest.* Minneapolis: University of Minnesota Press, 1936.

SPEARMAN, FRANK HAMILTON. *Whispering Smith*. New York: Charles Scribner's Sons, 1906.

SUBLETTE, CLIFFORD MACCLELLAN. *The Golden Chimney*. Boston: Little, Brown, and Company, 1931.

VIDAL, GORE. "The Death of Billy the Kid," in *Visit to a Small Planet and Other Television Plays*. Boston: Little, Brown, and Company, pp. 173-216.

WISTER, FANNY KEMBLE (ed.). *Owen Wister Out West. His Journals and Letters*. [Chicago:] University of Chicago Press, [1958].

WISTER, OWEN. "The Gift Horse," in *Members of the Family*. New York: The Macmillan Company, 1911, pp. 159-206.

————. "How Lin McLean Went East," *Harper's New Monthly Magazine*, LXXXVI (December, 1892), 135-46.

————. *Lin McLean*. New York: Harper & Brothers, 1898.

————. *The Virginian: A Horseman of the Plains*. New York: The Macmillan Company, 1902.

Index